Mock the Haggard Face

MOCK THE HAGGARD FACE

A Canadian War Story

Edward Mastronardi MC CD

Library of Congress Control Number:		2014908048
ISBN:	Hardcover	978-1-4990-1274-3
	Softcover	978-1-4990-1275-0
	eBook	978-1-4990-1273-6

Rev. date: 06/03/2014

To order additional copies of this book, contact:
Xlibris LLC
1-888-795-4274
www.Xlibris.com
Orders@Xlibris.com
619525

CONTENTS

PART 1
The Volunteers

PART 2
Fort Lewis

PART 3
Korea

Lt. Edward Mastronardi, Second Platoon ("The Deuce") A Company, Second Battalion, the Royal Canadian Regiment the late morning after his platoon of twenty-eight heroes successfully fought off the attacks by a very determined battalion of Chinese (nearly one thousand men) for almost ten hours on the night and early morning of November 2 and 3, 1951, at an isolated outpost located on the Songgok spur in the Samichon Valley in North Korea

This book is respectfully dedicated to the volunteers of the Canadian Army Special Force who served in Korea.

Help me, O God, when death is near,
To mock the haggard face of fear,
That when I fall—if fall I must,
My Soul may triumph in the dust.

—Unknown

PART 1

The Volunteers

CHAPTER 1

The Special Force

Why don't you join up,
Why don't you join up,
Why don't you join old Rocky's Army,
Two bucks a week,
Nothing to eat,
Great big boots and blisters on your feet.

The birth of the Canadian volunteer infantry brigade in August 1950 for United Nations service in Korea created a state of mounting confusion at the understaffed recruiting depots across the country. Thousands of volunteers from every province began converging on the enlistment centers. The halls and corridors of the depots reeking with the stench of stale sweat and tobacco smoke were filled with long lines of shuffling recruits waiting to be processed into the new force, the force that had been referred to as "Canada's foreign legion" by some enterprising newsman.

The motives of the volunteers for enlisting to fight an unknown enemy on an obscure Asian peninsula were as varied as their backgrounds. Among the large proportion of Second World War veterans, one reason for volunteering predominated: their failure to adjust to civilian life during the postwar period. The war in Korea provided a heaven-sent opportunity to escape the present, to recapture the time-faded glories of their war experiences, remembering the good times, the comradeship, the excitement of seeing new places and people, forgetting the discomfort, pain, the desperate fear of death. The motives of the young enlistees were uncomplicated and quite natural, welcoming the challenge and possible danger of fighting in the Far East with youthful enthusiasm.

The Special Force, flushed with the happy agony of "the soldier's farewell," was jammed into dimly lit, overcrowded troop trains dispatched to its far-flung training centers. A new song, its origin obscure, its lyrics catchy, was enthusiastically taken up by veterans and young soldiers alike, appropriately called Rocky's Army after Brig. John Rockingham, the force's dominating commander.

Meanwhile, the military camps and training centers across Canada were hurriedly reorganizing their training personnel and facilities in a frantic effort to meet their overwhelming new commitment. Additional stores of uniforms, boots, berets, webbing, weapons, and the many other articles of clothing and equipment required by the modern solider had to be demanded, feeding facilities needed enlarging, old barracks had to be renovated. The harassed members of the training units prepared to train, quarter, feed, and outfit the great numbers of Special Force personnel arriving with alarming regularity. In most instances, the complicated buildup carried out with remarkable efficiency.

One of the most unique problems resulting from the creation of the predominately civilian force was the bitterness many of the professional soldiers felt toward their "amateur" counterparts, objecting to training "a bunch of civilians" to do a job rightfully belonged to the regular army. In some training units, this unfortunate attitude created a wall of antagonism between the members of the volunteer force and the regular army, and this particular animosity reached its greatest intensity at the training camp of the Royals.

Capt. Cecil Smythe, adjutant of the newly formed second battalion of the Royals, was standing on the battalion's military camp railway platform, impatiently slapping the calf of his right leg with his silver-headed swagger stick. His military grooming was impeccable, he was of average height, he was of slender build, and his erect carriage gave the impression of tallness. Smythe, one of the small group of regular force officers, transferred from the First to the Second Royals, forming the nucleus of the recently created battalion. His deeply tanned face, sharply pointed, carefully waxed mustache, the apparent ease with which he endured the broiling August sun, exemplified his lengthy service with the British Army in India prior to migrating to Canada. A small group of maroon-bereted first battalion regulars were standing behind the dapper adjutant. They, along with Smythe, detailed to meet the first of a series of troop trains carrying Special Force volunteers due to arrive in the afternoon. It was Smythe's responsibility ensuring the new recruits were disembarked in an orderly fashion then transported to their living quarters.

He was about to check the arrival time of the first train with the station master when the unmistakable blast of a train whistle reverberated up the valley. The blinding afternoon sun forced Smythe to squint, looking critically over the motley group of men stiffly descending the steps of the troop train.

"Good lord, what an appalling spectacle!" he muttered to himself. "I've never seen the like of this before in my life. Heaven help the army!"

"Were you speaking to me, sir?" one of his sergeants queried.

"No, Sergeant. Just making a few remarks to myself."

"Horrible-looking bunch, aren't they, sir?"

"Yes, Sergeant, they certainly are. There's one consolation, however."

"I can't imagine what it could be, Captain Smythe."

"Well, old chap, anything that we can do for these people is bound to be an improvement."

Smythe's conversation with his sergeant was suddenly interrupted by a loud drunken voice belonging to a lone figure swinging precariously from the top step of the end coach, a partially emptied wine bottle clutched in his free hand.

"Hey, Cap'in! How about having a drink with the boys?"

For a brief moment, the shocked adjutant was too amazed to speak. Regaining his composure, he barked at this grinning sergeant, "I don't see anything amusing in that man's behavior, Sergeant. Place him in close custody immediately!"

The first contingent of the Second Royals had arrived.

Chapter 2

Paul

Entering the Second Royals orderly room, Paul Anderson shifted his suitcase to his left hand.

"Excuse me, Sergeant. My name is Anderson, Lieutenant Anderson. I was instructed to report to the adjutant on my arrival."

The orderly room sergeant looked up from his desk to the grey-eyed blond subaltern from Hamilton, examining him with a critical eye, and answered curtly, "Captain Smythe is very busy at the moment, sir. I'll tell him you're here."

As the sergeant disappeared into the inner office, Anderson seated himself on a narrow wooden bench, expecting to wait only a few minutes.

In the course of the next hour, the loud laughter-punctuated conversation coming from the inner office indicated that Smythe's serious business consisted of his entertaining one of his friends from the First Royals. After the adjutant's visitor finally departed, Smythe kept Anderson waiting another five minutes before admitting him.

"Come in, Anderson," Smythe ordered sharply without any attempt to apologize for the delay.

As Paul entered, the adjutant, looking at him critically, snapped, "Surely you've learned some of the normal military courtesies in the course of your training, Anderson."

Surprised at the rude introduction, he replied, "I'm afraid I don't follow you?"

"Don't follow me? To begin with, you always pay compliments by saluting or coming to attention when you enter another officer's office.

Secondly, you do not address me as 'you'—you address me by either my rank and name or 'sir.'"

"I'm sorry if—"

"You can dispense with the apologies, Anderson. Just remember the advice I have given you. You'll find life in the regiment a great deal easier if you do. We have ways of instilling discipline into ill-educated subalterns in the Royals."

Later, Paul Anderson wearily dropped his bulging suitcase on the sand-encrusted floor of his dingy room, a look of disgust distorting his handsome features seeing the cracked discolored walls of his cramped quarters. The excessive late August heat and the long walk he had made through the sprawling military camp carrying his heavy bag caused him to be overly critical of the shabby accommodation provided for the officers of the newly formed Second Royals. As the tall young lieutenant began unpacking his suitcase, he felt his irritation at his indifferent reception returning. Remembering Smythe's overbearing attitude at the interview, his small stuffy room seemed hotter than ever. Paul was perspiring freely from the exertion entailed in unpacking his clothes, rivulets of sweat staining the back of his shirt; his blond hair, bleached a corn yellow by the broiling sun, clung damply to his high-set tanned forehead. He absentmindedly wiped his face with one of his rolled shirtsleeves as he looked around his room for a place to put his books, consisting of three volumes on modern philosophical thought, a history of English literature, a study of Chinese history and customs; an anthology of poetry and an English dictionary carefully selected represented the essence of the arts course that he had taken at university.

After stacking his books on top of the small rickety writing desk situated beside his cot, he carefully opened a large manila envelope, gently removing the studio photograph of a lovely young woman, his wife, Barbara. Her delicately styled hair was as fair as her husband's, her lips sensually full; her features, though refined and classically molded, lacked the sensitiveness evident in Paul's face. The picture held tenderly in his hands appeared to him so lifelike; he easily imagined that her smiling lips were speaking to him. His thoughts drifted back to an incident that had occurred a few months earlier.

Barbara Anderson had been laughing as she opened the door of their apartment for her tired husband.

"Paul, dear, I have a surprise for you! Which hand do you choose?"

Although spending a trying day at his office, Paul couldn't help smiling at his pretty wife's childlike antics as she stood expectantly in front of him, blocking his entrance into their comfortable Hamilton apartment.

"I'll take the left hand, dear," he replied, kissing her gently on the bridge of her nose.

"Well, Mr. Anderson, you have just won yourself a prize!"

Barbara proudly presented her photograph to her husband, waiting excitedly for his reaction. Paul, looking intently at the attractive picture-portrait of his wife, was filled with two emotions, one of pleasure, the other annoyance. It was obvious the photograph must be expensive; his long detailed lectures on the need to follow a strict budget and to avoid unnecessary expense seemed lost on his luxury-loving wife.

Barbara quickly detected the look of annoyance on his face, her temper flaring up. "Aren't you pleased? I went to a lot of trouble to have it taken just for you."

"It's lovely, dear, but it must have been expensive. I wish you had waited for a while—at least until the end of the month."

"Money, money, money! That's all you ever worry about. You certainly have changed. You never seemed concerned about money after we met. Besides, I don't know why you keep that miserable little adjuster's job anyway. You know very well my father would be more than willing to find a decent-paying job for you in his firm. At least think of me once in a while, not just your foolish pride," she complained bitterly.

"Darling, we've been through this thing so often I'm sick of discussing it. I know my job isn't much, but at least I got it on my own. Besides, I'll only need it until I finish my thesis. After that, I'm bound to find a lecturing spot at one of the universities."

"Oh sure, finish your thesis! I'm sick of your damn thesis. I scarcely see you anymore. You spend your days at work and your nights and weekends at the university library. I haven't seen any of my friends for months—not that I want to see anyone. I haven't a decent thing to wear, I'd only feel ashamed."

"You have a lot of lovely clothes, Barbara. Just because I can't hand out hundreds of dollars so that you can get all dressed up doesn't make you a social leper, you knew very well the first few years would be difficult. I thought you understood that?"

"It looked different, somehow, our last year at school."

"Be patient, Babs—another six months or so and I'll be finished."

"Even if you do get your master's and find a university job, what kind of salary will you get? Daddy says that university teachers are horribly underpaid. I think you should direct your intelligence into better-paying channels and forget this teacher nonsense."

"Please, dear, let's not discuss it anymore. I've had a rough day. It's a wonderful picture, Babs," he finished lamely.

Paul, still staring intently at his wife's photograph, was completely lost in his thoughts when an unexpected voice startled him.

"I say but she's a real smasher! Wife or girlfriend?"

This admiring comment came from a towering lean figure stopping unnoticed in Anderson's doorway.

"Incidentally, old chap, my name is Carr-Wilson, Montague Carr-Wilson, but of course, everyone calls me Monty. Glad to have you aboard."

Smiling broadly, he extended his right hand toward Paul, who accepted it after a moment's hesitation. Anderson's unpleasant experience with Smythe was still fresh in his mind, making him wary of the affable blond-mustached Englishman.

"My name is Paul Anderson. Pleased to meet you, Wilson," he finally countered.

"Carr-Wilson, if you don't mind, old chap. Double-barreled name, you know, bar sinister or something equally dramatic. But I say, please call me Monty."

Somewhat surprised at Anderson's apparent coolness, Monty thought for a moment, his eyes narrowing shrewdly, asked, "You haven't, by any chance, met that horrible little man, Smythe?"

"Yes, as a matter of fact, I have," Paul replied dryly.

"Oh, then that explains it. I hope you won't judge all Englishmen by him. He makes me ashamed of being English. When I heard some of the other chaps refer to him as Teabags, I damn nearly swore off tea for life," Monty said in a joking tone.

"Just because I forgot to salute when I entered his office, he tore a strip off me," Paul replied.

"Don't let that pompous ass depress you, old chap. He's merely trying to impress upon us poor misguided amateurs. He's a professional, and we're blessed to have an officer of the First Royals as our adjutant. If it's any consolation to you, old man, he tried his nonsense on me when I first arrived. I'm very familiar with his type. He didn't get very far with me, I assure you. Say, Paul, that's quite an impressive collection of ponderous tomes you have there—you must be one of these 'thinking' chaps!"

"Well, no, not really. They're just some old friends I've kept with me since university."

"You needn't look so embarrassed, old chap. I wish I had attended a university. I did intend to go to Oxford, my father's old school, but the war intervened, among other things. I never did make it. I say, it's well past lunch, the ruddy bar is closed, but just by chance, I happen to have a bottle of excellent scotch in my digs. Care to join me?"

"Best offer I've had today, Monty. Let's go!"

A few days after his arrival at the Royals' training camp, Paul was informed by the adjutant he was to be interviewed at eight o'clock that evening by the recently appointed commanding officer of the Second Royals, Lt. Col. John Chapman Graves.

John Graves, a competent and justifiably confident career officer, made it his policy to interview his officers as soon as they settled in after their arrival. He was a big man with an infectious grin and a ready laugh. He seemed to have very little in common with the tradition-bound commander of the First Royals. Graves scrupulously avoided the pseudo-British mannerisms affected by many of his caste. Prior to the Second World War, the broad-shouldered officer from Northern Ontario spent two years in Scotland playing semiprofessional hockey. When war appeared inevitable, he returned home, joined his local militia unit, receiving his commission as a lieutenant. During the war, his natural leadership ability and aggressiveness had earned him rapid promotion and several decorations. When the war ended, he was accepted in the regular army with his wartime rank, quite an accomplishment for a man who had spent his post-high-school years laying railway ties and playing hockey. It seemed natural he should be selected to command one of the battalions destined to participate in the Korean campaign.

Colonel Graves was in the process of writing to his wife when Paul Anderson knocked at his door punctually at eight.

"Come in," he ordered in his deep bass.

Paul entered the unpretentious quarters of his CO, saluted smartly, and stood rigidly at attention before the pipe-smoking Graves. The Second Royals' commander looked over Anderson's lean figure carefully, studied his face closely. Rising from his chair, extending his right hand, he said warmly, "Glad to have you with us, Anderson. Please sit down—no, over here. It's more comfortable. In fact, it's the only comfortable seat in the place."

Graves returned to his desk, picking out Paul's personal history folder from a stack of some forty or more that piled on his desktop.

"I see from your service record that you were commissioned in the Hamilton Light Infantry two years ago."

"Yes, sir, I joined the regiment during my last year in the university."

"What course did you major in?"

"Philosophy and English, sir."

"That seems to be a rather unusual choice. What did you intend to do on graduation?"

"I had intended to do postgraduate work and then teach at a university, if possible. I got married, sir, and decided to combine working and school until I completed my master's."

"You decided, eh?"

"Why, yes, sir, I did."

"How does your wife feel about you joining the Special Force?"

"Well . . . ah . . . fine, I think. She more or less left the decision up to me."

"Oh, I see," Graves said quizzically then changed the subject. "Are you interested in sports, Anderson?"

"Yes, sir. I like tennis and swimming. I used to do a fair amount of track and field work when I was in high school."

"What about at university?"

"My studies kept me pretty busy, sir. I'm afraid I didn't spend very much time participating in sports, but I kept myself in pretty good shape."

"What do your friends call you?"

"Paul, sir."

"Fine, Paul. I'm going to outline the program that we'll be following during our stay here. Our training will be carried out in two phases. During the first phase, our men will be trained exclusively by the officers and men of the first battalion. During this period, all our officers, including me, will be put through intensive training, drill, other related subjects. Major Roger Harcourt, our 2 I/C, is responsible for carrying out the program. When I decide our officers have reached a satisfactory standard, we will take over command of our men from the first and carry on from there. It's the responsibility of each officer to train as diligently as possible for the job ahead.

"I'm warning you now, as I have warned and will warn every officer under my command, slackers will not be tolerated! I intend to keep only the best. Changing from civilian to military life is difficult at the best of times—it will be more difficult in our situation because we have so little time. My experience has taught me good officers save lives. Any questions Anderson?"

"No, sir, I don't think so—well, perhaps one. Will we have an opportunity to see our families?"

Graves smiled to himself. "Oh, yes. The weekends will be short, of course. We've been working Saturdays and Sundays. But as the training progresses, I intend to dispense with Saturday afternoon and Sunday sessions. Any other questions?"

"No, sir."

"Well, good night, Paul, and good luck. We'll be seeing a lot of each other during the next few months. Our course will start as soon as the rest of the officers arrive, which should be by the end of the first week in September. In the meantime, the adjutant will see to it that you're kept busy."

"I'm sure he will, sir," Paul replied sarcastically.

Graves looked up quickly and said curtly, "Captain Smythe knows his job, Anderson, and you'd be well advised to learn what you can about soldiering from him."

The two weeks that followed passed with excruciating slowness for Anderson. Fortunately for him, his growing friendship with Carr-Wilson made up for the friction that had grown between Smythe and himself. He admitted ruefully to Monty one afternoon, "Teabags may not be the most pleasant guy in the world. I have to agree with the old man—he certainly knows his job!"

Late one evening, as he was writing his daily letter to Barbara, he suddenly threw down his pen in a fit of temper. Rising quickly from this chair, he put on his tie and jacket, left the quarters, and walked across the broad lawn toward the officers' mess.

"I can't take this any longer," he muttered to himself. "I'm going to call Babs and ask her to come up here for the weekend."

Paul waited impatiently in the stifling telephone booth as the long-distance operator kept ringing his apartment.

"Surely she can't be out at this hour," he grumbled, looking at his watch, noting that it was after midnight.

As he was about to the cancel the call, he heard his wife's voice.

Barbara Anderson's body and mind became tense when the operator's impersonal voice identified the source of her late call. Before speaking, Barbara, a picture of desire in her form-clinging nightgown, frantically signaled "Quiet!" to a handsome dark figure laughing insolently and standing in her bedroom doorway. Then casually, she said a throaty "hello" to her eagerly awaiting husband.

"Why, this a surprise, Paul, dear. I was sound asleep when you called."

"I'm terribly sorry to have awakened you, darling, but I just had to hear your voice."

"Silly! I don't mind in the least," she replied, concealing her annoyance. "Is everything all right?"

"Well, yes—I just have to see you this weekend, dearest."

Barbara paused for a moment before replying, looking intently across the room toward her closed bedroom door.

"I don't know how I could possibly manage it, Paul. I promised Mother that—"

"I just have to see you, dear, but if you don't want to come, I suppose there isn't much I can do about it."

"Now you know very well that I want to see you. I'll come up this weekend. Do you have any idea of the connections?"

"That will be wonderful, Babs. If you catch the midnight train out of Toronto on Friday night, you should arrive here at the camp by noon on Saturday. I'll arrange a room for us in town."

At this point, the conversation was interrupted by the operator's voice. "Three minutes are up, sir."

"I'd better say good night now, darling. I haven't any change left."

"Good night, Paul."

Later, climbing into bed, he looked lovingly at his wife's picture, saying softly, "Good night, my darling. We'll soon be in each other's arms and end this terrible loneliness."

He then turned off his reading lamp, falling into a deep contented sleep.

Chapter 3

Mike

Michael Reardon, picking his way through the crowded tables of the hotel's dimly lit cocktail lounge, finally located an unoccupied table and settled his stocky frame into one of the chairs, sighing wearily as he did so, beckoning to a red-jacketed waiter serving a nearby table. The deeply tanned uniformed army lieutenant ordered a double rye on ice and lit a cigarette, stifling a jaw-cracking yawn.

"Damn those guys," he cursed softly. *A fine deal, they get the so-called guest of honor loaded, letting the poor bastard pass out. Can't blame them, I guess, done the same thing myself many times. Should have known better, I suppose. Must have been a hell of a fine party. Sure can't remember much about it,* he mused and began to chuckling out loud, recalling the astonished looks on the faces of some of the regular force officers on learning he, a lowly reserve army lieutenant, selected for the Special Force.

"That made their bloody mustaches twitch." He laughed.

After ordering his second drink, he was speculatively looking over the women sitting in his vicinity. "Good lord, what an optimist! Here I am with a paralyzing hangover, having to catch a train in two hours, yet I'm still damn fool enough to look around for a doll on the make! Mike, my boy, you're not well."

Reardon let his mind wander to his wife, Janice, and their constant battling over her mother's interference in their marriage.

Maybe we shouldn't have broken up, he mused. *I might not have flunked my year if we'd stayed together. Oh well, it's too late to worry about that now.*

His reverie was broken by the waiter. "Ready for another, sir?"

"Yeah, sure . . . Thanks."

After the waiter had returned with his drink, Mike raised his glass in a mock toast, philosophizing for the benefit of the startled occupants at the adjacent tables, "Booze may not be the answer to life's problems, but it sure as hell helps."

Reardon now watched a tastefully dressed, tall, lithe young woman wend her way carefully through the maze of tables. In spite of the smoky atmosphere, subdued lighting, it was apparent she was beautiful; he was fascinated by the almost feline grace with which she moved.

As she approached, his alerted senses whispered to him, *"Mike, you're in luck! She's going to sit down right beside you."*

He began to tingle with sensuous anticipation as she moved uncertainly toward his table, obviously looking for a place to sit. For a brief moment, he was afraid that the statuesque blonde beauty was going to pass him by; much to his relief, she stopped, asking in a throaty well-modulated voice, "Do you mind if I sit at your table? All the others seem to be occupied."

Mike stood up quickly, butted his cigarette, replying eagerly, "Of course, my pleasure." As he seated his attractive companion, he added, "I was thinking just before you arrived how lonely one can feel in a crowd . . . Cigarette?"

Hesitating a moment, she accepted one of Mike's proffered cigarettes, but when he offered to buy her a drink, she replied coolly, "No, thank you. I'll order my own."

Mike flushed and stammered, "I'm truly sorry—I meant no offense. I seem to be doing this badly, don't I?" Standing up and making an exaggerated bow, he continued, "Permit me to introduce myself. My name is Mike Reardon. I'm a native of this fair city, and I'm on my way to join the Royals Regiment second battalion, one of the outfits being recruited for Korea."

"Oh, then you've volunteered for Korea too?" Reardon's beautiful companion commented, her interest aroused. On seeing the perplexed look on Mike's face, she said, laughing, "Pleasure, excuse me, but you see, my husband is serving in the Royals. In fact, I'm on my way to see him. Perhaps you've met? His name is Paul Anderson."

"No, I'm afraid I've never had the pleasure. Incidentally, would you mind telling me your name? By very keen deduction, I've concluded your last name is Anderson."

"How very clever of you, Mr. Reardon. It's Barbara." She smiled, offering Mike her gloved hand.

"Now that we've been introduced after a fashion, will you let me order a drink for you?"

Laughing good-naturedly, she accepted, saying, "Well, I suppose I can't refuse now."

Chapter 4

Weekend Reunion

Barbara Anderson was tired, completely bored, finding the train trip from Hamilton uncomfortably hot, irritated by the creases the hard benches in the station made in her flattering white suit. Paul's wife thoroughly regretted her decision to make the long tiring trip, spending the weekend with her insistent husband; the prospect of an uncomfortable sleepless night in a train berth depressed her. She pretended not to notice the admiring glances of two men seated on the bench opposite her; Barbara's only acknowledgement of their obvious stares was to casually lower the hem of her skirt after carefully crossing her shapely legs. As she listlessly turned over the pages of a fashion magazine, her thoughts went to Paul.

Barbara was in her last year of university when she met Paul at a Christmas party, attracted immediately to the handsome young man standing alone in a corner of the room nursing a drink. After their first meeting, she thought that Paul was the most intelligent man she had ever known. His idealism, his love of the arts, his burning desire to explore the human conscience so completely captured her young imagination. After knowing him for only a few months, she decided to become part of his dream. Ignoring her parents' protests, she married Paul immediately after their graduation. For a few months, they lived an idyllic existence, and then the dream began to shatter. Much to her annoyance, Barbara discovered intellectuals have a limited commercial value in the business world; in addition, the thin intellectual veneer she had so carefully cultivated at the university soon wore thin in the face of financial insecurity. Paul's wife had come from a very comfortable home, unaccustomed to scrimping and saving to make ends meet. She had felt humiliated at the thought of her intelligent husband working for a small downtown business, angry at this stubborn refusal to accept a position with her father's firm. She began to shun his friends, imagining that they thought her frivolous, insincere, and mentally inferior. She begged him to give up his ambition to teach at a university and to concentrate on earning a better living for them by working for her father. Barbara felt pangs of remorse as she recalled ridiculing Paul in front of her friends, even to the extent of questioning his manhood. In her heart, she knew that it was to prove himself to her, he gave up everything joining the Special Force. Of course, there was Craig, her father's young legal advisor— handsome, unscrupulous, more than willing to provide his own particular brand of diversion for her. She flushed with embarrassment as she recalled Craig's presence in her apartment the night Paul telephoned.

Barbara closed her magazine and tossed it on the bench beside her, deciding to spend the two hours that still remained before her train was due to leave in the cocktail lounge located across the street. She rationalized that a cocktail or two might help ease the discomfort of the all-night train ride.

When she entered the crowded smoke-filled lounge, she felt a wave of annoyance sweep over her, looking vainly for a vacant table. Thinking she spotted one across the thickly carpeted room, she threaded her way toward it through the closely packed crowd; she was too late. About to retrace her steps and leave, she saw a darkly attractive deeply tanned army officer sitting alone at the next table.

On impulse, she asked, "Do you mind if I sit at your table? All the others seem to be occupied . . ."

Barbara slowly sipped her drink and coolly appraised the broad-shouldered, beribboned young officer sitting opposite her. She was amused by his obvious attempts to impress her, couldn't suppress a feeling of sensual excitement, Michael Reardon's nearness awakened in her, deciding he was a passionate man, his full lips framed his strong white teeth, his green eyes exhibited a smoldering quality as he openly admired her.

"Definitely an interesting type but so damn sure of himself," she concluded.

One drink later, he was busy telling Barbara the story of his broken marriage.

"Our big mistake was marrying too young. It was stupid for a guy, nineteen, and a girl, eighteen, to think they were made for each other. Everything was great the first year. Then one thing led to another until finally—bang! And it was all over. Mind you, Janice is a nice kid. Nevertheless, when I look back on the whole mess, I realize it was a big mistake," Reardon mused, looking alternately from this glass to Barbara's face then back to his glass again.

"Waiter! Two more of the same, please."

"No, Mike, I really shouldn't . . . Well, just one more then."

"At first, I thought Janice was jealous of my going to university when she had to work, but I soon found out it was more than that. We just didn't click anymore. I guess the right term for it is incompatibility."

"You're not the only one with that problem," she said impulsively.

"Are you speaking from experience, Barbara?"

"Oh no, I wasn't thinking of myself. As a matter of fact, some friends of mine are faced with a similar situation," she replied lamely, regretting her comment.

"Yes, I see . . . Well, enough of my trials and tribulations. The important thing is that I am fortunate enough to meet a very lovely lady. Therefore, I shall bury the past and concentrate on the very pleasant present. I really must congratulate your husband on his excellent taste, Mrs. Anderson. You are without a doubt the most beautiful woman in this establishment, if not in the entire city."

"Why, Mr. Reardon, either you've had too much to drink or else you're a shameless flatterer."

"Neither, lovely lady, I'm merely expressing what I am sure is the opinion of every man who has been fortunate enough to meet you. I could be trite and say our meeting is more than coincidence, perhaps the fates have intervened on our behalf."

"I suppose you could, but it wouldn't be exactly true now, would it? After all, there weren't that many seats. I'm sure that fate had nothing to do with it."

"Don't shatter me, Barbara. Let me enjoy the illusion of romance we've created!"

"That you've created, you mean. Your approach isn't very original, but it sounds rather nice coming from you. Say, I'm beginning to think I've already had too much to drink. Are you sure that my last drink was a single? You wouldn't be trying to take advantage of a young lady in a strange town, would you, Mr. Reardon?"

"Oh yes, I'm a bad one. I always prime my women with alcohol before I seduce them. It's the secret of my charm."

"There's probably more truth in what you're saying than you'd care to admit."

"What a thing to say, Barbara! I don't believe you'll have to worry about me. I seem to remember an expression that the talkers are seldom the doers."

"That may be true, I don't think I'll take any chances where you're concerned," she countered, laughing.

"My dear, you are perfectly safe with me. I shall be the epitome of gentlemanly behavior."

"Good heavens, Mike! It's nearly midnight. I haven't confirmed my berth yet. I really must go. It's been very nice meeting you. Goodbye."

"Look, Barbara, since we're taking the same train, why not let me confirm your berth for you? Besides, I'll gladly volunteer my services as the best redcap in town."

"That won't be necessary, Mike. I only have an overnight case with me. Besides, I doubt if you could ever find the locker."

"Try me, lady, just try me!"

"Oh, very well, Sir Lancelot, I'll let you be my knight in shining armor."

After they left the lounge, Barbara instinctively took Mike's arm as he led her through the marble-lined subway tunnel connecting the hotel with the station. Their footsteps and easy laughter echoed down the long corridor. On reaching the passenger waiting room, Paul's wife handed her locker key and berth ticket to Mike, who left to confirm her reservation and pick up her overnight case. Mike was in luck. Barbara's sleeping car was nearly empty, and the cooperative porter willingly changed Reardon's berth for one located directly across the aisle from that of the striking Hamilton beauty.

"These things just don't happen," he murmured happily to himself, striding back to the waiting room.

Barbara looked archly at Mike when he told her of the amazing coincidence of their being berthed in the same car. To his great relief, she agreed it was indeed a coincidence, added, smiling, "You seem to be a man of many coincidences, Mr. Reardon!"

There were only four other berths occupied in their car, their curtains drawn. As Barbara and Mike said good night, their hands touching briefly, their eyes met.

Later, when the train had jerked to a shuddering start, Mike lay awake in his berth, his body taut, and every nerve seemed violently alive. His mounting excitement almost choked him as he heard Barbara return from the washroom, climbing into her berth. When all was dark and quiet, he silently opened his curtain, took a deep breath, saying to himself, "Well, here goes nothing!"

"Barbara . . . Barbara," he whispered hoarsely.

He seemed to wait an eternity, about to give up, when Barbara's curtain parted slightly, and her voice answered huskily from within, "Yes, Mike?"

Reardon quickly stepped across the aisle and climbed into Barbara's berth, closing the curtains after him. All was quiet, except for the throbbing vibration of the train, lurching through the night.

Paul Anderson was pacing impatiently up and down the station platform as the train whistled its way around the final bend, thundering into view. The engine, belching steam and smoke, braked its shuddering coaches to a squealing stop. Paul half walked, half ran to the two passenger coaches in the rear. Seeing his wife more radiantly beautiful than ever, he barely noticed the uniformed figure descending the steps behind, carrying her bag.

"Thank heaven you're here, Babs!" Paul blurted breathlessly, crushing his wife in his eager arms. "I thought your train would never come."

Paul was hurt as he felt his wife stiffen in his embrace. "Paul, stop it! People are looking at us. Careful . . . Oh, Paul, you're creasing my suit."

It was then Anderson noticed the broad-shouldered figure of Mike standing uncomfortably behind his wife.

"Paul, dear, I'd like you to meet Mike Reardon," she said quickly. As the two men reluctantly shook hands, she continued, "I met Mike on the train this morning. He's been ever so friendly and helpful."

Paul brightened perceptibly, his twinge of jealousy gone. "That was very nice of you, Mike, I certainly appreciate it. I have a taxi waiting to take us to the hotel in town. Can we give you a lift anywhere?"

"No, thanks," Mike replied, forcing himself to smile pleasantly.

"We'll undoubtedly be seeing a lot of each other at any rate, so thanks again for helping my wife."

"Yes, Mike . . . Thanks for everything!" Barbara softly added, offering him her hand, her face expressionless, except for a smoldering look in her eyes.

Reardon watched the attractive couple walk arm in arm toward their waiting taxi, an amused smile creased his face. He turned his head away.

"Poor bastard!" he exclaimed to himself, turning around, giving the Andersons a parting look. "You're rotten, Reardon, rotten to the core . . . but so damn lucky!"

CHAPTER 5

The Men

"I can't understand, Bruce, why you be so determined to go against your own father by joining the army to fight a bunch of yellow-skinned heathens!" Mrs. Ida Mackenzie, a short dumpy woman in her late forties, shouted angrily at her tall angular youngest son. "After all your father has done for you, doing without to put you through school, speaking for you so you'd get taken on at the mine!" she continued in her Scots burr.

Mrs. Mackenzie was about to continue her tirade against the grey-eyed youth sitting, brooding in the corner of the kitchen, running his strong fingers through his thick black wavy hair. He suddenly raised his downcast eyes and said bitterly, "That's real good, Ma. Sure, that's really good! I'm supposed to spend the rest of my life in the pit just because I'm the only one left at home, and Pa wants me to work in the mine with him. Well, it may be good enough for him, it's not good enough for me! Look, Ma. I'm nineteen years old and, what have I ever seen besides Glace Bay, Halifax, and one trip to Fredericton five years ago? You didn't try to stop Jock when he joined up last wart."

"Aye, son. But if we had, he might still be alive today. It was different then, it was the thing to do, for you to run off with the chance that you might get yourself killed fighting the—"

"I'm sorry, Ma, I've made up my mind, and that is that. I'm going to Halifax this afternoon to enlist."

"Surely you'll wait till your father comes home, telling him of this terrible thing? What will he say? What will—"

"No! I won't wait to tell Pa, you know very well what would happen if I did. Ma, please stop crying! A man has to do what he thinks is right. There'll be only a lot of harsh words if I wait for Pa."

Unable to reason any further with his sobbing mother, he left the kitchen and went to his room to pack.

"Bruce! Oh, Bruce!"

"Yes, Ma?"

"Moira is here to see you."

"Oh. Would you mind coming upstairs, Moira? I'm packing my things."

Moira Campbell, a short pretty girl with deep brown eyes and long chestnut hair, was a friend of the Mackenzie family all her life. She and Bruce had been constant playmates as children. Now seventeen and changing from a slender girl to a full-breasted woman, her feeling for the handsome childhood friend was changing from friendship to love. She ran quickly up the narrow stairs, her shapely sun-browned legs covering the steps two at a time. She stood shyly, a little breathless, at Bruce's bedroom door, and then he turned around, grinning at her.

"For heaven's sake, don't stand there, Moira. Come in."

"Oh, Bruce! Tell me it isn't true. You're not going to do this foolish thing your mother just told me."

"Yes, I'm afraid I am. In fact, I'm leaving for Halifax this afternoon."

"But you never told me that you were going to join the army. Surely you weren't going away without telling me?"

"No, of course not. I was going to stop by your place before I left."

"But why didn't you tell me before?"

"I couldn't very well, Moira. I didn't make up my mind until last night."

"Then you didn't mean the things you said to me last week?"

"Of course, I did. When I said you're the sweetest, most wonderful girl I had ever met, I meant it."

"Oh sure. Now you're going away to a lot of strange places, among a lot of strangers. You won't ever think of me!"

"Don't be so daft. Of course, I'll be thinking of you. I'm only joining for eighteen months, not for the rest of my life. Then when I get back, I'm sure that I'll be ready to settle down like the others did after the war."

"Will you write to me, Bruce, and let me know how you are?"

"You know darn well that I will, but you must write me too."

"Oh, Bruce, you know I will—every day, if you like."

"Well, you don't have to write every day but regularly, mind you."

The young couple talked through the next half hour, sometimes of the past, sometimes of the future, carefully avoiding the present.

"I must be going now, or else, I'll be late. Well, goodbye for now, Moira. I'll write just as soon as I can."

"Goodbye, Brucie, dearest!"

Moira threw her arms around Mackenzie's neck and kissed him passionately, her eyes were brimming with tears, clinging tightly to him. As they reluctantly broke their embrace, looking wordlessly into each other's eyes, they knew they were in love.

The weight of young Mackenzie's troubled conscience began to lighten as the mileage between his family and himself increased. He had been deeply hurt by his father's refusal to speak to him when he had telephoned home to say goodbye. To make matters worse, both his mother and Moira had cried during the three minutes he had tried to speak to them, but his youth and burning desire to see the world soon supplanted his guilty feeling. He was understandably excited at the prospect of seeing places and people whose only reality had been in the pages of an outdated geography text, recalling with a smile how openmouthed he had been listening to the fabulous stories the last war vets, working at the mine, had told of their experiences. Now he was going to be on equal terms with them, no longer just as envious kid.

I might not see Paris or Rome or places like that, but what's wrong with Japan and Korea? None of the guys in the mine were ever in the Far East, he thought smugly.

Bruce's seat companion was a stocky barrel-chested grizzled fellow Cape Bretoner, who had joined the twenty-man draft just as the Montreal-bound train started pulling out of the station. Although not drunk, the brawny islander, reeking of booze, wasn't much company for Mackenzie at first, spending the first few hours of the trip sleeping. Finally, awakening with a prodigious yawn, he immediately struck up a conversation with his younger companion.

"I hope you're not minding my stink, lad, I was partying at the Legion last night with some of me old buddies from the Cape Breton Highlanders, and I ain't had no chance to clean up. It's a pity they ain't forming my old outfit, we was a real fighting outfit. Let me tell you, we sure as hell scared the blazes out of the Jerries more than once. My name be McHaskell, Jock McHaskell. I be known as the big Scotsman with an Irishman's name," he growled in a husky, grating voice as he extended a massive gnarled hand in a friendly greeting.

Bruce shook Jock's hand firmly, although he had expected the big man to crush his hand with his vice-like grip.

"My name's Bruce Mackenzie, Jock. I hail from Glace Bay," he replied cordially, lapsing into the idiom of the east coast miner. "My brother served with the Cape Bretoners. He was killed in Germany in '45. His name was Jock too. Did you ever run across him?"

McHaskell thoughtfully scratched his grey-streaked close-cropped head before replying in a somewhat gentler tone, "Sorry, bucko. I don't have no recollection of him. We had so many lads clobbered in '45—in fact, I even got shot up myself. No, I can't recall the name. He must have been a good man and pleased I am to meet the brother of a fighting highlander."

After telling Bruce about some of his Second World War experiences, which usually finished by Jock doing all the work and someone else getting the credit, he began telling this intrigued Nova Scotian about his postwar life.

"I was doin' pretty good for a while until I took up with this here woman that run the boarding house I was livin' in. The lyin' tart told me her husband had run off and there would be no trouble. Not that I blamed him, mind you, she had a face like a can o' worms, but she was pretty good company that first winter. It was almost like being married. Then the trouble come. First, I catches her in bed with a bloody sailor, but that wasn't too bad. Then her old man came home—that was bad! Keerist, what a fight we had! 'Course, it was me got thrown in the digger 'cause he was her husband and I was the guy that had broken up their happy home, or so they said at the courthouse. From then on, me boy, Jock McHaskell no longer prospered—aye, I fell on bad days. Never take a drink, Brucie, me boy. It's been the ruin of many a good man, not to mention women," he added with a leer.

"Mind you, now, I'm not an alky—I drink only the odd time, which means whenever I get the bloody chance," laughing, punching Bruce soundly on the back.

Mackenzie quickly concluded that the most beautiful women in the world lived in Montreal. As he stood in the middle of the new station, he found it impossible not to stare at the numerous shapely women seemingly filling the crowded terminal; one of the girls he was staring at caught his glance, returned it with a friendly smile, and he flushed deeply with embarrassment.

"The girls in Glace Bay would never do that, not the nice ones, anyway. Imagine Moira smiling at a stranger like that girl did!"

To his surprise, the thought of Moira smiling at anyone else, stranger or not, caused him an unaccustomed twinge of jealousy, promising himself he would write to her just as soon as he arrived at the military camp. Bruce, along with the other members of the east coast contingent, were waiting the arrival of the Montreal draft of Special Force recruits; the two groups were to be combined and transported to the Royals' camp by a special train. After their conducting officer met with the local movement control officer, he informed his draft that they had three hours "to kill" before train time but were to stay in the immediate vicinity of the station. Jock was enthusiastically in favor of following a somewhat different course.

"Hey, Brucie, let's you and me pick up a couple of those luscious lassies, get a bottle, and shack up for a few days."

"You must be crazy to think of a crazy stunt like that, Jock. You'd never get away with it!"

"Aye, me bucko, we'd have ourselves a real time, they wouldn't be too hard on us the first time."

"No, Jock. Count me out. I've got a nice girl at home. Besides, I haven't got the kind money you need for that kind of operation. I'm quite sure you don't either."

"You're a hell of a friend to let me down at a time like this. Oh look, Brucie, over there in the corner, ain't they the most beautiful creatures God ever made? That big dark-haired one is for me! Come on, Brucie?"

"Sorry, Jock, no!"

"Gawd, it's a crying shame to pass up beautiful stuff like that there. Look, kid, couldn't you let me have just a few . . . ?"

"Can't you wait for a weekend, Jock? You're in no condition to get chasing women now, and you'd only get yourself into a lot of trouble."

"Will you come and have a beer with me then?" McHaskell persisted.

"No harm in a beer, I guess, but I don't feel like one right now. Okay, here's a few dollars, don't miss the train. We only have about two and a half hours before we leave, be sure you get back in time."

"On my honor, Brucie. After all, a man can't get into too much trouble on a few measly bucks, but don't get me wrong, I ain't complaining. Thanks, kid!"

"Remember what the conducting officer said, Jock. We're under military discipline now."

"I heard him, I heard him. Would you mind looking after me kit bag until I get back?"

After leaving Mackenzie, the thirsty Cape Bretoner rushed out of the station, heading for the nearest tavern.

Sitting at a corner table in a dirty run-down tavern located a few blocks from the terminal, two men were having a heated beer-punctuated argument over the relative merits of their Second World War infantry units, obvious from their conversation they were Special Force volunteers filling in time before their train was due to leave for their training base. The taller older member of the arguing duo, his face and neck flushed a deep red from both beer and temper, was speaking loudly to his heavyset dark companion when McHaskell spotted them and headed for their bottle-crowded table.

"Look, Blackie, why in hell won't you admit it? Your outfit spent most of the bloody war in reserve. We had three times the casualties you guys did. Ain't that so?"

"So what, Curt? What in hell does casualties prove anyways? Just because you had a crummy bunch of officers and chicken-livered NCOs letting you poor clots get butchered doesn't mean you saw more action than anyone else. Why, you had a whole damn company captured lock, stock, and barrel just because one of your damn fool company commanders couldn't read a map, leading D, his company, smack bang into the Jerry lines. Ain't that so?"

Jock stood by for a few minutes unnoticed, listening to the argument; then unable to contain himself any longer, he pulled up a chair and interjected good-naturedly, "Hell! You guys don't know what you're taking about. Why, the Cape Breton Highlanders saw more action than the rest of the Canadian Army put together."

Startled, the two men looked up at the unwelcomed intruder. They were about to tell McHaskell to shove off and mind his own business when, with perfect timing and an ingratiating smile, he ordered a round from a nearby waiter, sitting down, saying, "Come off it, you guys. Ain't no use fightin' the last war again when the time can be spent better drinkin'. My name's McHaskell—me friends call me Jock."

Curt was first to reply. "I'm George Curtin, Curt to most people. This here is Blackie Balaski."

The three men shook hands congenially, started rehashing the Normandy campaign, agreeing fighting the North Koreans would be a "piece of cake" after their experiences with the Germans in Europe. Once again, the discussion between Curt and Blackie threatened to explode.

Curtin, pushing back his chair violently, jumped to his feet, shouting, "Okay, you SOB! I'll show you how to fight!"

Blackie jumped up kicking his chair over, ready to accept the challenge. Suddenly, he felt himself clutched by one of Jock's powerful hands. McHaskell's other hand simultaneously grabbed one of Curt's arms in a paralyzing grip.

"Come, come, now—this ain't no time for fighting! Let's bottoms up and change the subject or I'll hammer the hell out of both of ye. Waiter, another round for me friends!"

Blackie had tried a number of jobs after his discharge from the army in 1945 but without success, his lack of education, refusal to take a rehabilitation trades course, forcing him to return to his prewar occupation as a laborer. He never married, not remaining in one location long enough to carry out a courtship. His main outlets consisted of picking up prostitutes, getting drunk on pay nights. His failure, developing some form of stability during the years following the war, made him bitter, querulous, and argumentative. Not wanting particularly to join the Special Force, it was a way to escape his unpleasant existence.

Curtin's problem of postwar adjustment had been impossible from the start. During the war, becoming a confirmed alcoholic, he returned home to his wife and family unable to master his overpowering craving for drink; his pitiful weakness not only cost him numerous jobs but also his wife and daughters. He was on the verge of becoming a permanent inhabitant of Montreal's skid row when the Korean crisis occurred. Fortunately for him, he was able to stay sober long enough to pass the sketchy medical examination given to the Special Force recruits at the height of the enlistment period.

Curtin was looking hazily at the figures of his two companions, his jaw slack, his eyes bloodshot. He was feeling good, really good. "Just like the old days again," he mumbled to himself. "Friends, comradeship, that's the answer, comradeship. I'll beat the bloody booze, just wait and see. I'll show Mary and the kids, I'll get in good shape and give up the damn stuff, they'll come back. Then I'll make them proud of me."

"You saying something, Curt?"

"Naw, Blackie," Curt said, hiccupping, raising his head slowly from the sopping table then dropping it hard into a pool of stale beer. "You got the time, Blackie?"

"I ain't got no watch—damn thing's in hock. Hey, Curt! Get your head up, it's time to go."

Jock checked the time with one of the waiters then suggested, "Come on, you guys, time to shove off. We've got just enough time to buy some grape and make the train. Hey, Blackie! Give me a hand with this clown."

Bruce Mackenzie was becoming increasingly worried at Jock's absence as he anxiously scanned the crowds of people entering the station.

"The other guys are starting to form up already, and Jock isn't here yet, Bernie," he said nervously to the short stocky youth standing beside him. "I knew it was a mistake to lend him money—it'll be my fault if he misses the train."

"McHaskell is a grown man. You can't hold yourself responsible for his actions. Besides, he won't be able to do much on a few bucks in this city, that's for sure," the Second Royals' recruit from Montreal commented, smiling.

"I hope you're right. In any case, we'd better get a move on. They're starting to call the roll."

"Hey, Brucie, me boy . . . Wait for me!"

Startled by the booming shout that reverberated across the wide station, Mackenzie quickly turned, relieved to see Jock elbowing his way through the crowd carrying a paper bag in one hand, supporting a very drunk-looking individual with the other. Following behind, completing the incongruous picture, was the forlorn figure of Blackie dragging two large kit bags across the station floor.

After boarding the train, it didn't take Jock long to sample the contents from his precious paper bag, Mackenzie trying unavailingly talk him into putting the bottle away, getting some sleep.

"Never mind worryin' about old Jock, Brucie boy, I be perfectly capable of looking' after meself. No, now, don't frown so, have a drink on, Old Jock."

"No, thanks . . . Take it easy, will you? At least keep the damn bottle out of sight, or else, you'll get all of us in trouble."

"Well, me bucko, if that be your attitude, I'll be joining me friends in the rear," he replied, miffed at Bruce's refusal to drink with him.

McHaskell left the seat, joining his two drinking cronies sitting at the back of the coach. Unfortunately for the booze-saturated trio, the drinking didn't end with the end of Jock's bottle; Curt had hidden two bottles of cheap wine in his kit bag for just such an emergency.

All might still have gone well for the three celebrants, except for two unfortunate incidents occurring on their arrival at the Royals' camp. Blackie and Curt passed out; Jock, tottering, still on his feet, decided that it would be hospitable for him to offer the smartly dressed captain standing on the station platform a swig from his bottle. Jock, Curt, and Blackie had the dubious distinction of being the first members of the Second Royals to be thrown into the camp jail, an experience soon sobering them up.

Chapter 6

Training Accident

Mackenzie, McHaskell, and Balaski soon adjusted to the rugged training schedule imposed on them by the demanding hard-nosed instructors from the first battalion. It was Curtin who was having the most difficulty adapting himself to the rigorous routine, drinking heavily. Surprising his three friends, he suddenly stopped drinking. The following weeks passed very quickly, Mackenzie proving to be a natural soldier, having a consuming interest in learning, a tireless capacity for work, benefiting from his friends' previous military experience, the knowledge of his instructors; he became the first of the younger soldiers to be promoted. Although Jock and Blackie kidded the young Nova Scotian unmercifully about his new whitened lance corporal's stripes, they were very proud of their young protégé, not resentful for having no desire to be responsible for anyone else besides themselves. It was Curtin who was embittered by Mackenzie's promotion, badly wanting the same recognition for the sake of his self-esteem.

Resting on their bunks after a particularly hard day, the members of Mackenzie's nine-man section were gently nursing their swollen feet.

"Look at these goddamn blisters!" Jock cursed, pointing to two large fluid-filled sacs cushioning the bottom of the toes of his right foot. "I swear by all that's holy if that SOB of a first battalion sergeant yells at me once more, I'll punch him right in the head, throw my bloody rifle away, and soldier no more," he growled.

"You wouldn't have blisters if you'd take the trouble to mend your socks."

"Well, listen to God's gift to the Canadian Army! Our own Lance Corporal Mackenzie giving me, Jock McHaskell, the good word on how to take care of me feet! My god, man, it was me that taught you all you know."

"You can stop right there, Jock. I was only trying to be helpful. Sure, you gave me the word on how to prevent blisters, but why in hell don't you follow your own advice?"

"I'm sorry, Brucie, me boy. No need of me taking me sore feet out on you. It ain't you that's pushing us around, and that's for sure. Wouldn't be so bad if that damn parade square didn't get so blasting hot. How's your feet, Blackie?"

"No blisters but they're as sore as hell. Say, did you see that little jerk of a PT instructor running the butts of the officers? I thought I'd split a gut at the way some of them was heaving. Some of those officers look in pretty rotten shape to me. There's one young guy there, though, I hope we don't get for a platoon officer. Keerist, he was running along like it was nothing. I think his name is Riendeau or Reardan, something like that, anyways."

"I hate athletic officers—they're always trying to show you what tough guys they are," one of the other members of the section commented.

"What's the deal for tomorrow, Bruce?" Blackie asked, yawning.

"Let me see . . . second platoon ranges all day."

"What time are the trucks picking us up?" Blackie continued.

"No trucks, my boy. We ride on our fat feet in full marching order, and then we pad our way back."

"Oh no, not again!" the men chorused.

During the verbal bantering between the members of Mackenzie's section, Curtin, the only one to remain quiet, found each succeeding day increasingly hard to bear. The combination of tough physical work and his constant fight against the bottle was slowly crushing his weakening spirit. When he heard Bruce announce they would be marching the six long miles to the ranges, the last remnants of his overstrained willpower gave out. He painfully put on his boots without a word and left the barracks, heading for the men's wet canteen.

Nearly two hours had passed before Curtin's absence was noticed by his friends.

"Anyone see Curtis?" Jock questioned loudly.

"Saw him leave a couple of hours ago," Bernie Viau replied, looking up from the arduous task of cleaning his webbing.

"Come on, Blackie, we'd better find him. He ain't been himself lately."

"Aw, he's okay, Jock. He's probably taking in a show or something like that."

"One gets you three we'll find him in the wets."

"Get off it, Jock! You know damn well that Curt's off the booze so he can get straightened out with his wife."

"Blackie, me boy, once a lush, always a lush. After all, I oughta know." Jock chuckled then became serious once again. "Come on, Blackie, let's go."

Wearily, the two men put on their boots and went in search of their comrade. Entering the smoke-filled confines of the wet canteen, they spotted Curtin sitting alone in a far corner, obviously very drunk.

Finally seeing them walking through the haze of smoke, he shouted, belching loudly, "Hey, you guys, come over here, the drinks are on me!"

"Keerist, has he ever got a load on!" Blackie snapped at Jock.

"Yeah! We'd better get over there and keep him out of trouble—the joint's crawling with first-battalion types. Look at all them blasted maroon berets!"

Sitting down with their friend, it did not take them long to discover Curtin's bitter mood.

"The rotten army stinks, and the bloody Royals stink the worst!" Curt snarled loudly.

"Lord Jesus, man, cut it out! Do you want us to get our fool heads knocked off?" Jock hissed.

"I don't give a damn about those red-hated bastards. They sure as hell don't worry me. I can lick the whole bloody bunch by myself."

"Don't be such a damn fool! Sit down, Curt," Blackie demanded as Jock grabbed one of Curt's arms.

"Let me go, damn you! I know what the two of you are thinking—you think that it's the booze in me doing the talking. Well, I'll show you!"

Before either Jock or Blackie could stop him, Curtin broke free of McHaskell's grasp, lurching over to a table crowded with First Royals. He stopped a few feet from them. The room became quiet, tense. Addressing the hostile upturned faces before him, he shouted in a loud sarcastic voice, "You guys hire civilians to cook for you, clean up your rotten camp, fix up your crummy buildings—why, you even had to hire a bunch of civilians to do your goddamn fighting!"

That tore it to the man, the angered firsts threw back their chairs, rushing toward the startled seconds. True to his promise, Curtin, trying to fight the entire group, was quickly laid low by a single vicious punch. Without a moment's hesitation, Jock and Blackie were on their feet, driving into the center of the mêlée to retrieve the unconscious body of their friend, rolling him under a corner table, joining the fight. The greatly outnumbered members of the second battalion were taking a terrific beating. Soon, the fight centered on Jock and Blackie, separated from the main group by nearly a dozen opponents. Although McHaskell's massive fists were taking their toll, he was also taking a bad beating. Blood was streaming down his big head, his horny knuckles split and bleeding, his breath coming in painful, hard gasps.

At first, his system worked wonderfully; he would grab a luckless first with one hand, belt him with the other then pass the man's stumbling form over to Blackie who would administer the coup de grace. Blackie suddenly went down, the fight centering on Jock's powerful bearlike figure, still managing a semblance of a smile through his torn bloody lips, gloried in the smashing contact his driving fists were making on the heads, faces and stomachs of his oppressors, spitting at his challengers, defying them to come to him. The men of the 1st believing, if they could beat down this giant standing before them they could win, Jock didn't go down, the fight was broken up, the big Cape Bretoner became a legend of fighting courage among the members of both battalions.

The night of the fight proved to be Curtin's last in the Royals. Unable any longer to stand the killing pace of the training, he quietly disappeared from camp never to return. Jock was not surprised at his friend's desertion. He, more than the others, appreciated the painful struggle Curtin had put up, thought none the less of his friend for his failure.

In the middle of October, the brigade commander authorized a four day embarkation leave, allowing the members of the Special Force to visit their homes before proceeding to the United States to complete their training. Most of the members of the Second Royals, including Mackenzie, utilized the leave to visit their families; a few, including Jock and Blackie, deciding to spend their four days in Montreal. McHaskell and Balaski, pictures of eager anticipation, arrived in Montreal's Union Station. Their black boots gleamed with a mirrorlike finish, their khaki-colored battle dress uniforms were cleaned and pressed to military perfection, their jackets emblazoned with their Second World War campaign ribbons, the striking scarlet, gold, and white Special Force shields neatly sewn on the shoulders of their battle dress jackets. Swinging their small packs over their shoulders, they happily headed downtown.

Mackenzie was in high spirits when he returned to camp after finishing his leave. It had been a wonderful four days for the young maritimer; his proud parents were fully reconciled to their son's enlistment, and he had become engaged to Moira. Bruce, whistling, entering his barrack block, was surprised seeing the dejected figure of Jock sitting hunched over the edge of his bunk, staring fixedly at the floor.

"Hey, Jock, you fall in love or something during your leave? I don't think I've ever seen you look this brassed off," Bruce said laughingly.

"I'll thank ye to mind your own damn business, me bucko . . . And you can take that damn smirk off your face too!"

"That's a fine way to greet a friend, Jock. I meant no offense."

"I'm sorry I bit your back, Bruce, I had me a rough go in that bloody Montreal."

"It must have been bad to make you so damn bitter. What happened?"

"Well, I'll tell you, Brucie boy, but don't you go telling no one else for I be mortified enough as it is."

"Of course, I won't tell anyone else, Jock, you know that."

"It all started the first night. Me and Blackie decided to get primed up, pick up a couple of women, and then take them back to the hotel. Blackie, damn his soul, talked me into visitin' one of these places where queers hang out. I went along into his here joint on Dorchester Street. We spots these here really good-looking broads. No kidding, Bruce, they was real knockouts! I took what I thought was the best-looking one, took to me right away. Making a long story short, we gets them to the hotel. Me and Blackie had those kind of rooms that share the same bathroom.

"I starts right away to take off my clothes as soon as Blackie and his dame went into his room. My broad don't want to take off her clothes, which made me sore. Well, I finally gets her and started to . . . Well, it turns out that she ain't no broad! Yeah, a goddamn fairy! I punched the SOB in the head and threw him out o' me room. Then I went to give Blackie the word that we'd picked up a couple o' queers. I shouts through the door at him, and to you know what the ungrateful bastard did? He laughed at me and told me it was my tough luck, his was no 'queer,' and to leave him alone because he was busy."

Bruce, having difficulty controlling his laughter, was about to speak when McHaskell cut him off, saying, "And that ain't all! The next night, we goes to a regular joint. I was bloody sore at first, but Blackie bought the drinks, so I cooled off. This time we picked up two real broads, nice French stuff. They talked nice and were dressed real good. They didn't look like no whores. We had us a few drinks and then went to this here place to dance. Brucie, this broad I had making me forget the first night. Well, when we was dancing, I didn't fool around at all, and I asks her right out, 'Do you or don't you?' She gives me that I'm-not-that-sort-of-a-girl routine then says that for a big guy like me, maybe. That was all I needed.

"I said goodbye to Blackie and his dame quick like then takes off with my broad for the hotel. After a while, she says to me that she has a headache and wants to get an aspirin from her purse. She gets up, fixes up a drink for her and me, takes the aspirin, and then hands me my drink. I don't know how she did it, Bruce, but I got slipped a mickey, and I passed right out cold until Blackie gave me a shake the next morning. Yeah, that's right, me, Jock McHaskell, was rolled like a bloody greenhorn! I had enough then, so I came back to camp."

During the early part of November, the Second Royals, now under the command of its own officers, were preparing for the long trip to Fort Lewis, Washington, the advanced training site. The men of second platoon were being kept busy on the small arms-and-mortar ranges most of the time because their platoon commander, Mike Reardon, felt they needed more practice in weapon handling and range practice. Mackenzie's section was busily preparing for an all-day session of rifle firing on the camp's six-hundred-yard range; at the same time, the section's members were discussing their pending trip to the United States.

"There should be multi dames down there. I heard the camp we're going to is right between Tacoma and Seattle," Balaski informed the others with a leer of anticipation.

"That's for sure, and I'm just the bucko to give them a real thrill too."

"Keerist, what a dirty old man you are, McHaskell! Are you sure you'd know a dame when you see one?"

"Damn you, Balaski! I got a good mind to—"

"Dummy up, you guys. Here comes the sergeant," Bruce ordered.

"What's the beef, Corporal?" Sergeant Cross asked.

"Nothing at all, Sergeant. Just the usual thing, women at the new camp."

"No sweat there from what I hear. Some of the boys in the advance party have written back, saying there's more than enough to go 'round and that they're crazy about Canadians."

"That sounds like the place for me! What do you say, Bruce?"

"No use asking him a question like that, Blackie. He's engaged. Why, his girl, she writes him every day," Bernie Viau interjected.

"Incidentally, Mac, program change—we're going on the mortar range instead of the rifle range," Cross informed his youngest section commander.

"After all the bloody trouble we went to getting our rifles ready?" McHaskell complained.

"An old soldier like you should know you should always have your rifle in perfect condition, McHaskell," Cross curtly replied. "Mr. Reardon wasn't satisfied with our last mortar shoot mainly because a few members of your section were slack," he added, looking pointedly at McHaskell.

"What in the hell does Reardon know about what we should do?" Jock muttered under his breath.

"What did you say, McHaskell?"

"Nothin', Sergeant, nothin' at all."

"Then watch your tongue, or else, I'll let you pay your compliments to Lieutenant Reardon yourself," Cross warned the grumbling Cape Bretoner. Turning, he continued speaking to MacKenzie. "Sergeant Murphy of the first battalion mortar platoon will be supervising the shoot. Oh yes, another thing—you're to wear full marching order. Mr. Reardon was very unhappy over your turnout at this morning's inspection. Any questions?"

"No questions, Sergeant," Bruce replied in a terse voice.

After Cross had left the barrack block, Jock exploded angrily, "Who in hell does Reardon think he is? He'll probably try to run our butts off like he did the last time."

"That's enough of that kind of talk, Jock! Come on, gang, let's shake out the lead," Mackenzie commanded.

Outside the barracks, the men of second platoon quickly formed up into their sections, helping each other adjust their equipment, answering roll call. Starting their long march out to the mortar range, Jock pulled his beret down over his eyes.

"Straighten your beret, McHaskell!" Cross ordered.

"I was just trying to keep the sun out o' me eyes, Sergeant."

"Never mind the sun. Wear you hat properly."

Jock was about to object but, after taking a quick look at his sergeant's grim face, straightened out his hat.

The road that the men of second platoon were following was typical of the roads that traversed the Royals' sandy training area—rutted, full of axle-breaking potholes, generally unsuitable for any means of travel. The brisk November air served as a tonic for the marching singing men making their way down the steeply graded evergreen-lined road to the long narrow plain that bordered the wide sparkling blue Ottawa River. After marching for nearly two hours, they arrived at the Royals' mortar range.

Sergeant Murphy and his staff were waiting for the second platoon at the range's firing point. After the men had rested, split the platoon into its three sections, detailing Mackenzie's section to fire the mortar first, the remaining two sections were detailed to watch the firing from a safe vantage point. Bruce's men stood in a rough semicircle around the impressively mustached mortar sergeant as he began lecturing them on the main characteristics of the light two-inch portable platoon mortar. The section's members could not help looking bored; it was only the fourth time they had heard Murphy give the same talk.

When he had finished, he addressed Bruce, "Corporal, I want you to select one man and demonstrate the proper firing of the mortar for the benefit of the rest of your platoon. The rest of you lads, join the others behind the firing point. Okay, Corporal, you and your number two will act on my orders."

Mackenzie looked at Jock. "I guess you and I might as well do the honors, Jock."

"Very well, Brucie, me boy."

Mackenzie knelt behind the mortar, holding the deadly tube in his left hand, keeping his right hand free in readiness to trip the firing lever. Jock took up the loader's position on Bruce's right, ready to drop the explosive bombs down the weapon's smooth short bored tube. Sergeant Murphy was standing directly behind the mortar team, ready to give the firing orders.

"Prepare bomb," Murphy bellowed in his best parade square voice.

Jock picked up the nearest bomb and checked its charge.

"Fire!"

On the command "Fire," Jock dropped the bomb down the mortar barrel, putting his hands to the side of his head to protect his ears against the explosion. At the same instant, Mackenzie tripped the firing lever. There was an ear-shattering detonation as the mortar barrel burst into hundreds of fragments.

Mackenzie and Murphy were killed instantly by the premature explosion. Their torn twisted bodies lay in unrecognizable heaps beside the blasted mortar. Big Jock managed to stagger to his feet, a look of indescribable horror etched on his contorted face. He turned with a swaying motion, facing the terror-stricken members of his platoon, clutching convulsively at the gaping hole in his abdomen with his huge hands, crashing to the blood-soaked ground dead.

Two weeks later, on a cold, wet November day, the first of the six fully loaded troop trains carrying the Second Royals left the camp bound for Fort Lewis, Washington, where the Canadians were to complete the final phase of their training prior to going overseas. As the last train left the rain-swept platform, the faint strains of band music seemed to linger in the air, the faint echo of strong male voices singing the plaintive words of the currently popular "Good Night, Irene" slowly drifting away.

Chapter 7

Monty

"Ms. Bigelow! Tell Mr. Carr-Wilson that I want to see him immediately!" the authoritative voice of Harold Forsythe, president of Forsythe Insurance Agencies, snapped over the intercom.

Myrna Bigelow was momentarily startled by the big voice booming out of the little box beside her desk. The attractive shapely receptionist quickly recovered herself, acknowledged her employer's command in her nasal high-pitched voice, directing her attention to the tall tweedy Englishman lounging comfortably in a deep leather chair directly opposite her desk.

"You may go in now, Mr. Wilson," the attractive redhead stammered, unnerved by the amused searching stare Monty had been directing at her since his arrival some ten minutes earlier.

"Mr. Carr-Wilson, my dear," he corrected with a bored smile, nonchalantly left his seat, walking toward Forsythe's door.

Passing by Myrna's desk, he stopped, giving her arm an affectionate squeeze. When he leaned over, whispering into her ear, she blushed furiously, quickly pulling down her skirt. Later that morning, she confided to one of her friends, "I have never met anyone like that man Wilson, June. Why, he positively undresses a girl the way he stares at her, and on top of that, you'd swear that he can read minds. Why, this morning he made me feel as if I'd forgotten to wear a skirt! He's kinda cute, though, for an Englishman, that is. You know how stuffy a lot of them are. But not Mr. Wilson. He's always kidding around, and he says some of the most outrageous things sometimes! He's married too. I've never seen his wife. I bet he gives her a difficult time, though, the way he flirts with every woman he sees. Why, most of the clients that call him at the office are women. Some of them are really stuck on him too. He told me he was going to ask me out sometime, when he gets around to the Bs, that is. Can you imagine the nerve of him?"

After Monty had knocked on his employer's door, Forsythe ordered sternly, "Come in, Wilson!" When Monty had entered, he continued, "Sit down, Wilson."

"Carr-Wilson, if you don't mind, sir," he wearily corrected, seating himself by the large window overlooking Toronto's Bay Street.

"Wilson, Carr-Wilson . . . it really doesn't matter at the moment! I'll get to the point, young man—I've received another complaint about you, this time from the wife of one of our most important clients. To be more explicit, Mrs. Owen Prescott! Not only is Mr. Prescott one of Toronto's most influential business figures, but he also happens to be one of our largest policy holders!"

"I certainly agree with you there, Mr. Forsythe. Old Prescott must weigh at least eighteen stone."

"This is no time for your silly humor, young man. This is serious! Mrs. Prescott phoned me early this morning to tell me that you've been bothering her constantly to go out with you. Of all the colossal nerve!"

"I say, steady, old chap! That isn't the whole story, you know. I was merely trying to promote some business for the firm," Monty replied lamely.

"Promote business for the firm? It sounds to me as if you were far more interested in promoting Mrs. Prescott!" Forsythe raged. "No, don't interrupt me. This will not—this most definitely will not continue. I've spent the best part of my life establishing this business, and I'm certainly not going to let an irresponsible, unprincipled individual like you ruin its good name. Have you anything to say for yourself?"

Monty, turning his attention away from his angry employer, stared out the office window, creating the impression that he was thinking of a reply but actually thinking about Rita Prescott. *Why, that pompous hypocritical old windbag*, he mused, more in indignation than in anger. *If I tell him the truth about his precious Mrs. Owen Prescott, he won't believe me. It's my own damn fault. She warned me I'd be sorry if I carried out my threat not to see her again. I didn't think that she would go this far. Oh, well a woman scorned!*

"Well, young man, I'm waiting."

Monty pulled thoughtfully at his long aquiline nose before replying. "First of all, old chap, I'm well aware that you're going to give me the sack no matter how plausible my explanation may be, so I shall begin by saying that I am terminating my services here as of now! Please, Mr. Forsythe, it is my turn to speak. Therefore, I'd appreciate it very much if you would keep your odious comments to yourself."

"How dare you!" Forsythe spluttered, half rising in this seat.

"Good lord, Forsythe, sit down and shut up! As for your comments about my morals, you lecherous old hypocrite, surely you must realize that everyone in your office is aware of your affair with that brainless doxie you loosely refer to as your receptionist. Or is it merely coincidence that she's frequently away sick on the same days you go on your so-called business trips? Look at yourself! A fat pop-eyed caricature of a man living under the fantastic illusion you cut a romantic figure. Shall we call in your precious Ms. Bigelow to bear me out?"

Forsythe, completely deflated by Carr-Wilson's unexpected attack, sat down in frightened confusion.

"That's better," Monty continued. "I don't intend to lower myself with the likes of you by discussing my relationship with Rita Prescott." He arose and walked easily to the door then turned around and faced his indignant employer. "But I should like to conclude this rather unpleasant interview informing you there is only one woman of late who has enjoyed my most intimate attentions more than dear Rita. You know her quite well, my cuckolded friend . . . your own priceless wife! And well, it serves you right."

Before the completely flabbergasted Forsythe could recover himself, Carr-Wilson slammed the door behind him then, confronting the very pale Ms. Bigelow who had obviously heard everything, paused long enough to say to the frightened receptionist, "My dear young woman, if you must play the tart, why waste your time on a fat old man, especially when there are so many handsome vigorous men like myself about who could help you enjoy your sinful compulsions?" He bent over and chucked her under the chin as she twisted her head away. "Don't worry, my dear, I won't reveal your indiscretions to anyone."

"You . . . you Englishman!" she hissed at Monty as he left.

Carr-Wilson's period of unemployment was quite short, catching the Special Force's enlistment fever. His application for a commission in the new force was accepted on the basis of his service as an officer in a British regiment during the latter part of the Second World War.

Montague Carr-Wilson had emigrated from England to Canada in the summer of 1946. In the course of the four years that had followed his arrival, he had managed to accumulate a wife, a child, a dog, a quantity of furniture—unpaid for, a long succession of assorted mistresses, and a reputation as a ladies' man. Despite his obvious lies and weak deceptions, his wife, Ellen, refused to recognize him for what he actually was; instead, she cherished the image of her first impression—the charming handsome young Englishman who swept her off her feet at their first meeting. Monty, despite his many extramarital affairs, loved his wife in his own peculiar way, never seriously considering leaving her.

Carr-Wilson's arrival at the Royals' training camp was uneventful, with the exception that the caste-conscious Cecil Smythe had gone to particular pains trying to cultivate his countryman's friendship. At first, Monty had been amused by Smythe's gullibility, but he soon got tired of the game of testing the easily impressed adjutant's credulity. On one occasion, he had suggested darkly to Smythe that he was the illegitimate son of a very powerful English political figure and that he had been sent to Canada to avoid a family scandal.

"You know, Cecil, old chap, I shall be heir to a very great fortune one day—once I establish my birthright, you know. Incidentally, old man, I certainly hope that you'll treat this matter in the strictest confidence. I'd be terribly embarrassed if any of the other officers found out. You understand, of course."

"Oh, you can trust me, Monty. I shan't breathe a word. A most remarkable story, though. You must miss your family very much?"

"Well, yes, I do, especially my mother and sister, but one must accept his fate."

"Your sister? I thought that you were the only child involved."

"Well, ah . . . You see, old chap, my mother did marry an old family friend. Celia is actually my half sister."

"I think your father, whoever he may be, is an outright bounder!"

"He wasn't such a bad scout, really. He did pay generously toward my keep and even went so far as to have me registered at his old school, Oxford."

"I thought you told me that you had attended Cambridge?" Smythe queried suspiciously.

Monty realized that he had gone too far weaving his fairy tale about himself. "Well, you see, old man, I was bent more toward the sciences, arranging, through my mother, to have my school changed."

Monty discontinued the conversation, making a point of avoiding Smythe whenever possible. Unlike the caste-conscious adjutant, he genuinely liked Canadians, the Canadian way of living, never heard to refer to "the way we do it in the old country," quite content to accept his new life.

Although the amiable Englishman made many friendly acquaintances, among the officers of the second battalion, only two, Paul Anderson and Mike Reardon became his close friends. They made a strange trio. On casual observation, they appear to have nothing in common, Carr-Wilson serving as the common denominator between his two friends. Paul was intellectual and idealistic, while Mike was physical and fundamental. Monty possessed some of the characteristics of both men.

The officers of the Second Royals didn't spend all their tie working, spending many pleasant evenings in the luxurious Royals officers' mess.

"Hey, Monty! Paul! You two characters coming over to the mess for a drink before dinner?"

"Good lord, Mike! Why don't you get lost and leave us to our beds of pain."

"Come of it, Monty. It wasn't that bad. We ran only for a half an hour in PT, and the CO let us get away with only two tours over the obstacle course. Why, it was a cinch today."

"Okay, okay, muscleman, it may be a cinch for you, it's different for us," Paul complained.

"A couple of drinks and you'll forget all about it," Mike coaxed.

"You know, Paul, I think our friend here makes a very good point. Shall we up and away?"

After dinner, the three friends were sitting together reading when Mike's attention became diverted to a small group of officers shooting crap on a card table in the games room.

"What do you say we make a small investment in the crap game going on in the games room, Monty?"

"I'm afraid you'll have to count me out, old cock. I'm almost completely strapped. In fact, I'm down to my last tuppence."

"All I have is a quarter. It looks like they're playing for small change. Well, I might just as well be broke as the way I am. Be back after the first roll, fellas."

Reardon didn't return after the first roll; he had a remarkable streak of luck. As the stakes grew, his good fortune kept pace, parlaying his quarter into $300 by the next morning. On a succeeding occasion, Monty and Mike cleaned out the entire complement of gamblers in the mess to the tune of $500. The gambling fever suddenly became intense, some playing far over their heads in desperate attempts to recoup their losses. Finally, the commanding officers of both battalions, alarmed at the heavy losses of some of their officers, forbade gambling in any form in the mess.

Monty and Mike didn't mind, clearing nearly a thousand dollars between them in less than three weeks.

CHAPTER 8

Farewell Party

One quiet evening, early in November, Paul and Monty were sitting in front of the officers' mess fireplace, enjoying the warmth of the fire and each other's company. The two friends, inspired by a succession of hot rum toddies, began discussing the underlying causes they felt were responsible for the war in Korea.

Monty, in an uncharacteristically serious frame of mind, commented, "It's quite obvious to me, old chap, the Soviets are following a deliberate plan of exploiting the weaknesses in the West's Far Eastern policy by playing on the nationalistic feelings of the Eastern people. After all, North Korea isn't the only place that has felt their influence in this manner. The same thing is happening in Malaya and Indochina on a smaller scale. In fact, you will find a strong communist influence wherever you have a discontented native population."

"You feel then, Monty, the rise of communist-inspired nationalism is due strictly to the external influence of the Russians? Don't you think the actions of these people could be the result of their own deductive reasoning? That like the Chinese, they hope to find a reasonably quick solution to their economic problems through communism?"

"That might well be, Paul, but the case in point is North Korea versus South Korea, a clear-cut case of a well-armed minority attempting to force its will on a very unwilling majority. The same could be said for Indochina and Malaya, for that matter."

Monty was about to continue his discussion with Paul when he was interrupted by the entrance of Mike Reardon.

"What's up, fellas? Sounds kind of deep to me."

"I don't think you'd be particularly interested, old cock. We didn't get around to women. What do you say, Paul, old man, shall we educate this mesocephalic barbarian?"

"No, I think we should leave our nature boy unspoiled," Paul replied.

"Okay, okay, wise guys. How about knocking it off! I may not be an Einstein, but it'll take a hell of a lot more than a lot of big words to impress commies when we get there."

"Come off it, Mike. Don't be a sorehead, we're just kidding you. Say, it must be about time for me to buy a round. Same as usual, Mike? How about you, Monty?" Paul asked as he put his arm around Mike's shoulder in a friendly gesture. "I know that I'll always be able to depend on you when the going gets tough."

Reardon flinched at Paul's words, the image of Barbara Anderson flashing through his mind. "Sorry I lost my temper, Paul—no problem."

Later, in Anderson's room, the three young officers were discussing the farewell dance being given for the officers of the second battalion by the first battalion the following Saturday night, Monty and Mike complaining about their lack of dates for the event.

"Gad, what a revolting development!" Monty groaned.

"Oh, I don't know, Monty. Your physique isn't as bad as all that," Mike jeered.

"Very funny indeed, my clownish friend. You know very well that I've been seeing a positively delectable little thing in town the past few weeks. She's absolutely mad about me too—you know, old world charm and all that sort of thing. The difficulty is her husband will be home this weekend, husbands have a perverse talent appearing at the most inconvenient times."

"I'm in the same fix," Mike condoled. "I had everything set up with Renee, you know, the little French schoolteacher from Ottawa, the one that gives me French lessons every weekend."

"Oh rather! Isn't she the one who holds her classes in the bridal suite of the Hotel Henri on the Quebec side?" Carr-Wilson asked, winking knowingly.

"That's absolutely no business of yours, my lecherous friend. At any rate, she can't make it for the dance."

"I suppose we could invite our wives," Monty suggested unenthusiastically.

"Well, why don't you? Barbara is coming, and it would be a wonderful opportunity for our wives to become acquainted," Anderson added hopefully.

"I'm sure it would," Reardon snapped curtly.

"That's a fine attitude to take toward your wife, I must say."

"Look, Paul, I've said my goodbyes, and I intend to leave matters stand that way," Mike retorted, irritated by Anderson's comment.

"Mike is quite right, old chap," the Englishman affirmed. "As you are well aware, both Michael and I are laboring under marital difficulties that preclude us from asking our wives to the farewell celebrations. I know that I would heartily dislike spending what might prove to be my last night in Canada for some time engaged in verbal combat. In fact, the last party my wife and I attended together was a most distressing affair—I had to spend the entire evening holding her hands."

"Well, that certainly doesn't sound so very unusual, a husband and wife holding hands at a dance?" Anderson replied quizzically.

"My dear fellow, I certainly was not holding my wife's hand for anything so mundane as a display of affection! The truth of the matter is a young lady was present and my wife suspected us of having an affair—I was holding my frau's little pinkies to keep her from strangling me!"

"Oh, come now, Monty. It can't be as bad as all that?"

"Seriously, old chap, I think that I'll take potluck at the dance or, as you Canadians say, go stag. Anyone for a nightcap before turning in?"

"You can count me out, Monty. I'm going to write to my wife," Anderson replied.

"I'll keep you company, Monty. Wait a minute till I go to my room and put on a tie," Mike said.

After arriving at the mess, Carr-Wilson looked searchingly at his companion and asked, "I say, Mike, I know this is none of my business, mind, but . . . is there anything between Paul's wife and yourself?"

Caught off guard, Mike didn't reply immediately then countered with "Whatever made you think a ridiculous thing like that?"

"I really can't say, perhaps my fertile mind is working overtime, but you do have a most peculiar expression on your face whenever Paul mentions his wife."

Mike was tempted to tell Carr-Wilson about his brief encounter with Barbara on the Ottawa train but thought better of it, instead forcing himself to laugh, replying, "Monty, my boy, I'm afraid your imagination is working overtime. Now what about the potluck you were talking about in Paul's room?"

On the night of the farewell party, Monty, impatiently waiting for Reardon to finish combing his unruly black hair, took a quick look at his watch, demanding in an urgent tone, "I wish you would hurry. We were due in the mess five minutes ago. You know how sticky the old man is regarding punctuality."

"Okay, okay, keep your shirt on! I can't go over to the damn party looking like a blasted Zulu," Mike retorted then, shrugging his shoulders, said, "Oh, to hell with my hair. Let's go, Monty."

An angry Major Dearing was waiting for them. "What in blazes kept you two? You know damn well it was nine o'clock, not ten minutes after! The CO has been waiting for you two so he can have a group picture taken of all the officers before the dance starts."

"My fault, sir. I kept Monty waiting."

"This is no time for excuses. Let's get inside," Dearing commanded impatiently.

"That tears it! Extra orderly officer for both of us, you clot," Carr-Wilson hissed at his friend as they entered the main lounge of the ornately decorated mess.

Approaching Colonel Graves, holding court by the elaborate fireplace, Monty nudged his friend's arm, saying, "Look over by the patio, Mike. There's Paul and his wife. Isn't she lovely?"

Reardon looked quickly in the direction indicated by Carr-Wilson. For a moment, he was completely speechless; Barbara never before looked more radiantly beautiful and desirable than she appeared at that moment. She was dressed in an expensive blue evening gown, highlighting by her long blond hair, falling in a tumbling cascade about her bare shoulders.

Chuck Dearing could not help but smile as he watched his two young platoon commanders offer their belated apologies to Colonel Graves. He was very pleased with both of them, Monty for his steadiness and remarkable self-control, Mike for his daring and physical aggressiveness, feeling his only weak link was Anderson. Though he was trying very hard, dependable, to the battle-wise major, he lacked the spark he felt essential in a first-class infantry officer.

The prematurely grey-haired commander of the Second Royals A Company chuckled to himself. "If I had a wife as lovely as Anderson's, I suppose I'd have a hell of a time keeping my mind on soldiering too!"

The Royals officers' mess, situated on the edge of a broad plateau overlooking the Ottawa River, was grandly decorated for the dance on the night of the Second Royals farewell celebration. At the bottom of the plateau, the glistening dark Ottawa River was serving as a ribbonlike reflector for the moon and stars shining brightly in the clear November sky. The mess consisted of an anteroom, a large expensively furnished main lounge, an elaborately equipped dining room, a long patio stretching the entire length of the building facing on the river. The dance music played by the Royals band floated out over the vast Ottawa Valley toward the Gatineau Hills lying beyond; from the river below, the dazzling figures of the officers and their ladies could be seen dancing on the enclosed patio.

Inside the mess, the combination of music and good liquor taking effect, inter-battalion rivalries and animosities were temporarily forgotten. The officers of the first battalion tried to make the evening as pleasant as possible for their departing counterparts, encouraging their wives to dance with those officers of the second who had been unable to bring their wives or girlfriends.

From the moment he had learned that Paul's wife would be present at the party, Mike had dreaded the prospect of meeting Barbara again. When their reunion finally occurred, it turned out to be an even more uncomfortable experience than he had anticipated. Reardon's embarrassed, subdued manner was in direct contrast to Monty's suave, confident, almost intimate approach to Anderson's young wife. Mike fully realized the reason for his troubled feelings, guilty having betrayed the man with whom he had exchanged friendships. His attempts to be pleasant failed miserably, only succeeding in making himself sound taciturn to the point of rudeness. A leering devil was whispering to him, *"How many others since you?"*

After finishing a courtesy dance with Paul's wife, during which little was said, Reardon mumbled his apologies to the surprised couple, grabbed the bewildered Carr-Wilson by the arm, and steered him to the bar.

"I say, Mike, old man, steady! Whatever has gotten into you? I wasn't ready to leave," spluttered Monty angrily. "Why, you lecherous old remittance man, you! I could read your mind from the other side of the room, or was it just friendship prompting you to start spiking Paul's drinks? He's a good friend of ours, and I think that we'd better leave it that way. What will it be, rum or rye?"

"Ah . . . Oh, make it rum this time, old chap. I suppose you're right, but she certainly would be a tasty morsel," he finished lamely, annoyed he'd been so obvious.

"Don't be too sure, Monty. It just isn't worth it. Believe me, I know," Reardon curtly retorted then changed the subject.

Major Treleaven of the camp headquarters staff was enjoying himself immensely as he always did at a free party. He and his wife Joyce made a point of accepting all social invitations, feeling that by doing so, they were enhancing their social standing among the military hierarchy of the camp. Unfortunately, during these affairs, their behavior followed an unvarying pattern. The major became hopelessly drunk, his usually proper wife becoming an outrageous flirt. Joyce, a vain, flighty woman in her early thirties, couldn't stop herself from encouraging men's attentions in a childish attempt making her husband jealous, at the same time bolster her own ego. The unique pattern followed by the Treleavens became an accepted thing among their friends. Consequently, their conduct was seldom a source of comment. Although the Treleavens rarely went home together, no one, not even the officer becoming the object of Joyce's harmless flirtation, ever seriously consider taking advantage of the situation.

Monty was watching the infantile antics of Joyce Treleaven with amused indifference when she spotted the attractive-looking Englishman standing alone by the fireplace, deliberately making her way toward him. Monty had just enough time to whisper to Mike, arriving from the opposite direction with two drinks, "Well, old cock, wish me luck—here comes my potluck!"

Mike turned unsteadily toward the object of his friend's attention, chuckled drunkenly, returning to the bar.

"When I saw you standing all by yourself, I couldn't help feeling you would like to dance. My name is Joyce Treleaven. I bet you're a wonderful dancer."

"What about your husband, Mrs. Treleaven? Won't he object?"

"Oh him!" she replied, making a wry face, tossing her brunet waves disdainfully in her husband's direction. "George doesn't mind, really. Besides, I always ask good-looking men to dance. Come on, they're playing one of my favorite pieces."

Dancing with his attractive partner, Monty stooped over slightly to nuzzle Joyce's long soft hair, humming the strains of the tune the band was playing. Joyce was dancing on her toes in an attempt to match Carr-Wilson's towering height as she softly caressed the back of his neck in tempo with the music.

"You're a marvelous dancer, Monty. I'm so glad I asked you to dance with me," she breathed heavily in his ear.

"The pleasure is all mine, my dear," he replied gallantly, giving her slim waist an affectionate squeeze.

Completely unaware of the gentleman's game played, where Joyce Treleaven's flirtatious conduct was concerned, Monty began following a pattern typical of him in such situations, becoming deceptively attentive to George Treleaven, plying him with double-strength drinks, at the same time encouraging Joyce to drink up a constant succession of strong cocktails, ending his campaign borrowing a car from one of the officers of the First Royals.

"Now to select the right moment," he muttered to himself as he rubbed his hands together in nervous anticipation.

While they danced to an undulating tango, the lights of the patio were turned out. Immediately, Joyce pressed her body tightly against Monty's as her mouth searched hungrily for his lips.

"Darling, let's leave this place and go somewhere, anywhere, so that we can be alone! I want you so," Monty whispered, his voice trembling with passion.

Joyce suddenly became rigid in Carr-Wilson's arms, angrily breaking off their embrace. "Of all the colossal nerve! You certainly make a big thing out of a kiss, mister. Please take me back to my husband."

"You must forgive me, Joyce! I behaved like a cad, you look so lovely, I'm about to leave to fight, perhaps never to return. I . . . but that isn't an excuse. Oh, Joyce, dear, I don't know what to say! Please say that you'll forgive me?" Monty begged artfully, a trace of desperation in his voice.

"Of course, I'll forgive you, Monty, I understand, but we really must go back to George," she replied gently.

Monty left Joyce with her husband and went to the bar to order another round of drinks. Waiting to be served, he mopped his brow in relief, saying under his breath, "You damn fool—you almost ruined everything!"

After a few more congenial rounds, George Treleaven slipped away completely into alcoholic unconsciousness. "Looks like your husband is no longer with us," Monty said laughingly to Joyce. "Shall we dance?"

"Sure, honey, I'd love to. Look at that damn husband of mine—passed out like a light. Does it all the time," she answered drunkenly.

Firmly supporting her unsteady figure, Monty led Joyce to the darkened patio. Once there, they gave up all the pretext of dancing; their lips met passionately.

Joyce broke off her embrace, mumbling, "I'm going home now . . . I feel terrible!"

"Are you sure you won't have another drink, Joyce, dear? It might just be the thing to pick you up," Carr-Wilson urged, worried at the prospect of losing his quarry after his nightlong sustained effort.

"Good god, no! I couldn't stand the sight of another drink," she retorted in disgust.

"I'll take you home then, if you like?"

"Fine, fine. Just get me out of here before I get sick—please!"

"Right, my sweet. You get your coat and I'll meet you outside," he ordered.

When Joyce stepped out into the cool early morning, the fresh air proved to be too much for her, collapsing into Monty's willing arms. He started the car, didn't head toward the married quarters as he had promised, instead driving her down the steep hillside road, leading to the deserted officers' beach.

In the meantime, in the mess, the party finally breaking up, two of George Treleaven's closest friends found him snoring loudly in an easy chair in the games room.

"Poor Old George potted again! Take his other arm, will you, Charlie?" The taller of the two men sighed.

The wives of the two men looked briefly for Joyce. Unable to find her, they rejoined their husbands who were staggering under the weight of George's inert form.

"I suppose Joyce, poor dear, must have become disgusted."

"Can't say that I blame her either," her friend added patronizingly.

PART 2

Fort Lewis

Chapter 9

Preparing for War

Gen. Douglas MacArthur's successful surprise offensive during September-October of 1950 created a sudden change in the Korean War situation, proving embarrassing to the Canadian government. After the American landing at Incheon, the resulting string of military successes enjoyed by the UN Eighth Army seemed to make Canada's contribution of a brigade unnecessary; plans were made to change the destination of the Special Force brigade from Korea to Germany where it would fulfill the dominion's NATO army commitment. In the meantime, it was decided that a token force of a battalion of Canadians would be sent to Korea, remaining there until the military and political situations in the Far East clarified. The remainder of the brigade, supplemented by a new battalion, was sent to its Far East staging area at Fort Lewis to carry out collective training pending final disposal. Fort Lewis was selected for this task because its extensive training area was ideally suited for winter exercises.

The majority of the ten-thousand-man brigade was dispatched to its American training base during the first three weeks in November. In general, the training area and training facilities proved to be very adequate: the area was suited for infantry exercises up to brigade level; the weather was never too severe. Consequently, maximum use could be made of the training time available.

The training of the men progressed rapidly through the various levels of section, platoon, company, battalion, and finally brigade. Many training exercises were held. Some were designed to test the efficiency of battalion and brigade communications; others were held to test the degree of mobility of the various components of the brigade. The exercises were held and carried out to test the leadership capabilities of the brigade's officers and to build up and test the physical stamina of the men. The concluding exercise was spectacular. Appropriately called Fire War, it consisted of a coordinated brigade attack, including tanks and artillery, across a vast plain overlooked by the majestic ice-capped Mount Rainier.

A unique feature of the exercise, a feature that greatly impressed the U.S. Army officers observing the mock attack, was the use of live ammunition by all the Canadian units taking part. The training and discipline of the men were excellent; not a single serious injury or fatality resulted from the Fire War in spite of the thousands of live rounds fired. This stirring finale held late in February resulted in the proud brigade commander's announcement, "My brigade is ready for action."

The six troop trains carrying the members of the Second Royals sped across the Canadian west toward the American training base at Fort Lewis, Washington; the trip was uneventful. The special trains seldom stopped, except for coal, to take up water, or to allow the troops to exercise. Most of the members of the Royals were from Eastern Canada; many of them had never seen the Canadian west. They found the early stages of the trip exciting. As the hours passed, the long monotonous ride began to pall on even the most enthusiastic passengers. At first, there had been a lot of discussion about the mortar range accident. Later, the men spent most of their time playing cards, reading, sleeping, or staring out of the windows at the scenery flashing by. Finally, much to everyone's relief, the four-day trip ended; the much anticipated moment of being the members of the first large contingent of Canadian troops ever to train on American soil had arrived.

The first of the six crowded trains squealed to a shuddering stop. Inside the packed coaches, the travel-weary Canadians were busily assisting one another in the awkward task of fitting their cumbersome web equipment over their bulky greatcoats. Outlined against the fall mist covering the station platform stood the massive yellow-helmeted figure of an American movement's control officer, standing a little behind him was a small group of Canadian soldiers forming part of the Royals' advance party.

The gravel-voiced American captain began bellowing at the disembarking Canadians, "Come on, you guys! Shake the lead out. Get a move on, we haven't got all day. Next train is due in ten minutes."

Muttering their resentment at the crude welcome, the Royals were led in a single long file to a shadowy line of yellow buses waiting half-hidden in the Pacific mist. A short bespectacled U.S. Army sergeant monotonously counted off the Canadians, one to thirty, and loaded them onto the chartered vehicles. As each bus filled up, its bored driver slammed the door. Clashing the idling transmission into low gear, he let out the clutch, jammed down on the gas pedal so that the bus jerked forward with an angry roar, driving along the intricate network of roads traversing North Fort Lewis's vast area until they reached a group of faded white two-storied buildings bordering the south end of the biggest parade square the Canadians had ever seen. When they arrived in front of the barracks, the men quickly debussed, formed up into their respective platoons, and were led to their quarters by guides from the advance party.

Colonel Graves, accompanied by his staff officers, stood in the drizzling rain supervising the housing of his men until the last trainload of Royals had been looked after, only then did he go to his room in the officers' quarters. A short time later, the officer in charge of the advance party, Major Harcourt, reported to Graves, giving him a complete breakdown of the facilities available to the Royals in the camp. When Harcourt finally left, the weary colonel couldn't help feeling discouraged; there seemed to be a tremendous amount of work to do, very little time to do it. The initial problems of housing and feeding his men were in hand. The more complex problems of training—selecting and utilizing company training areas, obtaining transport vehicles, finding suitable office facilities for the many battalion training and administrative functions—appeared, at first sight, to be insurmountable.

Graves was faced with a more immediate problem, having to decide whether to let his men leave the camp the first night. Originally, his intention was to confine all his officers and men to barracks for the first few days. After carefully considering the matter, he changed his mind, announcing to his company commanders half the battalion would be given the opportunity to visit Tacoma the first night, with the remainder having the same privilege the following evening, if all went well. That evening, the buses commuting between the camp and the city of Tacoma, ten miles south, were filled with jubilant Canadians eager to sample Washington nightlife.

CHAPTER 10

"You Can't Get Drunk on American Beer"

When the three platoon officers of A Company finished supervising the housing of their men, they reported to Major Dearing, the company commander, for further instructions.

"Sit down, gentlemen," Dearing requested as he stifled a face-contorting yawn. "The CO had decided to let half the battalion have an evening pass into Tacoma. Our lads, D Company, and support company get the first nod. The others will get their chance tomorrow night if our bunch behaves. Now hold on, don't get too excited, there's a small catch—each company must provide a night duty officer."

"What about the orderly officer, sir?" Mike queried.

"This duty is in addition to the regular orderly officer. The CO wants to make damn sure that no unpleasant incidents take place because there aren't enough duty officers to handle the situation. He hasn't forgotten that nasty incident in the wets back at the camp."

"I'll wager that you and I are the first two orderly blokes, Mike. At last, Teabags has us," Monty groaned.

"Oh, I wouldn't worry too much for a while, Monty. I think Red Saunders has the job monopolized for at least a week. The old man took a very dim view when he caught him with that bottle on the train," Dearing commented.

"Couldn't happen to a nicer guy," Mike interjected, smiling.

"We still have to draw up a company roster, chaps. I suggest that you flip a coin to decide the lucky one for tonight."

"Put your money away. I'll take the first duty," Paul Anderson volunteered, amused by the broad grins that creased the faces of his two friends after making his offer. "Don't expect me to make a habit of it."

"This is damn nice of you, Paul. I'll do the same for you sometime," Mike thanked him.

Arriving at their quarters, the three friends were pleased to find that their batmen had cleaned up the rooms, unpacked their gear, and pressed their good uniforms. After taking time to clean themselves up, they proceeded to the small mess adjacent to their quarters made available for the Royals' officers. Finishing their dinner, the three young subalterns sat in front of the mess fireplace, sampling their first taste of American Pacific Coast beer.

"That feels a hell of a lot better—nothing like a hot shower, a good dinner, and a drink to settle the nerves," Reardon commented as he nursed his glass of nut brown ale.

Monty looked at his watch then quickly rose from his chair, saying, "I say, Mike, old chap, we had better hurry if we want to catch the eight-o-clock bus."

"Yeah, you're right. Oh damn! I forgot my swagger stick. Hold on for a minute, Monty. I'll have to go to my room to get the damn thing."

Reardon and Carr-Wilson cheerfully made their way to the North Camp bus depot where they were met by two other Second Royals officers, Capt. Jungle Jim Phillips, a tall rawboned Australian, and Bill Purvis, a battle-experienced officer from Kitchener, Ontario. When the four officers had boarded the bus, they decided to forgo visiting Tacoma, instead agreed to stop at the first suitable roadhouse they passed. As their bus droned southward, the mist-shrouded night became illuminated by an exciting sequence of brilliant multicolored neon signs advertising everything imaginable. Finally, their attention was arrested by a huge flashing sign seeming to shout at the steady stream of traffic roaring ceaselessly by Rocco's Tambourine.

"What do you say to our trying Rocco's, chaps?" Phillips suggested in his booming voice.

"Should be a pretty good spot, Monty. Sign says liquor, food, and dancing," Mike added.

"True, old chap. And where there's dancing, there's bound to be that other important commodity . . ."

"For instance?" Purvis cut in.

"Women, of course," Monty snapped impatiently.

Phillips pulled the signal cord, and the bus came to a swaying stop a short distance down the highway from the roadhouse. The eager quartet crossed the busy four-lane highway, walking quickly back to the brightly lit tavern.

"Gad! What an oasis in a neon wilderness!" Carr-Wilson exclaimed, obviously impressed.

On entering, they were met by a very pretty hatcheck girl. The four Canadians eyed the shapely young girl appreciatively. She, intrigued by her first sight of Canadian uniforms, stared back at them with more than casual interest.

A congenial dark Italian American, his round face beaming, came toward them. "Welcome, Canada! We've been expecting you. My name is Rocco. I'm sort of the boss around here."

After the five men had exchanged introductions, the owner of the cabaret continued in his rasping voice, "I've been saving one of our best tables for you, and the first round is on me. By the way, boys, I hope you won't take offense—would you mind checking your belts along with your hats? We've had trouble with belts from our own boys, especially the marines. They have a bad habit of using them in fights. I'll take you to your table as soon as you're ready."

When the smiling girl finished checking the Canadians' hats, sticks, and belts, she brought an oversized pair of dice from underneath her counter and began rolling them casually on its felt-covered surface.

"Anyone like to take a chance?" she asked pleasantly. "Fifty-cent limit."

"I'd like to take a chance with you, baby. But not using dice," Mike countered, grinning.

"I just bet you would! But you'll have to line up, buster," she parried expertly.

The tables surrounding the small elevated dance floor were nearly filled; wispy tendrils of smoke had begun to hang in the darkened corners; a small combo was playing a nostalgic collection of old favorites reminiscent of the Second World War. As soon as the four men had been seated, they were each presented with a large foaming pitcher of beer and a glass by a tired-looking waitress. When she left, the Canadians toasted their arrival.

Mike grimaced, saying, "Is this stuff ever weak! I wish we had some Canadian brew. You sure as hell can't get drunk on American beer, and that's for sure!" Ignoring the glass placed before him, Reardon began to drain the entire contents of his pitcher.

"Take it easy, cobber," Phillips warned. "This weak stuff, as you call it, has a nasty habit of sneaking up on you."

As the four-piece combo commenced playing the haunting strains of the currently popular song "Be My Love," Carr-Wilson nudged Mike, directing his attention to two young women sitting alone at a nearby table. "What do you say, keed? Shall we try?"

"Right-o, old chap, let's give them a go!" Mike replied, imitating his friend's pronounced accent.

The two girls spotted Monty and Mike approaching their table, looking quickly at each other, deciding wordlessly to accept the dance invitations their intuition told them were sure to come. Both Mike and Monty had the same girl in mind, the attractive blonde of the duo. Reardon, anticipating Monty's intentions, distracted his attention to the jaded redheaded vocalist singing on the bandstand.

"Say, Monty, she may not be able to sing but take a look at that figure."

As Carr-Wilson turned around, Mike moved quickly to the girls' table, addressing the blonde, "Pardon me, may I have this dance?"

Annoyed by his friend's deception, Monty hissed, "That was a rotten thing to do, Reardon."

"All fair in love and war and all that sort of rot." Mike laughed, leading his attractive partner to the dance floor.

Carr-Wilson then turned to the other girl, flashed his best smile, speaking pleasantly, "I was afraid that my friend was going to ask you to dance. I would have been completely shattered if he had. May I have this dance, my dear?"

As they danced, Mike began questioning his partner. "The music is awful, isn't it?"

"Well, actually, it's a lot better on weekends. They have a special group on Saturday nights," she replied softly with a noticeable German accent.

"Then you must come here quite often?"

"No, not really," she replied, flustered by the directness of the Canadian's question. "My husband is in Korea with the army. My girlfriend and I go out once in a while to have a few drinks and dance a little, but that's all," she continued defensively.

"I hope you don't think I'm being nosy, but from the color of your hair and accent, I'd say you are German, right?"

"Yes, I'm German. I met my husband after the war. He was stationed in Munich, my home city."

"Incidentally, my name is Mike Reardon, and I'm a lieu—"

"You are a lieutenant in the Canadian Army," she interrupted him, laughing. "My name is Tina, Canada."

"You certainly know a lot more about Canadian ranks than the rest of the Americans around here. Why, one of them came up to me and said I looked awfully young to be a two-star general."

"Back home, I kept company with a British officer before I met my husband. I believe your army is very similar to that of the English, is that not so?"

"Yes, quite similar, Tina, in some ways, that is," Mike acknowledged. "You know something, Tina? You're really very lovely. In fact, you have the most beautiful hair I've ever seen."

"You're a shameless flatterer, Mike, just like the English," she retorted, although s secretly pleased by Reardon's admiring comments.

"No, honestly, I really mean it," he breathed huskily as he pulled her yielding body closer to his.

Big Jim Phillips had been invited by a group of Americans to sit at their table. In a surprisingly short time, a large number of people grouped themselves around the handsome Australian captain with the flowing red mustache, enthralled by his endless anecdotes about his Pacific War service.

"The war in New Guinea was a bleeding hell. I can tell you. Why, I can remember one occasion when five cobbers and I were cut off by a whole battalion of Nips for two days. Mind you, the little beggars thought there was a much larger force, and impression we went to great pains to give them. It developed into a deadly game of hide-and-seek until the crafty little bastards—excuse me, ladies! I meant to say beggars—until they caught on to our deception and began to comb the jungle systematically foot by foot until they had driven us into the center of their perimeter. We finally managed to secure a footing on a small hillock where we made our last stand. They didn't wait very long to come at us either. Screaming at the top of their bloody lungs, about forty of them came charging up the ruddy ridge at us. While my cobbers were cutting them down with their submachine guns, I was busy picking up the grenades they were tossing at us and smartly tossing them back. Then the main group decided to have a go, and about a hundred more came charging at us, yelling, 'Banzai! Banzai!' I gathered all my cobbers' grenades and began to roll them down the hill into the very center of the blighters.

"Let me tell you, my friends, the result was unbelievable! Scores of them were either killed or wounded. What, my grenades didn't stop, our bullets did. Well, the slant-eyed little bas—I mean, beggars—finally had enough and ran like devils, possessed back into the stinking jungle. Our fire attracted the attention of a large patrol sent out by our CO to look for us, and we were saved. Fighting in New Guinea was war!"

Phillips concluded his story by letting his head fall forward as if in silent thanks for his "miraculous" escape; his tense, quiet audience stared at the big Australian in awe.

Bill Purvis was busy talking to the hatcheck girl, who never ceased to roll her dice during their conversation. Although he was losing 50¢ pieces at an alarming rate, he had convinced himself she was interested in him.

"How about letting me take you home when you're finished?" he suggested hopefully.

"Oh, I couldn't do that. I mean, you're nice and everything, but I never let fellas pick me up when I'm working. How about another roll?"

Purvis automatically placed another half dollar on the counter. "When can I see you then? How about tomorrow night? You said Thursday is your night off."

"Gee, I wish I could . . . No, I mean it, honest, but I got to go to a shower for my girl friend tomorrow night. She's getting married next week."

"Are you busy on Sunday? Surely you don't work on Sunday. You could show me the town," Bill suggested.

Instead of answering his question, she asked, "How about another roll? Your luck's bound to change."

"Yeah, sure," replied Purvis ruefully. "I've been about as lucky with your dice as I've been with you. Well, how about Sunday?"

"Gee, I'm sorry, but if you're not going to play anymore, I'll have to look after one of the other customers. So long."

The combination of beer, sentimental music, and soft lights had succeeded in making Monty's brunet look considerably more attractive to him. As the evening progressed, he began to find her quite desirable. During one of their turns on the dance floor, he held his sharp-featured partner very close and whispered lovingly into her right ear as he gently bit the lobe in an attempt to arouse her passion.

"My dear, you need a man's love. I know that you must be very lonely. I could make you forget your loneliness if you'll let me," he crooned huskily.

"Oh, for god's sake, cut that out, will you?" she snapped angrily. "What do you think you're doing anyways? I want to sit down. No! Right now."

When they returned to the table, the irate brunette signaled her blonde friend to join her in a trip to the powder room. Tina excused herself, joining the other girl. After they left, Mike ordered another round of beer, began singing some of the words of the song the band was playing.

"You know something, Monty? This group isn't bad at all. No kidding, I really feel like dancing," he mumbled in a beery voice. "I think I'll ask them to play 'Sentimental Journey' again. Scuse me." He rose unsteadily to his feet and wove his way to the orchestra stand.

When Mike got back to the table, Carr-Wilson commented nervously, "They haven't returned yet, Mike. I wonder whatever could be keeping them this long. Do you think they've left?"

"No-o-o . . . You know dames, Monty," Reardon replied indifferently, taking a large gulp from his fresh pitcher of ale. "They always spend hours in the can powdering their noses, gabbing, and what have you. They're probably deciding what they're going to do about us taking them home. Tina's kind of cute, isn't she? I'll bet my bottom dollar she's a real blonde too."

"You certainly pulled a fine stunt on me, Mike. A fine friend you are. I suppose it really doesn't matter though. They all look the same in the dark," Monty mused philosophically.

Meanwhile, the two girls were having a heated discussion in the powder room over the two Royals officers. "Now look here, Tina, we agreed to go home together," the tall dark girl complained angrily.

"I can't understand why you're so angry. It certainly wouldn't do any harm to let them take us home. Why, the Englishman seems to be quite nice," Tina replied, her annoyance causing her accent to become more pronounced.

"Maybe your guy is okay, Tina, but mine's a real creep. My god, he's been trying to make me right on the dance floor. The way he started to bite my ear and stroke the back of my neck with those long fingers of his made me want to scream! And I thought all Englishmen were gentlemen . . . It just goes to show you."

"All right, I'll go home with you," the German girl agreed. "But Mike is rather nice," she added wistfully.

"Oh, damn it all, give him your phone number if you're so stuck on him. Let's get out of here."

Mike could not help laughing at the amazed look on Monty's face as the two women left them after bidding the briefest of goodbyes. He began to taunt his friend mercilessly, "Whatever happened to the great lover? I thought you said you had the brunette eating out of the palm of your hand. You and your corny line!"

His ego sorely wounded, Carr-Wilson glared at his friend and said, "I don't know what in hell you're laughing at, Reardon. You didn't do any better than I did!"

"Don't be too sure about that, old cock," Mike announced triumphantly as he produced a note Tina had slipped into his hand before she left. He began reading it aloud, "*Dear Mike, I'm sorry I had to leave as I enjoyed meeting you very much. In the event that you might be interested in seeing me again, I am enclosing my address and telephone number. Affectionately, Tina.*"

"Well, I'll be damned! Of all the fantastic luck," Monty exclaimed jealously, and then recovering himself, he clapped Reardon on the back. "Good for you, keed. I'm glad that at least one of us had some success. She's a lovely girl. Say, Mike, what do you think of the little hatcheck girl? I'll wager she'd be an interesting little partner for some nocturnal dalliance."

"I don't know about that, Monty. I was talking to Bill Purvis in the washroom, and he said he struck out. According to him, she's only interested as long as you keep losing your money. Then when you get serious or quit playing, well, it's 'So long, sucker!'"

"Steady now, old chap. Just because a crude fellow like Purvis fails to gain the attentions of a pretty girl, it certainly doesn't preclude a gentleman with *beaucoup savoir faire* from succeeding."

"Meaning yourself, I suppose?"

"Naturally, my friend. However, I don't feel the time is right for me to, as you Canucks say, make my play."

It was Jim Phillips and his imaginative tales of his war exploits that saved the evening for the Canadians. Surrounded by eager listeners, his table was laden with pitchers of beer, spotted were Monty and Mike sitting alone. Purvis was nowhere to be seen.

"Come on, cobbers. How about joining our party and meeting some of these marvelous people?"

"Shall we join Jungle Jim, Mike? Looks like a good party brewing over there."

"Oh lord, no, Monty. I don't think I could stand another of that bull swinger's stories."

"Come on, don't be an ass. Surely you're not going turn down all that free beer," Monty shrewdly suggested.

"My friend, you've made a point. Well, don't just sit there, Monty. Let's go!"

Mike Reardon lost all count of the number of pitchers full of beer he had emptied. The combination of alcohol, dense cigarette smoke, throbbing music, and loud voices became a huge nebulous floating mass in his befogged mind. He laughed when the others laughed, he sang when the others sang, and he drank constantly. Rocco gave up the futile task of trying to quieten the noisy Canadian-American party and joined it; the orchestra members joined the party. Finally, everyone in the cabaret joined the celebration.

Suddenly, Jim Phillips climbed up on one of the tables, making an impassioned speech about the brotherhood of Canadians and Americans, recklessly waving a full pitcher of beer above his head. Completely carried away by his own eloquence, he called for attention from the entire assemblage in his loud booming voice.

"My American friends, I beg your attention," he demanded solemnly as he balanced himself on his precarious platform. "I propose a toast to His Majesty, the King, leader of our Commonwealth!"

An unusual event followed: Americans stood up with the Canadians, perhaps the first time since the revolution, American citizens spontaneously toasting an English sovereign.

One person in the group failed to rise. It was Mike Reardon; he had passed out quietly in his chair. Phillips, annoyed at what he considered to be inexcusable conduct, completed his toast by pouring the contents of his pitcher over Reardon's nodding head.

Monty half walked, half carried his friend's inert form outside, hoping the fresh air would clear Mike's head. "Easy now, keed. You sit here for a minute, you'll feel better. I'll be back in a short while."

When he returned some ten minutes later, Mike was not to be seen. "My god, Mike's in no condition to be wandering about. If he decides to cross the highway, he'll be killed!"

As he searched anxiously for his friend, the lights of a passing car revealed Mike's recumbent form curled around the far corner of the building, slightly shielded by a lone straggly piece of shrubbery, which had somehow survived the rigors of growing in a gravel parking lot.

Monty ran over to where Mike lay, began shaking him vigorously, saying, "Come on, Mike, old man. You can't stay here, you know. It looks positively ghastly to see a Canadian officer lying on the ground like a drunken derelict. Come on, keed! Straighten up, for god's sake!"

Mike raised his head slightly and began to chuckle. "'S okay, Monty. No one can shee me. I'm hiding in the bushes!"

CHAPTER 11

Tacoma Hospitality

The citizens of Tacoma, Washington, soon became accustomed to the novelty of having a large group of Canadian soldiers in their midst; they realized there was very little difference between the Canadians and their own soldiers, except for the uniforms they wore. With characteristic American hospitality, they welcomed the Canucks into their homes and clubs. There were a few isolated incidents involving Canadians and Americans during the brigade's six-month stay. On the whole, the members of the Korea-bound brigade enjoyed their visit. More importantly, their hosts enjoyed having them in their city.

A few weeks after the Royals' arrival, Don Standish, a young subaltern in D Company, met a young Tacoma socialite at a local golf and country club. During a subsequent meeting, Don's attractive companion suggested it would be nice if she and a group of her sorority sisters from the College of Puget Sound arranged a party for about ten single young officers from the Royals. Standish, thinking this would be a splendid idea, accepted on behalf of the officers of the battalion. However, Standish was faced with two major problems: he could not find ten single officers in the battalion, few of the single officers available showed any interest, one expressing it, "Attend a sorority party? My god, man, I haven't played post office for years! Sorry, no dice."

Finally, after much coaxing, Standish was able to persuade five eligible lieutenants to agree to attend the sorority party and, reluctantly, in desperation, asked Monty and Reardon to join the group. After Mike and Monty accepted the invitation, they tried to convince Paul Anderson to join them on the basis that it was a social gathering. It would be bad manners if the officers did not make a good showing. Anderson thanked his friends but declined.

Paul, sitting alone staring ruefully at his wife's photograph, a bundle of her old letters strewn haphazardly on his writing table, couldn't understand not receiving a letter from his wife in over two weeks. Unable to contact Barbara at their apartment by telephone, desperate, he called her mother's home, asking about his wife's whereabouts. Her mother became evasive, sounding quite annoyed with her son-in-law for bothering her. The only consolation he had from the call was learning Barbara was well, but on thinking, an old suspicion returned, *Could there be someone else? What utter nonsense! There must be some other explanation* . . . His thoughts were interrupted by the entrance of his two friends.

"Paul, we know you said you didn't want to go. We put your name on Don Standish's list anyway. Be a sport, pretend you're single for a night, you can claim you're separated from your wife, separated by about three thousand miles."

"I agree with Mike, old chap," Monty added. "I'm sure that spending a night out in the presence of some young women will do you a world of good. After all, old man, you're the only real intellectual in the crowd. Why, these impressionable young college girls are bound to welcome you with open arms. You owe it to the rest of us to come along, Paul. Rather bad form if you don't."

"Don't you two ever give up?" Paul asked. "Just because your marriages are a mess, you chase every woman in sight, doesn't give you the right to corrupt everyone else."

"You don't have to get so damn sore, Paul. We're only trying to be helpful. All you ever do is sit around here writing your wife or, else, reading some brain-twisting book with an unpronounceable name. Instead of reading about life, why in hell don't you live a little?"

"What I do, Reardon, is my business. Now will you two stick to your skirt chasing and leave me alone?" he demanded, his face flushed with anger. "I'm going over to the club to make a long-distance call home. Excuse me."

As Anderson passed Reardon standing by the doorway, Mike asked, "Nothing wrong, I hope? Sorry to have bothered you, Paul."

"No, there's nothing wrong. I'm sorry I lost my temper. I know both of you mean well. I'll see you later at the mess."

After Paul left, Mike turned to Monty and asked, "What in hell has come over him? God, he's touchy lately." Monty replied, "These scholastic chaps are rather temperamental as a rule."

"I wouldn't say that Paul is temperamental, Monty. Why, he used to be one of the most even-tempered guys you'd ever want to meet. There must be some other reason."

"I'll let you in on a little secret, Mike, but for heaven's sake, keep it to yourself. I'm quite sure that his wife hasn't written him lately, and you know how that would affect the poor dab. He positively adores her."

"So that's the score! Can't say I'm particularly surprised though. The little bitch!"

"Why, Mike! What a rotten thing to say." Then narrowing his eyes, Monty asked shrewdly, "Do you know something about her I don't?"

"Of course not! Let's change the subject. Say, isn't it about time for dinner?"

Later that evening, Paul dropped in on Mike getting ready for a date with his German girlfriend Tina. Paul said casually, "If the invitation is still open, Mike, I'd like to be one of the gang going to the house party tomorrow night."

Mike was surprised and was tempted to ask Paul the reason for his change of heart but thought better of it, saying instead, "That's great, Paul. I'll drop by Don's room on my way out and tell him to include you. Anything else I can do for you?"

"No, nothing at all, thank you. Incidentally, who is the unlucky girl tonight? Tina?" When Mike nodded his head, Paul continued, "In that case, I suppose we won't see you until morning parade?"

"Paul, my boy, you're so right!" Reardon replied suggestively, a pronounced leer on his face. "Never let anyone try and tell you that German women are cold."

When Colonel Graves learned of the party invitation to his officers, he decided to detail one of his field officers to accompany the group of young men in the role of an unofficial chaperon, feeling he had enough trouble on his hands without having to worry about his junior officers creating problems with the daughters of some of Tacoma's most socially prominent citizens.

"After all, with young hell-raisers like Carr-Wilson and Reardon present, almost anything is possible," Graves mused. Sighing deeply, the greying colonel recalled his days as a young junior officer early in World War II. "I wonder whatever became of that cute little redheaded chorus girl I picked up in London in '40?" he asked himself.

The palatial home of the party's hostess was located in the exclusive Tacoma suburb of Lakewood, an elite country club community bordering the northern shore of American lake. The house, appropriately called Shore

Manor, a magnificent example of the architect's art, was built in three distinct levels on a steep bluff that overlooked the lake.

John Martin and his wife, Martha, were justifiably proud of their beautiful home, but Martin was prouder of his two beautiful daughters, Anne and Margaret. Anne Martin, an honor student, was president of her college sorority, the one suggesting to Don Standish her sorority organize a party for a group of Royals officers.

As prearranged, the other girls arrived at Anne's house an hour before their guests were due, assisting the Martin girls to make final preparations for the party. Mrs. Martin and her husband were visiting friends for the evening. The Martins, remarkably generous hosts, arranged for an ample supply of liquor and a lavish buffet for the girls and their Canadian guests. Martin was not unduly worried about the conduct of the girls at the party, feeling they were old enough to take care of themselves. He had implicit faith in his daughters' ability to keep things under control.

Precisely at nine o'clock, two taxis filled with Canadian officers pulled into the entrance of the circular driveway fronting the Martin home. As Major Dearing paid the fare, the rest of the officers led by Don Standish walked up to the massive oak door, a few rude remarks passed by some of the young men present as Standish pressed the bell. The pleasant sound of chimes following, the door was opened by a startlingly pretty girl who ushered the men through the anteroom into a large luxuriously furnished living room; they were faced by ten of the loveliest girls the Canadians had ever seen. The young Tacoma socialites were ranging in age from nineteen to twenty-two, their beauty matched by their gowns. One of the young officers, a look of awe on his face, spoke to Standish in a hoarse whisper, "This is really great, Don, and to think, I almost passed up this trip."

During the extensive series of introductions that followed, Dearing and Anderson both felt embarrassed, Chuck Dearing because of his age difference with that of the girls, Paul because of a guilty conscience.

Anderson began to regret his decision to join the party the moment he entered the room and, once the lengthy introductions were over, quickly detached himself from the gaily chatting group. Seating himself by the fireplace, he began to listlessly poke the fire's crackling embers. One of the girls sat beside him, her attempts to arouse the blond Canadian's interest futile. Sensing his indifference, she excused herself, proceeding to look for a more congenial partner. Her next choice, much to his surprise, was Chuck Dearing.

Standish was irritated by the expert manner Carr-Wilson and Reardon monopolized the company of the two striking Martin sisters. Margaret Martin, although fascinated by Monty's charm, was not taken in by him.

"Better watch out for that smoothie, Magpie! Give him half a chance and your virtue will quickly become a cherished memory," she wisely warned herself.

Her elder sister, Anne, was listening politely to Mike's earnest, unavailing attempts to impress her. However, she was indifferent to the rugged Canadian's purely physical charm, valuing a man's mind far above his muscles, a rare attitude annoying the wealthy backseat Romeos in her social set. While chatting with Reardon, she found her attention straying to the handsome refined-looking Canadian who sat reading by the fire. Much to her surprise, she found her curiosity and interest in the solitary figure increase each time she looked at him.

Deciding she wanted to meet the Canadian by the fire, she turned to Mike, asking, "I hope you'll excuse my poor memory, Mike—who is the fellow sitting alone by the fireplace?"

"Oh, that's a winger of ours. His name is Paul Anderson. He's really a nice guy but a bug on philosophy, poetry, and that sort of stuff," Mike answered.

"Oh quite! He's the intellectual type which may account for his peculiar behavior at times," Monty added. "I hope you'll excuse his conduct, I'm quite sure he doesn't mean to be rude. He didn't intend to come in the first place. He feels uncomfortable at affairs of this kind for some reason."

"He doesn't seem to be enjoying himself," Anne commented. She stood up, tossing her long tawny hair as she turned her head to face Mike. "I hope you'll excuse me for a few minutes. Your friend, Paul, looks rather lonely. After all, as the hostess, it's my duty to ensure that all of my guests are happy."

Paul, completely engrossed, did not see the tall slender figure of Anne moving toward him.

"Must be a very interesting book you're reading, Mr. Anderson. I didn't think our party was that dull!" she chided.

Paul stood up in embarrassed confusion and replied apologetically, "Oh no, Ms. Martin. It's an excellent party, I'm not much of a party man, I'm afraid. You must think me awfully rude!"

"Not at all. Your two friends explained that you're quiet, dislike parties, and are a book worm. I'm pleased you managed to find a book that interested you."

"I can tell that you've been speaking to Mike." Paul smiled. "Books are not his main interest, I'm afraid. You do have an excellent selection."

"I understand you're interested in philosophy? No, I'm not psychic—your friend Mike again. Tell me, Paul, what branch of philosophy particularly interests you?"

Paul felt himself warming to the attractive young woman seated on the edge of his chair. During the ensuing conversation, he learned that Anne shared many of his academic interests, had developed an impressive knowledge of English literature and poetry. When she asked Paul about his life before joining the army, he seemed nervous and evasive.

She was tempted to ask if he was married but thought better of it, instead picked up the book of poems he'd been reading, commenting, "I see you were reading 'He Fell Among Thieves.' Are you fond of Noyes' poetry?"

"No . . . not particularly, except perhaps for this one," he replied.

Anne, staring into the flickering fire for a few moments, turned to Anderson and, in a voice full of emotion, said, "I think the young Englishman's death was a terrible tragedy. To die so young, when he was so full of promise . . ."

"I don't agree with you, Anne," Paul said quietly. "He lived and died by an inflexible code, fashioned in his consciousness all his life. When faced with death, he had the fullness of life to draw on to give him strength for his violent end. His last words and thoughts contained no regrets but rather an inspired appreciation of having lived."

"Oh, Paul, that may be true, but then again, all his rare appreciation for living, an appreciation so necessary among mankind, was lost when his head rolled in the dust."

"Again, I disagree, Anne! Mankind didn't lose anything when he was beheaded. Why, at that very instant, somewhere on the earth, a new life was born. He was able to see the immortality of life, which enabled him to master man's greatest fear—death."

When he finished speaking, Paul caught Anne's look of rapt attention. As their eyes met, she flushed with embarrassment, her excitement mounting as she looked at Paul's keen, sensitive face, his tousled blond hair, the brooding intelligence evident in his eyes. Taking one of his long slender hands, she stood up, saying, "I'll bet you are a wonderful dancer, Paul. Shall we join the others?"

While dancing, he found himself comparing her with Barbara, making him feel guilty, ill at ease.

Anne, immediately sensing the sudden change in his attitude, spoke, "Is there something wrong, Paul? You look so strange."

"No, of course not. Maybe I feel guilty at having given up my studies," he lied lamely, wondering, *Now why did I say that? Why didn't I tell her about Barbara? Oh well, it doesn't really matter. I won't be seeing her again. Not much sense spoiling the evening.* In his heart, he knew he wanted to see this sensitive girl again.

Reassured by Paul's explanation, Anne continued giving her views on the destiny of mankind, a subject always of interest to Anderson. It was his turn to stare at Anne with rapturous attention, admiring her quiet esthetic beauty, her long soft red-gold hair, the sculptured lines of her sensitive face, her flawless skin, her slender well-proportioned figure, her large luminous green-tinted brown eyes that, to the Canadian, seemed to reflect the beauty of her soul.

Not realizing Mike Reardon, by now a little drunk, had been standing behind them, listening for some time, they were startled when he spoke, "Hey, Monty! Come over here and listen to the professor's line. It's terrific," Mike interjected sarcastically.

Carr-Wilson, with Anne's sister in tow, joined the threesome, sensing hostility between his two friends. He skillfully cleared the air, saying, "Come on, you two intellectuals! How about descending to earth joining the sybarites? You two have dazzled each other long enough."

"Sure, how about mixing with the plebes? Mind if I dance with the hostess, Paul?"

"Sure thing, Mike. It's all right with me if Anne's agreeable."

"Why, Michael Reardon, I accept with pleasure," Anne chided Mike, at the same time winking at Paul. "But," she continued, "only one dance now. It's almost time to serve the buffet."

Dearing, prepared to spend a quiet dull evening, was standing by the piano, feeling quite paternal watching the young couples enjoying themselves. Having danced with most of the girls present, he felt intuitively a few of them wouldn't need too much encouragement to give up their partners and spend the rest of the evening with him. He wisely refrained from doing it, instead staying on the outer fringes of the party playing records and, of course, drinking, filled with a warm glow created by numerous shots of straight bourbon. He looked quite impressive standing alone—a picture of distinction. The silver steaks in his hair at the temples were reflecting dully in the flickering firelight.

Pamela Bartlett had been miffed by Paul Anderson's lack of interest in her company earlier in the evening, spending most of her time flitting from one group to another, at the same time mixing herself strong cocktails. Pamela was a product of money—pots of money. Her wealthy father was always indulging the whims of his lovely but temperamental only child. On her sixteenth birthday, he gave her a new car. He sent her on a tour of Europe when she was eighteen. At nineteen, she asked for and received a Caribbean cruise. Now at twenty, she was completely out of hand and did as she pleased, listening to no one.

She experienced her first serious love affair while attending a private school in Washington DC. Her lover was an associate of her father's in the State Department. The Bartletts had returned to their home in Tacoma when his work in Washington was finished. At her own request, they left Pamela behind to finish her year at the exclusive girls' school she was attending. Bartlett asked his friend of long standing to keep an eye on his daughter, which the friend did only too well, finding his young charge's inexperience and passionate willingness refreshing after the dull routine affairs he experienced with many career women in the Capitol. The end of the school year also ended Pamela's affair. She felt no regrets, enjoying the experience too much for regrets, leaving her with a weakness for older men, a weakness evident the moment she spotted the lone figure of Dearing standing beside the piano.

"Whatever is a handsome man like you doing standing by himself with so many girls around?" she laughingly asked the startled major. "In case you've forgotten, I'm Pamela Bartlett. I hope to God that you're not going to leave me standing here by not asking me to dance."

Recovering quickly from his surprise at the frank, unconventional approach used by the pretty brunette facing him, grinning, he replied, "Why, it will be a pleasure to dance with you, Ms. Bartlett!"

"Good lord! The name is Pamela, not 'Ms. Bartlett,'" she retorted impatiently, mimicking his words. "Some of you Canadians are as bad as Englishmen, honest to God. Well, aren't you going to tell me your name, handsome? Or am I supposed to have it inscribed on my heart as a result of our first introduction?"

"It's Chuck, Chuck Dearing."

It did not take Dearing very long to discover that, despite her obvious youth, Pamela Bartlett knew how to excite men. As they danced, she pressed her lithe, sensuous body in a bold rhythm against his; she gently flicked his right earlobe with her tongue.

A few dances and a few drinks later, she whispered huskily in his ear, "Chuck, darling . . . My car is outside. Take me for a drive? Please? I know a wonderful place where we can be alone."

Pamela directed Chuck to drive north on Highway 99. As the car careened along the super highway, they remained silent, both lost in thought. He sat quietly, driving with one hand, fondling her thighs with the other. He was about to slow up and turn back when Pamela directed him to make a turn into a secluded bush-lined side road. Unable to resist the urgency in her voice, he followed her instructions, pulled to the side of the deserted side road, cut the engine, turning off the lights.

Pamela's eyes glowed hungrily in the pale light reflected in them from the star-filled sky, her sensuous full lips parted, her breath coming in short passionate gasps. She tore at the clasp fastening her mink jacket, pressing her breasts against his rigid body.

Making one last desperate attempt to control the situation, Chuck said aloud, "Look, Pamela . . . This isn't right! I'm almost old enough to be your father. Besides, I'm married."

"I don't give a damn," she panted, throwing herself into his arms, stopping his protests with desperate kisses. A low animallike scream rumbled in her throat as she hissed, "Take me . . . for god's sake, take me!"

CHAPTER 12

The Deuce

Maj. Charles Dearing was sitting at his desk in his company office reading the battalion training directive his second in command, Capt. James Phillips, had passed to him. It was obvious, from his look of annoyance, Dearing was unhappy with the training program drawn up by Major Harcourt and approved by Colonel Graves. After he finished reading, he looked out his window at one of his platoons undergoing drill on the company's parade square.

Sitting this way for a few moments, his fingers drumming on the top of his desk, he turned to Phillips, saying, "Better round up the platoon commanders, Jim. Have them here in, say, a half hour. The sooner we get this bloody thing started, the better."

Reading the directive a second time, Dearing felt his anger rise. It was evident to him the commanding officer had chosen to ignore every one of his A Company commander's training suggestions.

"If he doesn't want our opinions, why in the hell does he bother to hold training conferences and ask for suggestions? That damn textbook-soldier Harcourt is behind this. I'd bet my bottom dollar on that," Dearing said aloud in his empty office. He made a motion to pick up his field telephone to contact Colonel Graves then thought better of it.

Chuck Dearing, thirty-eight years old, in excellent physical condition, began reflecting on the circumstances resulting in leaving his family, a successful business, volunteering for the Special Force, admitting to himself fortunate being asked to take over his father-in-law's real estate agency after the latter's death. Although not liking real estate as an occupation, it had provided his family with a good living.

Despite numerous disagreements with his wife during the early years of their marriage, they managed to share some happiness; their serious difficulties began with the arrival of his mother-in-law, Chuck agreeing to have her live with them on the condition she was not interfere in their private affairs, an arrangement proving satisfactory for a short time. Then unable to control her dislike of her son-in-law any longer, she began tearing the marriage apart, influencing her daughter to insist her husband give up drinking, his friends, his athletic interests, resulting in Dearing drinking heavily, starting an affair with his secretary. Grace Dearing found out about the affair. Acting on the advice of her vindictive mother, she decided not to separate from her husband, instead make him pay dearly for his indiscretion.

Grace Dearing's biting criticism of everything her husband said or did became more sarcastic, more unbearable, not letting him near her, except on rare occasions of satisfying her own physical needs. Finally, Dearing asked her for a divorce or at least a separation. At her mother's insistence, she refused. Dearing's nemesis wasn't going to let her son-in-law run her dead husband's business without her around to keep an eye on things. Chuck often considered walking out on the whole sordid mess but, for some strange reason, couldn't. The fear of having to start all over again was too great.

The announcement by the Canadian Army that they required qualified officers to volunteer for the Special Force gave Dearing a golden opportunity to escape his tormentors, keeping his self-respect. Volunteering for the Korean brigade, his excellent war record, his previous wartime rank of lieutenant colonel, would result in him being commissioned a major in the new force. Unfortunately, Dearing clashed with Graves soon after his arrival at the Royals' camp. The months following didn't alleviate the strained relationship between the two men, a relationship attributed to their dissimilar personalities. Graves was often forced to remind Dearing just who was commanding the battalion. Making matters worse, Major Harcourt disliked him intensely.

Dearing's reflective mood was jarred by the noisy entrance of his officers, laughing at Monty's lurid description of his date with the hatcheck girl from Rocco's place. Seeing the grim look on Dearing's face, they stopped laughing, aware of the conflict between their company commander and Graves, its resultant effect on Dearing's temper. When he had finished briefing them on the details of the latest training order, understood the reason for their commander's fit of bad temper, Graves had instructed A Company to continue basic training to bring it up to the required standard, while the rest of the companies were authorized to start advanced training. Dearing's hand shook, holding the damning directive, a slight he wouldn't soon forget. The officers of A Company knew some of the other company commanders deliberately exaggerated the capabilities and progress of their companies to look good in the eyes of the battalion commander. Unfortunately for Dearing, Graves spent so much time checking on his pugnacious A company commander, seldom noticing the failings or weaknesses in the other company leaders.

Reardon was the first to speak. "What's the big idea, sir? My platoon been ready for advanced training since we left Canada as far as I know, so are the other platoons in the company. Why, if something isn't done about that directive, we'll be the laughingstock of the battalion!"

Monty and Paul, nodding their agreement with their friend's angry remarks, said nothing. Consequently, Mike bore the full brunt of Dearing's pent-up anger.

"Who in hell do you think you're talking to, Reardon? You'll damn well follow orders and like it. Understand?"

Mike clenched his fists convulsively, a hot surge of rage rising in his body. A large vein in his neck began to throb from the violence of his anger. When he was about to speak out, Monty wisely cut him off by asking, "How long will we have to continue basic training, sir?"

"Until your platoons are bloody well ready!" Then ashamed at his outburst, Dearing apologized, smiling slightly, "Sorry I blew my stack. I feel just as badly about this business as you do, in fact, worse, because I know it isn't really your fault. Just the same, we have to follow orders even if they appear unfair. Let's show the old man what a real outfit can do. What do you say?" Feeling somewhat better after Dearing's apology, the three young officers readily agreed.

"Any questions? Okay then, that's it, except for you, Mike. I'd like a word with you in private."

When the other two men left, the major commenced to speak. "I'll be brief, Mike. Look, I know you're trying, trying very hard," he said slowly, "but you're pushing your boys too hard. We aren't trying to train a track team."

"I don't think I get you, sir. I'm only trying to get my guys in shape. Some of them are in lousy condition." Reardon continued more in surprise than anger, "Why, the old man is a bug on condition, you know that."

"That's fine as far as it goes, but isn't there more to it than that? Haven't you been trying to show your men what a tough guy you are by showing them up? Now be honest!"

"That's not true, sir, not true at all! I can't imagine how you ever got hold of a crazy idea like that."

"You may think it's crazy, Mike, but that's exactly what a lot of your boys are thinking. They feel you're trying to build up a reputation at their expense. Look, fella, I've been in this business a hell of a lot longer than you. Believe me, I know the score. I was a hairy platoon commander once myself. You've got the makings of a fine officer, kid. You're strong and have guts to spare. I know that, so do your boys. Now start showing them you're also clued up. Incidentally, Mike I'm sorry as hell I gave you a hard time earlier. I got a kick in the ass before you came in I just couldn't help passing it on. Well, what do you think?"

"I don't know quite what to say, boss, except I didn't know I was making such a horse's ass of myself. I guess there isn't much else for me to say except 'thanks for the tip'."

"That's the spirit, Mike. Come on! Don't look so glum. I'll tell you what, let's go over to the mess and I'll buy you a drink."

Reardon's men were disappointed, resentful, learning they had to continue basic training while the platoons of the other companies started on advanced work. They knew they were in for a lot of "riding" from other members of the battalion. Many of the platoon members, unaware of the friction between their company commander and the battalion CO, blamed their humiliation on Reardon's lack of experience, the resulting bitterness creating a difficult situation for the platoon sergeant, Eric Cross. It was Cross's responsibility to keep the tempers of his men under control, maintaining platoon discipline. One of his hardest tasks was stopping the men from calling their platoon commander "Running Reardon, the Marathon Marvel" behind his back.

The men of second platoon, nicknamed the Deuce by the other platoons, were dejectedly packing their gear for the long fourteen-mile trek to the training area. Most of them were silent, discouraged at the prospect of making a tiring hike in the rain.

"If it hadn't been for that damn Running Reardon, we wouldn't be in this rotten fix. The only good thing about it is we won't have to take any more crap from the rest of the apes around here," Al Johnson complained resentfully to his brother.

"Look here, Al, you were told by the sergeant to stop calling the platoon officer Running Reardon," Gus Johnson warned his younger brother. "If Cross ever hears you, it would serve you bloody well right if he punched your head in."

"Well, listen to Mr. High and Mighty! Didn't take long for that 'first hook' to go to your head, did it?"

"Cut out the bullshit, Al. Here comes the sergeant."

Sergeant Cross strode purposefully into his platoon's barrack room, scanning the area, a look of displeasure on his rugged face. His men were behind schedule in packing their gear, openly hostile, their sleeping area in disorder.

"Come on, you guys, get a move on! We haven't got all goddamn day. This place looks like a ruddy pigpen! Some of you get some cleaning materials and clean this place up. One and three platoons are almost ready."

"Isn't that just ducky?" An unidentifiable voice boomed from the far end of the room.

Cross whirled to face the origin of the unknown voice, irately demanding, "Okay, wise guy! Speak up! Sounds like it could have been you, Banks."

"Heaven forbid, Sergeant, it wasn't me," Banks responded with mock seriousness, trying desperately to keep from laughing.

"Never mind the funny business, you guys, and get going!"

Edward George Banks possessed a volatile, irrepressible wit, establishing him as the undisputed platoon clown. His never-ending attempts to be funny were perhaps 10 percent effective, being his own best audience, always laughing more loudly at his jokes than his listeners. Ed, a product of a financially comfortable Toronto family, was typical of the modern city-bred generation. His outlook on life was cynical and immature, his comprehension and interest in world issues almost nil. He teamed up with the Johnson brothers since joining the Deuce, making an unlikely trio—Ed taking the part of the wit, Al hot tempered, and Gus serious and taciturn.

Blackie Balaski sat on his cot, looking at the unpainted floor. Although he didn't believe in grieving, he found himself unable to make new friends after the deaths of Bruce Mackenzie and Jock McHaskell, still missing them, especially Jock. Shrugging his big shoulders, he stood up, continuing the arduous task of packing his kit. Several of the men of the platoon tried to team up with Blackie after the accident. Refusing their friendship, he preferred to stay by himself. He began drinking heavily, paraded for drunkenness in front of Dearing and Graves, unhappy and disillusioned, often considered "going over the hill." Fortunately, his unhappiness with civilian life, still fresh in his mind, stopped him from deserting. Blackie did take time-out from his self-imposed isolation to cheer up and help another member of the Deuce who seemed to be as lonely and discouraged as himself, another Montrealer, Bernard Viau.

Viau typified the large Anglo-French Canadian element growing up in the city of Montreal in recent years, learning early in his young life being the son of a tradition-bound French Canadian father and a domineering Irish Canadian mother created a peculiar set of problems, one being his mother's obstinate refusal to learn French, obliging him to learn to speak and think in two languages. At his mother's insistence, he was sent to an English-speaking school; at his father's insistence, he formed a group of French-speaking friends in their parish. To please both parents, he tried to make friends from both ethnic groups. Growing older, young Viau spent more of his time with his English-speaking friends.

Bernie's father was surprised, bewildered by his only son's decision to join the Special Force, particularly bitter by his son's decision to join the Royals in preference to the French Canadian battalion being formed for the Special Force. Bernie selected the Ontario battalion, feeling he would have more in common with the members of the Royals. His disappointed father chose to believe differently, certain his son was ashamed of his French Canadian blood. There were bitter words, heartbreaking recriminations between the two men the night before Bernie's departure for the Royals' training camp, his father refusing to contact the son since that unhappy night. His refusal to answer his son's letters made Bernie feel guilty and depressed.

Viau, finishing assembling his web equipment, was sweeping the area around his cot when he saw Blackie standing alone, looking out one of the windows.

"Hey, Blackie! You'd better hurry up, or else, the sergeant will be mad as hell at you."

"Yeah, sure, thanks, Bernie. Don't you worry about Old Blackie. I've forgotten more about soldiering than most of these clowns know."

Despite his words, he began speeding up his packing, his experience teaching him the soft-spoken Cross was no man to fool with.

At last, the men of the Deuce were ready, Cross forming them up in three ranks outside the entrance to their barracks, calling platoon roll.

Mike Reardon arrived as Cross was completing his roll call. Observing the impassive looks on their faces, he knew he had a tough job ahead of him. Cross called the platoon to attention, turned about, saluting his platoon commander smartly, saying, "All present and correct, sir."

Reardon, returning his sergeant's salute, stood the men easy, commencing to speak, "Men . . . I know that every last one of you is pissed off at having to go through phase 1 again. Well, so am I. Maybe I'm the one that's fouled up. Then again, maybe you're partly to blame. It really doesn't matter now. The important thing is to forget past misunderstandings and show the rest of the battalion what a real outfit can do."

After Reardon finished speaking, the men of the Deuce, including Cross, looked at him with a new respect, Blackie later expressing it, "Maybe he ain't so bad. I've seen worse!"

CHAPTER 13

Exercise Rattler

The tempo of the brigade's training increased considerably during January and February of the new year. The training of the Royals had rapidly progressed through platoon and company level until they were ready for their first big test as an integrated battalion. Exercise Rattler—this ambitious exercise was designed to test the Royals in battle situations they could expect to face in Korea. Colonel Graves realized Rattler was not only a test of the training standard and fighting efficiency of the Second Royals but also a test on his ability as the battalion's commander. This knowledge made him nervous and irritable during the last week prior to the start of the exercise, facing a number of administrative problems completely divorced from the organization and planning functions connected with the impeding scheme, including a serious morale problem concerning both his officers and men.

The fluctuating fortunes of the war in Korea created doubt as to the eventual destination of the Canadian brigade. A strong rumor suggested the Special Force might not be required in Korea, instead sent instead to Germany as part of Canada's NATO commitment. The uncertainty of their destination, coupled with the relentless intensity of their training, resulted in a sharp decline in his men's morale. Cases of AWOL, drunkenness, and insubordination were rising at an alarming rate. Oddly enough, the Canadians were relatively happy when they were training in the field. They accepted the discomforts of living outdoors in the penetrating cold of the wet Pacific Coast, the rugged field exercises helping the men rid themselves of their pent-up frustrations and excess energy. Graves managed to improve matters by enforcing a strict code of discipline in the battalion, holding his company commanders personally responsible for the conduct of their troops.

His punishments for lapses of discipline became more severe, resulting in his being nicknamed by the men February Graves because of frequent sentences of twenty-eight days' detention.

Some of Graves's officers were presenting him with a different type of problem, off-camp romances in a few cases, these casual affairs developed into serious romances which, in turn, broke up marriages and families. The problem of the morals of his officers was a touchy one. Uncertain as to the best way to handle the situation, he finally decided to use a direct approach, arranging to interview the officers concerned; his first interview was with Charles Dearing.

Dearing had become a serious problem for the CO of the Royals. By Graves's exacting standards, the major from London should have been his best company commander, finding Dearing to be an excellent tactician, a good leader of men, however finding his A Company commander argumentative, resentful of criticism, highly critical of other senior officers, including his own commander. Making matters worse, Graves had been contacted by Pamela Bartlett's father regarding Dearing's relationship with his headstrong daughter. Graves decided to settle the Dearing problem once and for all, picking up his field phone, asking the duty operator for A Company to ask the major to report to him.

Dearing walked into Graves's office, saluted smartly, and asked, "You wanted to see me, sir?"

"Yes, Major Dearing. Please be seated," he replied coldly. "I'll get right to the point. I'm not at all pleased by the way you've deliberately misinterpret my orders and—"

"I don't know what you're driving at, sir!" Dearing cut in sharply.

"So you don't know what I'm driving at, eh? Well, I'll tell you. My orders regarding the cutting of timber in the training areas were very explicit. Good god, man! When I visited your company area last Friday, I could have sworn I was in an Indian village complete with lean-tos and a log cabin! How in hell do you explain that?"

"I was carrying out sound training practices by encouraging the men to use their initiatives using any available materials to make themselves comfortable," Dearing responded sullenly.

"Well, you don't have to try to cut down the entire forest in the state of Washington to do it, man. Damn it to hell! You should have been with me when the brigade commander chewed me out the last time you did the same fool thing. Do you have any idea how much it costs the Canadian government every time your men cut down one of those damned trees? And what happened to the three prize steer the local rancher reported missing? Well, I bloody well know where they went—your men slaughtered them!"

"You should know, sir. You ate one of the best steaks."

"How in hell was I supposed to know they came from rustled beef! Then there's the business about the deer. You know what I mean, Dearing. In case you're interested, there's a fine of $500 and imprisonment for shooting deer on the Washington State preserves. It's about time that—"

"You're being—" Dearing began.

"That's enough, Major! I haven't finished. Let's get one thing straight once and for all. I'm commanding this battalion, and you'll bloody well do what you're told. I'm warning you, Dearing, if you step out of line just once more, I'll parade you in front of the brigade commander and have you relieved of your company. Do I make myself clear?"

Chuck Dearing could contain himself no longer. His voice trembling, he lashed back, "Look, Graves, I joined this outfit to do a job and not to be treated like a bloody puppet. I commanded a fighting battalion myself, as you damn well know, and did a hell of a good job! There isn't a goddamn thing you can teach me about leading men, Colonel. The only real difference between us is you stayed in and I got out after the war. You've given me a hard time since I joined the battalion. I can't seem to do anything right as far as you're concerned."

"The other company commanders haven't given me nearly the same trouble as you have, Dearing," Graves countered.

"Sure! You think they're wonderful just because they spend most of their time kissing your ass instead of speaking up . . . Well, I'm not built that way."

"You're getting mighty moral for a man who spends his time running around with a young girl—in fact, young enough to be your daughter," Graves snapped back.

"My private life is none of your business . . . sir!"

"It sure as hell becomes my business when the father of a nineteen-year-old girl goes to the trouble to phone me and threaten legal action against you if you persist on seeing his daughter."

"She's twenty, not nineteen."

"Nineteen, twenty—what in the hell difference does it make? In case you're interested, he had a private detective follow you and the girl to Seattle last weekend, and let me tell you, he was as mad as hell when he spoke to me."

"My god, you'd think I had seduced the president's daughter! I'll admit the whole affair may be foolish on my part, but believe me, she's been around."

"Bartlett admits to that. Nevertheless, he doesn't intend to let her throw herself at a married man old enough to be her father—those were his words," Graves replied.

"How did he find out I was married? From Pamela?"

"No, he went to the trouble of having you investigated. In fact, he even knows your wife's address and made it very plain, unless you stop seeing his daughter immediately, he'll contact your wife, telling her about the whole sordid mess."

Graves's last remarks completely subdued Dearing. The last thing in the world he wanted to happen was for Grace to find out about Pamela. Looking at Graves, shrugging his shoulders, he said quietly, "Well, I guess that tears it, sir. I admit I was wrong about the girl. I should have known better, you're actually to blame in a way."

"That's ridiculous! How could I be?"

"You detailed me to go to the goddamn party."

Dearing's reply made both men laugh, reducing the tension between them. He continued, "I guess you were right about the other matter too, Colonel. I can see where I've been difficult at times. I'll try my best to conform."

"I sincerely hope so, Chuck. You're a good officer. I need you as a company commander . . . not to run my battalion for me."

Graves stuck out his hand and stood up; Dearing followed suit. They shook hands, sharing a feeling of understanding and mutual respect for the first time.

The men of the battalion were preparing energetically for the impending ten-day exercise; every barrack block was a hive of activity, the occupants busy cleaning their weapons, mending socks, washing their dirty clothes, and assembling equipment. Cpl. Jack Harvey, leader of one section of the Deuce, carefully inspected his men's weapons, proud of his nine-man section; their spirit was good, worked well as a team. Admittedly, part of the reason the big strapping corporal from Collingwood, Ontario, received the full cooperation of his section was due to his bone-crushing fists. He was also a natural leader, his one serious weakness, his overwhelming desire to fight when he drank too much, a situation occurring all too frequently.

Jack Harvey was only sixteen when he joined the Canadian Army during the Second World War, shipping overseas as a member of the Queen's Own Rifles. He fought in Northwest Europe, was wounded, and was repatriated home. His father, a wealthy lumber dealer and prominent civic politician in the small Ontario town, was unsuccessful in convincing his son to enter the family business. Unsettled in mind, restless in body, Harvey decided to follow the uncertain life of a lake seaman, shipping on grain boats, oilers, and ore boats, completed the change in the hard-bitten youth the war had started. His heavy drinking, brutal conduct, becoming so unbearable to the people of the town, his father forced to tell him to leave, on pain of being jailed on any one of a number of serious charges. Surprisingly, Jack obeyed his father's request, spending the lake off seasons in Toronto and Montreal, much to the regret of the police in both cities. It became a common occurrence in city jails to have Jack as an overnight guest, sleeping off the effects of his long drinking bouts. During one of his frequent alcoholic excursions, he met and fell in love with a Toronto bootlegger's daughter, and after a short boozy courtship, they married to their mutual regret. Their marriage, punctuated with booze and violence, was short-lived; she left him, taking up with a team rider from a small American traveling rodeo.

Jack Harvey had been inspired to join the Special Force, standing in front of a judge in the Toronto city hall court. This time Harvey, charged for assault and battery, knew that he was going to "get the book thrown at him" unless he could think of some sort of reasonable defense.

After the charge had been read to the big-shouldered six-footer, the judge spoke, "What do you have to say for yourself this time, Harvey?"

"Nothing, I guess, Your Honor, except I didn't start the fight. It was the other guy started it."

"Yes, of course, Harvey. It's always the other guy who starts the fights, it seems," he commented sarcastically. "Anything else?"

Jack had a sudden inspiration. "Would it please Your Honor to let me go this time? I'd like to join this here Special Force to fight the communists. I swear I'll get in no more trouble if you'll let me do that, Your Honor, sir."

The judge looked thoughtful for a moment. "Very well, Harvey. Maybe we can put your fighting and hell-raising to some constructive use. I'm going to give you a suspended sentence on the clear understanding you make application to enlist and are consequently accepted in the army. Let me make this clear—if you do not make the attempt to enlist, or if you are not accepted, I'll see that you serve the full term of your sentence in the Don Jail."

Jack Harvey was ugly by a woman's standards. He had a badly misshapen nose, the result of innumerable fights, a square jaw, and a shock of unruly thick brown hair. Despite his frequent drinking bouts, his body was lean and hard, matching the flintlike blue in his eyes; his voice matching his manner, gruff and clipped; his mercurial nature manifested itself in many different moods; his laugh deep and infectious; his rages, black and forbidding; a devoted ally or a bitter, relentless enemy.

There was a lot of conjecture among the members of the Deuce as to the probable outcome of a fight between the soft-spoken sergeant and the boisterous corporal. On joining the platoon, Harvey had cockily asserted he could lick anyone in it, including the sergeant. His cocksure attitude was altered somewhat, witnessing Sergeant Cross systematically beat up then knock out a much bigger man than himself. Cross was one of the cleverest boxers and hardest hitters Harvey had ever seen.

Harvey was carefully examining the section's Bren light machine gun as the gunner, Pvt. Fred Frome, stood idly watching his corporal expertly strip the weapon. Frome, a native of Calgary, Alberta, contrasted markedly with the towering Harvey; he was short, stringy, appearing physically incapable of contending with the gun and its heavy magazines on long marches. Fred loved his weapon, giving him a feeling of power and equality. When he had his Bren gun in his hands, he felt like a big man.

Frome, of German extraction but looking Semitic in appearance, had the long hooked nose, full lips, sensitive brooding eyes, and dark complexion of an Israelite. Most of his eighteen years had been spent living on the fringes of society in run-down boarding houses, cheap hotels, in fact, anywhere his mother was able to find work. His upbringing had been haphazard, his education sketchy, having learned to compensate for his lack of size and formal education by exploiting the weaknesses of others, despising the weak, admiring the strong. His one tender characteristic was his steadfast love and devotion for his mother.

"Gun's in good shape, Fred. You may be a pain in the ass in a lot of ways, but I have to admit that you sure as hell know how to handle a Bren gun," Harvey admitted grudgingly.

One by one, Jack inspected his men's rifles, handing out criticism or praise, depending on the state of the weapon.

Gus Johnson, leader of the third section, had finished his inspection. He silently moved behind Harvey, who was too preoccupied looking down a rifle barrel to notice him.

"What in hell are you looking for, Jack, a bird's nest?" he asked, laughing at the incongruous picture the big corporal presented, looking down the barrel.

Jack whirled around, his face flushing with quick anger. Recognizing Gus, his anger disappeared, and he grinned back, saying, "Not in this section, Johnson. My boys don't fool around with their weapons like some other guys I could name."

Harvey was referring to an incident that had occurred a week previously when Cross had put two of Johnson's men, including Gus's brother Al, on charge for having dirty rifles. Jack and Gus were joined by the leader of the second section, Cpl. George Whitefoot, a mahogany-complexioned full-blooded Canadian Cree Indian.

"Listen to the baloney! If you guys want to have a look at some really good weapons, you'd better have a look at my section," Whitefoot drawled affably.

George Whitefoot's powerful, bulky, bowlegged frame was in direct opposition to the coordinated grace of his movements, never known to waste a word or motion. He controlled his men by his deceptively quiet manner, a manner that had been mistaken for timidity by a few unfortunates, for in a fight, he could move with the agility and power of a bear.

The three big corporals made an impressive sight as they stood talking together. Although having radically different backgrounds, utilizing different approaches in leading their men, they showed a number of common characteristics. The corporals of the Deuce were battle-experienced, knew how to give a good accounting of themselves in any type of fight, sharing a common loyalty toward their platoon, proud of their sections, respected Sgt. Cross, and were growing to respect their platoon commander, Mike Reardon.

The men of the Deuce were enthusiastic about participating in the battalion scheme, giving them the opportunity to compete with the platoons in the other companies on an equal basis. The members of A Company had not forgotten the caustic remarks and jibes directed at them by the men of the other companies when Dearing's company had been ordered to repeat the last phase of basic training. They were determined not only to do a good job, showing the rest of the battalion that A Company was the best company in the Royals, but the Deuce's members were also determined to prove that theirs was the best platoon.

The long awaited exercise started on a bright sunny morning in mid-February. The plush multi-green Washington vegetation, mottled by irregularly shaped patches of wet snow, the water-saturated, spongy, mossy carpet covering the vast area, was shielded from the sky by towering Pacific Coast evergreens, oozed cold puddles of water under the feet of the Canadians trudging over its yielding surface. The first phase commenced with the battalion moving in a long snaky column in a direction eventually taking them to the area supposedly occupied by a strong enemy force. Using a narrow dirt road as its axis of advance, the column moved in two groups. A company had been detached from the battalion sent ahead to probe the route of the main body for any signs of enemy resistance, while the remaining companies followed a safe distance behind.

Graves detailed Dearing's company to be the point of the column during the initial stages of the advance; Dearing, in turn, detailed Reardon's platoon to lead the company. The Royals' column advanced rapidly and without incident for a half hour when the lead platoon, the Deuce, was fired upon from a large copse of trees some two hundred yards from the road.

Reardon quickly located the origin of the blank-round fire directed against his platoon, indicating the enemy strength was approximately a platoon. Dearing moved up quickly to Mike's location. Looking over the situation, he carefully decided that a company attack was in order, calling a company orders group. While waiting for Carr-Wilson and Anderson to arrive, he radioed his information and intentions back to the battalion commander. Dearing decided to leave Mike's platoon where it was to provide fire support and to attack the enemy position from the right flank, using, as his start line, a drainage furrow that ran into the deep ditch bordering the axis road. He issued the orders and positioned his two assault platoons along the start line, with Anderson on his left and Carr-Wilson on his right. When his company 60-mm mortars commenced, laying a barrage of smoke under the command of the company warrant officer, Dearing ordered the attack to begin.

The noise of the blank fire became deafening as A Company moved in a large irregularly shaped arrowhead formation toward the enemy position. Voices of the NCOs could be heard above the deafening din, exhorting their men forward, "Keep in line . . . Move back . . . Move faster, damn you! Keep going!"

Graves arrived forward just in time to watch Dearing put in the final phase of his attack, sweeping over the enemy objective. It was obvious the colonel was pleased with the results; he was actually smiling.

This same procedure was followed many times during the next four days of the exercise, with each rifle company taking its turn leading the column. At the end of the fourth day, they reached a large clearing in a patch of woods, lying half a mile from the main objective, a low ridge bordered on either side by narrow treeless plains. Graves chose to utilize the clearing as his assembly area, moving his battalion to the edge of the woods before first light the following morning. At 4:00 a.m., the men were rousted out of their sleep, given a hot breakfast by their mobile company kitchens, formed up and moved to the attack start line. The Royals were cold and uncomfortable in the chill morning air, many of the men were hacking and coughing as they moved to the edge of the trees, the predawn quiet broken by the murmur of voices, the rattle of equipment. A and D Companies, the assault forces, were moved into position first. As soon as they had been strung out along the tree line in attack formation, Graves ordered Dearing and Buck Carson, commander of D Company, to attack along their preset axes. As A and D moved off, B and C Companies moved up into the start line positions vacated by the assault companies following them to the objective. When the attack had been successfully completed, Graves called an orders group of his company and supporting arms commanders to establish the battalion defense perimeter and their respective defensive responsibilities. In addition to setting his company's defensive task, Dearing was given the additional responsibility of providing a platoon for a night fighting patrol.

The men of the Royals, spending the remainder of the long hectic day digging and wiring, by nightfall, they were exhausted as the result of working steadily for nearly sixteen hours. While the three sections of the Deuce were digging for the night, Mike Reardon attended Major Dearing's orders group to receive final details of the defense stage of the exercise.

"God, I'm bushed! How do you two feel?"

"What an idiotic question," Carr-Wilson remarked with friendly sarcasm. "Tired? I feel like a shortsighted mare that married an elephant by mistake. I'm exhausted."

Paul Anderson was too tired to make any comment.

Meanwhile, the men of the Deuce were busy digging.

"If I lift another goddamn shovelful of dirt, I'll bust a gut, so help me!" Blackie groaned, throwing down his dirt-caked shovel. "I haven't felt this tired since I spent a weekend in '45 with a nympho in Paris, Bernie."

Bernie Viau jumped into the half-finished two-man slit trench after Balaski had wearily climbed out and took over where Blackie had left off. "How can you think of sex at a time like this?" he asked in disgust.

"Come on, you guys, get a move on. We haven't got all bloody day!" Big Jack Harvey ordered gruffly then shouted at the rest of the members of his section, "Get the lead out, you bunch of zombies, you look half dead. Get up off your butt, Frome, and get your goddamn Bren slit finished!"

When Sergeant Cross saw the black look on his platoon officer's face, he knew there was bad news.

"Better get hold of the section commanders, Eric. I've got a dandy to tell them," Reardon said to him. "Of the twelve goddamn platoons in this bloody battalion, we got the rotten job of taking a nice all-night stroll."

"Colonel Graves decided to send out a night fighting patrol, and we're it!"

"Goddamn it, sir, it isn't fair! Our boys have worked twice as hard as the other platoons. It wouldn't hurt for some of those other bastards to get off their fat butts."

"I agree, Eric, but you know the old expression—'Ours is not to wonder . . .'"

"Yeah, ours is but to do and work our asses off!"

"I'll tell the section commanders to take it easy and make sure the guys get some rest," Reardon replied, ignoring Cross's interruption.

Reardon was pleasantly surprised at the reaction of the members of his platoon hearing about the patrol. There were some groans and complaints but, on the whole, quite cheerful at the prospect of locating the enemy's new position that night. In fact, they adopted a motto: "If it's a dirty job, give it to the Deuce."

Two days later, the Royals carried out their withdrawal, making the long trip back to camp. Arriving at the camp gates, the proud members of the battalion straightened their backs, began swinging their arms, and sang enthusiastically despite their overwhelming weariness. Exercise Rattler was over; the Royals had scored a resounding success.

Wearily, Paul Anderson was removing his mud-caked boots when his batman handed him a letter; it was from Barbara. Eagerly ripping open the envelope, he eagerly began to read.

"My dear Paul, I don't know quite how to say this, but I've met someone else . . ."

CHAPTER 14

Lovers

Paul Anderson sat slumped over in his chair, his face white with shock, the damning letter from his wife held loosely in his trembling hand. Anderson's mind was in a painful turmoil as he reread the heartbreaking letter. When he finished, he looked up at the smiling picture of his wife; a mixture of grief, rage, and bewilderment etched in his tormented face, a deep sob in his aching throat. "Barbara in love with another man? Impossible! It just can't be true."

Hearing someone entering, he quickly averted his face as Mike walked in. Seeing Paul's tear-stained face, Reardon retreated toward the doorway in embarrassed confusion and said apologetically, "I'm damn sorry, Paul. I shouldn't have barged in like this. I'll be back later."

"No, please don't go, Mike. I'd like to talk to you . . . I've got to talk to someone," he pleaded, regaining some of his shattered composure. He picked up Barbara's letter from the floor where it had fallen from his nerveless fingers and handed to Reardon. "Please read it, Mike."

"No, Paul. It wouldn't be right for me to read your personal mail," he replied, pushing the letter away.

"I want you to read it, Mike, please!" Paul repeated, thrusting Barbara's letter into his friend's reluctant grasp.

As Mike read the contents of the crumpled pages, his face contorted in anger; when he finished, he looked at Anderson, flushed red and snarled, "The bitch . . . The dirty little bitch!"

Paul, shocked by Mike's violent reaction, instinctively defended his wife. "Mike! You have no business talking about Barbara that way. That's a rotten thing to say. You've no business insulting her like that! There must be some explanation. I'm going to phone her. She can't just throw away our marriage like this. I can understand her being attracted to another man after all our long months of separation. She's so beautiful, loves a good time. I suppose I shouldn't be surprised, but I'm sure once I speak to her, she'll change her mind . . ." Paul was almost babbling.

"Don't waste your time, Paul! She isn't worth it, believe me. I know." Mike cut in, his voice quivering with anger.

"What do you mean?" Paul asked, shocked.

"I was hoping I'd never have to tell you this because you're the last person in the world I want to hurt. Please remember what I'm about to tell you happened before you and I ever met. The only reason I'm saying anything now is because I like you too much to stand by and watch you eat your heart out over a woman who bloody well isn't worth it."

"Stop beating around the bush and out with it, Mike," Paul demanded, rising to his feet. "What are you trying to tell me?"

Mike stood in front of his friend, looking directly at him, and replied, "Remember the first day we met? The day your wife arrived for the weekend?"

Paul nodded, a suspicion gripping his vitals.

Mike continued, "Barbara and I spent the previous night together in her berth."

For a moment, Anderson looked at Mike with a look of utter disbelief. Then the full import of his friend's words finally struck home. He completely lost control of himself, screaming, "You're lying, you bastard! You're lying," leaping at Reardon punching him in the face.

Mike, caught off guard, stumbled over a chair, falling to the floor. Recovering quickly, he jumped to his feet, ready to drive his fists into Anderson's body but stopped.

Paul was standing in front of him, his hands clenched rigidly at his sides, sobbing, "Hit me, Mike. Hit me hard!"

Reardon looked at Anderson for a moment, turned on his heel, left the room without a word. Never before had he felt so despicable.

It was Monty Carr-Wilson who finally healed the breach grown between his friends after that night, managing to make Anderson understand Mike couldn't blamed for something happening before they met, reasoning with Paul that, after all, it was another man Barbara wanted, not Reardon who was just trying to be helpful. Monty had a sudden inspiration for curing Paul's depression over losing his wife, arranging dates for Anderson and himself with Anne Martin and her sister.

Anne's happiness at the prospect of seeing Paul again was genuine, though she was disappointed and hurt he had not bothered to call her after their first meeting at the party. As soon as she heard his voice, she completely forgot her earlier pique. When Anne first saw Paul again, she was shocked by his appearance; his face was drawn and pale, his eyes ringed with deep shadows. Anne was discreet enough to avoid asking Paul what was troubling him, feeling certain he would tell her when he was ready.

Paul and Anne met frequently during the ensuing weeks, taking long strolls in the woods bordering the lake, attending concerts, dining and dancing at the country club. Some evenings, they were just sitting quietly together by her fireplace, enjoying each other's company.

Anne was not greatly surprised learning that Paul was married, suspecting as much from the beginning. Despite this, his acknowledgment of what she had suspected hurt her deeply, so much so that she was tempted not to see him again, except realizing she was in love with Paul. Having fallen in love with him the first night, she couldn't bring herself to send him away. One evening, Paul, staring thoughtfully at the glowing embers in the fireplace, told Anne everything, showing her Barbara's last letter. Gently, Anne placed her hands on the sides of his head, pulling his face to hers, kissed him fully on the lips. Wordless, Paul took her in his arms, kissing her hungrily, almost desperately, feeling his bitter pain. His disappointment evolved into a tender love for the strange American girl who had come to mean so much to him. Anne lay languidly in his arms as Paul gently stroked her hair and neck. She absentmindedly fondled his cheek, thinking, then sat up slowly, looked at her watch, and turned to Paul.

Putting her hands on his shoulders, she said, "I love you, darling, and I want to be part of you. You're the one I've been saving myself for . . . No, shush, dear, and let me finish!" stifling his murmured protests by placing a hand over his mouth. "I love you and want you," she repeated passionately.

Paul stood up, pulling Anne close to him, kissing her tenderly, and then he asked, "Are you sure? My dearest, I love you too so very much, but I wouldn't want ever to hurt you. Are you sure?"

"I've never been more sure of anything else in my life." She paused for a moment then continued haltingly, "Please be gentle with me, dearest. I've . . . I've never been loved this way before."

The men of the Deuce were in high spirits when they returned to their barracks at the conclusion of Rattler. Their water-saturated, mud-covered equipment was strewn about the barrack room floor, the shower rooms filled with laughing, singing, whistling soldiers eager for a night out on the town.

Bernie Viau was determined to visit Tacoma despite his weariness. As soon as the Deuce arrived at the barrack block, Bernie had hurriedly removed his equipment, seeking the nearest telephone, wanting desperately to speak to a young Tacoma girl he had met before Christmas, Dorothy Butler, having a very important question to ask her.

Bernie's first meeting with the pretty little redhead had taken place in a Downtown Tacoma department store where she worked as a clerk. It had been an inauspicious occasion; he was doing some last-minute Christmas shopping for his family when he saw Dorothy busily arranging her purse counter, her long ponytail bobbing saucily as she moved her head, not aware of the presence of the young Canadian until he cleared his throat awkwardly. Looking up quickly, startled by his quiet approach, she was pleasantly surprised, confronted by a stocky clean-cut Canadian solider. Her immediate reaction was to say to herself, "He's cute," as Bernie began inquiring timidly about the price of the various purses offered for sale.

"I'd like something suitable for a woman who is attractive and very close to me."

"Oh, I see," she replied, losing interest. "We have something here that is very chic, ideal for the new styles. Any girl would be thrilled to receive a purse as lovely as this one for Christmas."

"Ah . . . Thank you very much, but you see I have an older woman in mind—my mother."

"No kidding?" she blurted then said, "I'm sorry, sir. Wait, let me see. Perhaps your mother might like this one?"

As he looked over the purses, Bernie wondered if the rest of the salesgirl's figure matched her attractive face. He was greatly relieved when he saw a trim shape and legs as she stepped from behind the counter to point out some purses featured in an aisle display. They chatted amiably, unmindful of the time, until a growing number of impatient customers and the ominous presence of the floor-walker forced Bernie to make a decision. He bought the purse suggested by the Tacoma girl, reluctantly stammered a goodbye, leaving for another part of the store. Standing by the escalator for a moment, he watched Dorothy serve her customers. His heart beat faster every time her ponytail bobbed as she moved around her counter. He must see her again.

The opportunity came two days later. Mike Reardon, his platoon commander, detailed him to help pick up Christmas decorations for the A Company mess. When they finished their task, Viau asked Reardon if he could visit the department store, promising to return shortly. Fifteen, twenty minutes passed without a sign of the young private. Mike, glancing at his watch impatiently, decided to look for Bernie and give him a blast.

Parking the jeep in front of the department store, he entered shouldering his way through the milling crowd. He finally saw Bernie standing beside the purse counter, talking eagerly to the pretty young girl standing behind it, pleasure glowing in both their faces. Bernie spotted Reardon striding purposefully toward him and hastily said goodbye to Dorothy, walking quickly toward his platoon officer. "Sorry to have been so long, sir. I didn't notice the time passing."

"This is neither the place or the time to carry on a romance, Viau," Reardon snapped, but seeing Bernie's worried look, he clapped him on the back and said, smiling, "Can't say I blame you, Bernie! She's a lovely-looking girl."

Bernie started seeing Dorothy whenever possible, her mother developing a liking for the shy Canadian from Montreal, insisting he spend Christmas with her family. It was a delightful Christmas for Bernie; he'd never been happier.

During the weeks that followed, a sweet, tender, and sincere love for each other grew between the young couple, and before leaving on Rattler, Bernie asked Dorothy to marry him, insisting that she not give him her reply until he returned from the exercise.

Bernie was tormented by misgivings as he nervously dialed Dorothy's number. It seemed to him an eternity had passed before the impersonal ringing on the other end of the line stopped. Then Dorothy answered, "Hello."

"Of course, I'll marry you, silly! I could have told you that the first time you asked if you had let me. Will you be long, dear?"

"As soon as I clean up and change. How does your mother feel about it? Did she object?"

"No, of course not. Mother likes you nearly as much as I do. She was very pleased when I told her you'd asked me to think things over before answering. She said it shows that you have a lot of common sense. Please hurry, darling!"

Their wedding took place a month later. It was small but not very quiet, for all the members of the Deuce were invited and showed up in force. Bernie's best army friend, Blackie Balaski, was best man, Major Dearing made a speech, Mike Reardon spiked the punch and made a pass at the maid of honor, George Whitefoot told some fantastic tales about his ancestors to an attentive American audience, Blackie got very drunk and sentimental. Jack Harvey and Frome started an argument which was quickly squelched by Sergeant Cross before reaching serious proportions. The small comfortable Butler home was overcrowded; there weren't enough seats to go around, but there was plenty to drink. Later, Mrs. Butler served a delicious meal. Everyone had a great time.

Bernie and his lovely bride, oblivious to the noise made by the celebrants, slipped away quietly from the reception after saying goodbye and started on their weekend honeymoon trip in Dorothy's brother-in-law's car. There were tears in Mrs. Butler's eyes, watching the car drive away, praying silently for their safety and future happiness, a shadow of cold fear gripping her heart.

CHAPTER 15

The Final Phase

The changing war situation in Korea had one favorable result; the fate of the Canadian Twenty-Fifth Brigade was finally decided. On February 21, it was announced that the original plan was to be followed; the entire brigade group would be sent to Korea.

The Royals' battalion, formed up on parade in a hollow square, was standing at ease as Colonel Graves approached. Major Harcourt, bringing the nine hundred men to attention, saluted Graves smartly, stepping one pace behind the CO. Graves, standing the battalion at ease, began speaking. "Men . . . We're going to Korea!" he announced, grinning broadly.

Immediately, every officer and man in the Royals began to cheer, the deafening roar reverberating off the buildings surrounding the battalion parade square, cheering themselves hoarse.

Finally quieting down, Graves continued. "We'll be sailing sometime next month. I'll pass on the details to your officers as I receive them so that you'll be kept in the picture. Now that we know for certain where we're going, it is the responsibility of every one of us not to let up in our training. In fact, we must work harder than ever, which means I'm confining both officers and men to camp, except for special reasons—and I do mean special!"

The first phase of the Royals' move to Korea consisted of preparing their vehicles for the long sea trip, selecting an advance party to precede the main body of the battalion to look after its transport, preparing a base camp outside of Pusan in Korea. After the advance party left for the Far East during the first week in April, the men of the Royals were seized by the growing realization that after the long weary months of training, the moment of truth was nearly at hand.

The CO's announcement had far-reaching effects on his men. Many short-term love affairs came to their inevitable conclusion. A few choose to ignore the finality of the situation, trying desperately to cram a lifetime of love into the few weeks still remaining. Paul Anderson defied Graves's edict, risking court martial, to see Anne. Her parents left on a month-long visit to her aunt's in Minneapolis, providing the lovers the opportunity to be alone together. Monty Carr-Wilson, understanding the situation between Anne and his friend, kept Anne's sister out of the way by taking her out regularly, a frustrating experience for him. The only satisfaction for his efforts was an occasional hot necking session with Anne's strong-willed sister. Knowing he was married, she was determined to protect her treasured virginity.

Margaret, speaking to her sister, very concerned over Anne's intense relationship with Paul, warned, "You can't keep on his way, you know. Despite his wife's behavior, he's still legally married! It just isn't wise. What about Mother and Dad?"

"We've decided to wait until he comes back, Marg, to straighten everything out."

"That's fine, Anne, if he comes back!"

"That's a terrible thing to say!" Anne replied, starting to cry.

"Anne, dear, don't carry on so. I'm just trying to be helpful. A romance like yours can be dangerous. Supposing he makes you pregnant! What then?"

"Why don't you leave me alone and mind your own business!" Anne sobbed as she ran out of the room.

The following weekend, in spite of her sister's heated protests and threats to write their parents, Anne left to spend the weekend with Paul at a ski lodge situated on the slopes of Mount Rainier. As the day of departure drew near, Paul and Anne were desperately making impossible plans for their future. When they were in each other's arms, nothing seemed impossible, feeling nothing could stop a love as strong as theirs.

All officers and men of the Canadian brigade were confined to camp the night before they were due to leave for Seattle to embark on their Korea-bound troopships. There were no exceptions; constant checks were made throughout the brigade to ensure that the order was complied with fully. However, a slight relaxation in the order was made by allowing visitors into camp.

Paul, waiting impatiently for Anne at their rendezvous outside the officers' club, was pacing nervously up and down in front of the club's entrance. He saw her car turn the corner, illuminating him in its headlights When the car stopped, Anne moved over to the passenger side as he got behind the wheel, driving to a secluded wooded area bordering the south boundary of the camp. The lights of oncoming cars revealed the clear-cut details of her face, still beautiful despite its pallor and look of silent suffering; her lips were bloodless, her eyes dark-circled from lack of sleep.

As he drove, Paul glanced briefly at Anne, feeling a rush of hot tears to his eyes. *My god, how I love this girl! It's not right that we should be separated now*, he thought, sighing bitterly.

Finding a secluded spot to his liking, Paul stopped the car and took Anne into his arms, embracing her for a few moments, and discussed their plans for the future. Anne's words flowed in a feverish torrent.

"I'll apply for a job in the city as soon as the school year is finished, dearest. Why, between the two of us, we should be able to pay for at least one year of postgraduate work. The cost of living in Vancouver can't be any higher than it is here in Tacoma. Oh, darling, I wish you could be here for my graduation! It would make me feel so happy and proud to see you there . . . Tell me, Paul, do you think there's any chance you could divorce Barbara while you're in Korea? It would make things so much simpler if you could."

Anne's mention of Barbara's name and divorce brought a cold wave of reality to Paul, replying, "As I tried to explain before, darling, it's not as easy as all that. Divorce laws in Canada are a lot more stringent than here in the States. There are fewer grounds open for divorce, and it takes a lot longer for one to go through. I'll probably have to go back to Hamilton for a short time to make the necessary arrangements."

"If you do, I'm coming with you!" Anne heatedly interjected.

"Of course, you will, Anne, dear," he soothed. "We agreed long ago we'd never be apart again after I return. Never!"

The morning of the Canadians' departure was bright and sunny; the heavily encumbered troops loaded on chartered buses similar to those that had transported them to the camp on their arrival. When the vehicles were loaded, they began moving in a long line toward Seattle thirty miles distant.

The pier, at which the Royals' huge twenty-thousand-ton troopship was berthed, was a bedlam of organized confusion. Movement control officers, both Canadian and American, were busy forming the Royals in line, shouting conflicting orders, checking off the numbers of troops, and loading them on board. Red Cross volunteers were passing out coffee and doughnuts to the seemingly endless line of soldiers; a large American brass band was playing a nonstop medley of military and dance music. One by one, the men shuffled along, some laughing, some singing, others quiet and thoughtful. In spite of the apparent confusion and delays, the monumental task of checking off, loading, and berthing over a thousand men was done with amazing rapidity and skill. Finally, the task was finished, the white transport cast off, slowly moving along the quay heading up Puget Sound toward the Pacific, its rails crowded with eager soldiers. As the ship disappeared down the sound, the people on shore could hear the Canadians singing, "So long! It's been good to know you . . ."

One week after Paul had sailed for the Far East, Anne Martin's suspicions of the past month were confirmed; she was pregnant. Sitting on the chesterfield in front of the fireplace, the same chesterfield on which she and Paul had spent so many pleasant hours together, she was trying to decide on what to do, regretting not having told Paul of her suspicions before he left, not wanting to cause him additional worry at an already difficult time in case her fears were unfounded. She had not been too apprehensive at the possibility of having a baby when they had been together, but now that Paul had left, she felt terribly lonely and frightened, a rash of confused thoughts racing through her agitated mind.

"What will I tell Dad and Mother? They'll never understand. What will they think of me? I'll tell Margaret first . . . It'll be easier that way."

A sudden horrible thought confronted her. "Suppose his wife changes her mind and refuses to give him a divorce, what then? Oh god, what will I do?" she cried aloud.

Then calming herself, she began concentrating on the happy prospect of their future together after Paul returned.

After all, a year isn't a terribly lone time, she thought brightly. *Paul's divorce will probably be through, and we'll be able to get married as soon as he comes home. Then we can get started, the three of us, someplace, somewhere. No one will need to know how long we've been married,* she concluded optimistically.

Anne instinctively clasped her breasts and abdomen. Closing her eyes, she lay back on the chesterfield thinking of Paul. "My darling, wherever you are," she whispered, "the world is such a desperately mixed-up place, but we have now something wonderful between us . . . Oh, my baby, my little baby, we'll love and protect you, my little sweetheart!"

Anne began to sob, a soul-shaking sob welling up from the depths within her, the cry of pain as old as woman as old as the world.

Later that evening, she wrote Paul: *"My darling, I have some news for you that is both wonderful and frightening . . ."*

PART 3

Korea

CHAPTER 16

The War in Korea

After its initial setbacks in the summer of 1950, the UN Eighth Army, under the command of Lt. Gen. Walton H. Walker, began building up its strength. The positions occupied by the North Koreans were pounded relentlessly from the sea and air. During the dark days of the Pusan Perimeter, the UN forces doggedly repelled repeated enemy attacks while preparing to launch an all-out offense designed to break the communist ring.

The counterblow, deftly planned by the Far East commander, Gen. Douglas MacArthur, fell on the North Koreans on September 15, 1950. It was a large task force carrying the Tenth U.S. Corps stealthily making its way up the west coast of Korea, anchoring off the port city of Incheon unobserved. A successful amphibious landing was made by the Americans under the cover of a terrific air and sea bombardment, their main objective being Seoul, the capital of South Korea. Encountering light resistance, the UN forces rapidly covered the twenty miles, separating Seoul from Incheon, recapturing the city.

As soon as the news of the successful Tenth Corps landing reached the communist forces besieging Pusan, they began a frantic withdrawal, ending up as a rout when the Eighth Army broke out of the perimeter, attacking the rapidly retreating North Koreans. The Eighth Army, advancing relentlessly, finally linked up with the Tenth U.S. Corps, General MacArthur broadcasting a demand for the surrender of the North Koreans. Despite their crumbling resistance and the deep penetration into North Korea by ROK forces, they refused.

Heated discussion between the Soviet and Western blocs took place in the political committee of the UN General Assembly. Finally, MacArthur was granted permission to carry on operations north of the thirty-eighth parallel. The North Koreans were in complete retreat. One by one, their major cities fell to the unfaltering advance of the UN forces. Pyongyang, the capital of North Korea, and Wonsan, North Korea's major seaport, fell in quick succession. The end of the spectacular advance occurred on October 26, when a small UN force actually reached the Yalu River, the border between North Korea and China.

During November, however, the resistance of the communists increased markedly. Unknown to the UN command, large numbers of men and great supplies of equipment were streaming across the border from China. On November 24, MacArthur started a general offensive designed to end the war by Christmas. On November 26, as the world waited expectantly for the results of the offensive, the combined Chinese army and the remnants of the North Korean army launched a large-scale attack in northwest Korea, followed by a massive attack in the northeast a few days later. Douglas MacArthur's ambitious Christmas offense had failed. Relentless large-scale communist attacks forced the UN forces to begin a long painful, heartbreaking withdrawal to the south through the snow-swept, bleak hills of North Korea. During the dark days of the retreat, under seemingly impossible conditions, innumerable epics of human courage occurred. The extremely difficult task of evacuating the entire Tenth Corps by sea was a saga of courage and sheer guts. The general withdrawal of the Eighth Army finally halted, and defensive positions, established along the Imjin River, were over two hundred miles south of the Chinese border.

Shortly after the New Year, the Chinese launched another overwhelming offensive in the east against the forces of the Republic of Korea. The South Koreans, responsible for the defense of the right flank of the Eighth Army, collapsed under the pressure, forcing the UN army to withdraw, once again give up Seoul. A line was finally established thirty-five miles south of the city; it was here that the Chinese winter offensive was stopped.

During February and March, the Eighth Army carried out a series of short battering offensives bringing them back toward the thirty-eighth parallel. Seoul was liberated on March 16; the Chinese began a general withdrawal. By the end of March, the UN line was just a few miles south of the disputed parallel. In spite of the cease-fire negotiations being held in the UN Assembly, MacArthur openly advocated continuing the offensive and, in fact, carrying the war by air into Manchuria to interdict the communist forces and supplies flowing into North Korea from Communist China to ensure complete military victory. As his ideas were in direct conflict to the policy being carried out by the president of the United States, MacArthur was relieved of his command and replaced by Lt. Gen. Matthew B. Ridgway.

CHAPTER 17

Troopship

The fourteen-day sea voyage across the Pacific was uneventful. The men of the Royals soon settled into a daily routine: early breakfast in shifts, cleaning up their domestic areas for inspection, weapon cleaning, supervised exercise on the broad foredeck; lunch, afternoon exercises and lectures; supper, antimalaria tablet parade, evening recreation, and finally, an early turn-in.

Colonel Graves set up an orderly room, conducting the business of his battalion as normally as possible, for he was responsible to the ship's captain for the conduct and discipline of his men. The captain's word was law; his daily morning inspections of the ship were thorough, painstaking, ensuring the lower decks where the men were housed were kept scrupulously clean. Seasickness was fairly common, especially during the first week, but the excellent discipline of the men prevented the effects of the sick from unduly upsetting others. The seasick soldiers were prevented from lying in their bunks and required to participate in the daily routine, which helped them considerably.

The Paludrine tablet parades for the prevention of malaria, a common affliction in Korea, were an innovation for the Canadians. Every night of the week, except Sunday, the men lined up in their quarters and were issued a tablet by their platoon officers. The object was to build up a resistance against the disease before the men came into actual contact with the mosquito-borne infection.

A common U.S. Navy expression, "Now hear this, now hear this," was heard constantly, punctuating every message passed by the ship's executive to the crew and military passengers.

A few enterprising soldiers started a veritable gambling casino out of sight of the ship's officers in the main lower deck passenger lounges. Here, crown and anchor, black jack, dice, and poker games flourished. When the evening operations were suspended before compulsory turn-in, the organizers of the illegal activities were careful to clear away all signs of their operations to prevent discovery by the captain during his exacting daily inspections. It was not long until the small shipboard pay, given to the men prior to sailing, was in the hands of a lucky few; the losers had the dubious consolation of watching the gambling "giants" devour one another's winnings in high-stake poker and crap games. This process of elimination continued until the lucky grand winner, a sergeant, had accumulated over $5,000.

The officers spent their leisure time either resting in their cabins or the lounge where they read, talked, played cards, or listened to music. A small group of officers, which included Steve Patrick, the battalion medical officer, and Monty Carr-Wilson, were busily conducting an almost perpetual poker game. In the course of the trip, Steve and Monty had managed to win most of the other players' money. Mike Reardon, a self-confessed "bones" specialist, won over $600 before meeting his match in the person of Red Saunders, an aggressive, cocky platoon commander from D Company. Red "got hot" and "cleaned" Mike out after a half hour of feverish activity.

"Oh well, it was fun while it lasted," Mike commented fatalistically as he got up from the floor, dusting off the knees of his trousers. "Make way for the last of the big-time spenders," he said ruefully as he left Red's cabin, heading for the main lounge.

As Mike approached the poker table, Monty Carr-Wilson was looking directly at Doc Patrick, absentmindedly stroking his cards. "Raise you fifty," he said quietly.

"Here's your fifty and fifty more, Monty," Doc replied, a trace of a smile on his lips.

Carr-Wilson sucked in his breath as he looked at the $400 pot. "I'll see you, Doc."

The spectators waited expectantly as Steve Patrick laid down his cards. "Three aces!"

"I'll be damned! Well, that beats me. Here are my openers," Monty said in disgust, throwing down his cards. "Well, old chap, I'm afraid that finishes me for the rest of the trip. Oh hello, Mike. I didn't notice you were standing behind me. How did you fare, old cock?"

"Three guesses and the first two don't count," Mike replied.

"Oh no! Not you too?"

"Yep, cleaned out. Incidentally, have you seen Paul around?"

"Why, yes, Mike. He was writing to his lady love the last time I saw him."

"How is he going to mail it, by seagull? What do you say we go and torture him for a while?"

"Wonderful idea, keed . . . After all, a little torture is good for everyone."

The war in Korea was still an obscure, vague prospect to most of the Royals members; their thoughts and conversation still centered on home and their stay at Fort Lewis. The lighthearted attitude toward the war, prevalent among both officers and men, became most evident during the lectures on enemy characteristics and tactics given to them by the battalion intelligence officer. He did his best to try to make the Chinese communist soldier seem real in the eyes of his listeners. When describing the tactics used by the communists, they merely laughed. They just could not visualize the Chinese attacking in waves, the first wave carrying automatic weapons, the second wave flourishing long bamboo sticks with bayonets strapped on the ends, the third and succeeding waves carrying nothing but grenades and small arms ammunition. The prospect of fighting a dogged, determined enemy in some of the most rugged terrain in the world seemed remote to the men of the Royals relaxing and chatting in the warm sunshine, reflecting off the white superstructure of the sleek ship. War was the farthest thing away from the minds of the men sunbathing on the decks, leaning over the ship's rails, staring at the azure waves of the Pacific Ocean.

The peaceful aura, settling on the Royals during their voyage, was quickly dispelled by a short terse news announcement on April 25:

> The combined communist forces of China and North Korea launched a major assault in the west-central sector of Korea, resulting in the withdrawal of the First and Ninth U.S. Corps.

The following day, the first information of the gallant stand made by the First Battalion, Gloucester Regiment, one of Great Britain's most famous fighting units, appeared in the ship's daily newsletter. The copies of the publication were seized quickly by eager hands.

> The first battalion, Gloucesters, of the British twenty-seventh brigade, after a gallant stand against an overwhelming enemy force, was overrun yesterday morning. There has been no communication with the battalion since that time.

The war had come much closer to the men of the Royals.

CHAPTER 18

Pusan

The most picturesque part of the long sea voyage occurred near its end when the small islands lying off the Japanese mainland were sighted. The excitement of the men aboard the ship mounted rapidly as their ship churned through the rolling ocean swells toward the faint purple shadows in the distance. Seagulls from the mainland began swooping and swerving in graceful circles around the ship, screeching their baby-like cries. A small Japanese fishing smack manned by a lone courageous fisherman was sighted. The captain of the doughty ship, looking ridiculously tiny on the vast ocean's heaving bosom, grinned and waved at the intrigued Canadians lining the rails of the troopship.

At last, the tiny islands came into clear view, a rare and beautiful contrast of bright oriental green and rich chocolate brown against brilliant ice blue sea; multisized fishing sampans, junks, trawlers, and canoes dotted the water's surface. The integrated picture of sky, sea, ships, green foliage, and dwarfed twisted trees gave the impression of an exquisite Japanese print suddenly come to life.

The southern extremity of the Korean coastline was sighted on May 3, thirteen days after the ship had left Seattle. To the inexperienced eye, the first sight of land revealed merely a low purple cloud set on the rim of the horizon. In fact, the only positive indication that the ship, cutting through the gentle swell of the Japanese sea, was indeed approaching landfall was the gradual enlarging of the purple shadow. The sea lost its rich blue and, instead, looked muddy and discolored.

The Canadians' ship approached the entrance of the channel leading to Pusan Harbor in the late afternoon. They were amazed by the heavy orange-brown pall of smoke hanging over the city. Although they were still several miles out of sea, their nostrils were assailed by an indescribable stench originating from the overcrowded city and blown out to sea by a stiff offshore breeze. The peculiar mist clung tenaciously to Pusan and seemed to consist of a conglomeration of the stink from countless unwashed bodies, the odor of open sewers filled to the brim with human refuse, the foul smell of disease, rotten food, and death.

As the troopship bumped gently against its jetty, hundreds of ragged young Korean urchins, looking like a collection of gnomes in their tattered brown clothing and pointed hats, swarmed out of a large shed lying along the length of the pier, fighting each other for the ship's lines, many of them begging in chorus, looking up at the grinning Canadian soldiers on the ship:

"Hey, Joe, me chop chop . . . Habba cigarette? Chocolate? Gum?"

"Hey, Joe, me habba pretty sister. You like? How much you speak?"

Many soldiers threw cigarettes down to the scrambling mob, amused by the pathetic exhibition of animal savagery, as the young Koreans fought one another desperately for the objects thrown on the pier.

The reaction of some of the officers to the antics of the Korean mob varied: Mike Reardon was amused, likening the scene to a circus. Carr-Wilson was revolted, remarking on the similarity of the Korean dock wallopers to a pack of unwashed animals. Paul Anderson found the pitiful sight sickening and tragic, flinching as he watched in fascinated horror the merciless beating of one of the Koreans by a burly gang boss.

Throughout the long night, as the Canadians slept, the brigade's supplies were haphazardly unloaded by the unruly dockworkers. Starting early the following morning, the Canadians were disembarked in a drizzling rain, loaded onto a fleet of ancient trucks driven by Koreans, undoubtedly the world's worst drivers, starting on their way to their staging camp located outside the city. After a wild drive through the downtown streets, a drive punctuated by loud blasts of horns, screeching brakes, screaming tires, passing through an odiferous tin, wood, and cardboard shack town called Little Chicago, the Canadians amused at the innumerable "Out of Bounds" signs to be seen everywhere.

"Keerist, there are more out-of-bounds signs in this burg than there are stop signs in Winnipeg," one wag commented.

The rain-soaked Canadians drove nearly an hour in open trucks to reach the assigned staging area, the site of an old Korean cemetery having been used until recently as a North Korean prisoner-of-war camp. The area, dotted liberally with burial mounds, enclosed by a high wire fence, now contained a tent city set up by the members of the Royals' advance party. Near the entrance of the encampment, a vehicle compound had been set up, in which the battalion vehicles were neatly lined up, waiting to be cleaned of their covering of protective grease. The advance party made excellent progress; there was still much to be done before the living conditions in the camp would be suitable. The Royals spent the next two days digging latrines, setting up additional tents and company kitchens. The enterprising members of A Company, with Dearing's blessing, even managed to scrounge a complete lighting system, including a gas generator, to light up their company area.

After his troops had settled in, Colonel Graves directed his company commanders to start conditioning training to help the men shake off the effects of the long sea trip. The conditioning program was carried out in a series of stages, including long marches, climbing steep hills while wearing full equipment, finally, carrying out backbreaking lung-bursting attacks up the sides of a particularly formidable hill. This last exercise, appropriately called Charley Horse, was designed to give practice to the rifle companies in the difficult tactic of attacking an enemy uphill.

The big day finally came. On May 14, the Canadians were ordered to move up to the front, the long awaited order been precipitated by a successful large-scale attack by the communists against the ROK troops on the eastern front. To bolster his sagging eastern line, the Eighth Army commander pulled some of his units out of the west-central front to reinforce the South Koreans in the rugged eastern mountains, in turn calling upon the Canadians to plug the gap left by the departure of these units.

Mike Reardon's platoon was in high spirits arriving at the Pusan staging area. As he lead his men to their platoon area in the A Company lines, their lighthearted mood quickly changed. A drainage ditch close to their tents had become blocked, causing the rainwater to back up flooding out the immediate area. Their tents were sagging, the floors filled with nearly a foot of muddy water. Sergeant Cross gave Jack Harvey's section the job of clearing the blocked ditch; the remaining sections were detailed to clean out the tents, tidying up the debris-littered area as best they could. Blackie Balaski, knee deep in the slime of the ditch, cursed bitterly as he shoveled out the heavy silt.

"Join the goddamn infantry to fight and what do they have me doing? Cleaning bloody sewers, that's what," he grumbled.

"I suppose you'd rather swim in your bed instead of sleep in it?" Bernie Viau chided his friend.

"Come on, you two, cut the gassing and get that damn ditch cleaning out. We haven't got all day!" Jack Harvey yelled. "Hey, Frome, get off your scrawny ass and give Viau and Blackie a hand! My god, I no sooner turn my back and you flake out somewhere. You're the laziest clot I've ever seen!"

Darkness had fallen over the camp before the Deuce had finished their difficult task exhausted. When they finally crawled into their rain-soaked blankets for the night, slept the deep sleep of worn-out men.

The following week, after a particularly strenuous day including a fifteen-mile route march with full pack, culminating in a climb up the steep hill, forming the northeast boundary of the camp, Reardon's men were in their tents wearily removing their web equipment, some massaging swollen feet, others just flopped on the floor lying still in an effort to forget the tortuous session they had just completed.

"I don't mind the rotten marches, but that goddamn hill is killing me!" Al Johnson groaned, his face a picture of misery.

"Remember, my boy, you volunteered, so quit your bitching," Gus Johnson reminded his brother. "Besides, what in the hell did you expect? You know damn well that you can't get into shape to fight the Chinks sitting on your butt."

"Sure, I realize that, but do we have to do it all at once? We've been going like hell ever since we got to this gook paradise. I don't mind working, Gus, but this is ridiculous," he complained.

"Don't feel so bad about it, Al. Just wait till the old man decides that we'd better run to the front to keep in shape after we've finished here. Then you'll have something to bind about!" Ed Banks added sarcastically. "Holy cow, are my feet ever killing me! You know something, fellas? Feet should start up a union so that they could protest over work."

"I didn't feel too bad until I saw how bushed Reardon was when we got near the top of that SOB of a hill. Did you see his face? I've never seen anyone sweat as much. I figured if our muscleman was that bloody tired, I must feel even worse, and from then on, I did, believe me," Al remarked as he pulled off his mud-covered boots.

"He was just sweating out the booze he soaked up last night. He went out on a big drunk in the city last night with his limey buddy. I heard it from Kalamazoo, his batman," Ed confided to his friends.

"Kalamazoo? You mean Kalmalachuck, don't you?" Gus queried.

"That's the guy, only Kalamazoo is easier to say. That's what the guys have started to call him. He doesn't mind," Ed replied.

Al was not listening to the conversation between Banks and his brother. Instead, he was working up a big hate over what he considered unjust treatment of the men. "The officers get all the bloody breaks, and what do we get? I ask you, what do we get? Nothing, that's what. Why, they keep us caged up here like a bunch of gook prisoners while the brass go off to town and get loaded! Boy, I'd like to write my member of parliament. I'd have a story to tell him!"

"Why don't you, Al? Sounds like a great idea," Ed suggested, trying to keep from laughing.

"Why don't you two dry up for a while? I'm damn sick of hearing you two bitching all the time. If you don't like the way the battalion is being run, why in the hell don't you go and tell the colonel? I'm sure he'd be just too happy to hear your suggestions," Gus commented caustically.

"Hey, you guys . . . Chow's on," a voice called from outside their tent.

From his position on top of the steep hill that bordered the Royals' camp, Mike Reardon could see on one side the white capped breakers of the Japanese Sea rolling up the sand beaches lining the east of the sprawling city, on the other side, at the base of the hill, an endless series of interlocked, overflowing paddy fields covering the valley floor. His exhausted men lay in a broken circle around him, resting and drinking in the cool air prior to making the long descent to camp. As he sat resting, his arms clasped around his knees, he began to think regretfully of the events that occurred the night before.

He had talked Monty into accompanying him to town the previous night to look for the fabulous United Nations Officers Club, where East meets West. After driving the jeep around a considerable part of Pusan's shabby downtown district, they finally located the ramshackle building housing the unique club. The freshly painted front of the establishment was boasting an illuminated sign, "United Nations Officers Club." The mounted a short shaky flight of stairs, arriving at a curtained doorway where they were greeted by a short sleek dressed in a dirty ill-fitting tuxedo Oriental, who, after much bowing and scraping, led Mike and Monty to a dirty cracked marble-topped table.

"My god, what a rat trap! Will you look at these chairs? They're filthy!"

"Mustn't be too fussy, Mike, old chap. We're not in the States now. I say, look at those two Americans in the corner. Why, they're wearing shoulder holsters. I was under the impression that the war was somewhat farther north, weren't you?"

"Never mind the Yanks. Look over in the corner opposite us. I think they're Greeks. That's right, the two dark-skinned types."

"Good lord! They certainly aren't shy the way they're mauling the two girls sitting beside them."

"Yes, but look at the faces of the girls, Monty," said Mike awed. "Not a trace of expression on either of their faces. Boy, are those two characters ever making a big impression."

"Don't look now, old friend. I think our oily friend has two of his best headed in our direction."

"My god, look at them! What a horrible pair of bags!" Mike exclaimed.

"Oh, I don't know about that, Mike. Mine doesn't look too terrible, but yours—"

"Where do you get this mine-and-yours stuff? Why—"

"We sit down here, yes?" the first of the two heavily made-up Korean girls asked in a lilting singsong voice.

"Why, of course, ladies! Please be seated," Monty gallantly replied then whispered to his friend, "Don't look so ruddy stunned, Mike. Seat the other girl."

The two girls, dressed in cheap Western clothes, appeared to be a mixture of Japanese, Korean, and Occidental bloodlines. They might have been considered pretty had they not worn such atrocious masklike makeup.

"Me, Mary, you like rye? Maybe rum, habbe yes?"

"And what's your name, my dear?" Monty asked the taller and prettier of the pair. She looked in bewilderment at her girlfriend who immediately spoke to her in Korean.

"Me, Phat, you like drink? He like maunti cotail."

"What in hell is she talking about, Monty?"

"Elementary, old cock. Her name is Pat, and she wants a martini."

It was soon obvious to the two Canadians that, although the girls spoke a few words of English, they understood very little of the language, resulting in a bare minimum of conversation between the hostesses and their escorts.

"Dancee?" Mary asked Mike, busy trying to decide the true identity of the murky liquid the establishment insisted was Canadian club rye.

"Yeah, sure, kid. Say, Monty, why don't you and your dream girl start contorting to this god-awful Korean version of a rumba?"

"Later on, Mike. I'm rather busy right now," Monty replied, pulling his willing partner closer to him.

Mike's partner danced jerkily, puppetlike, automatically pushing her passionless body close to his. He managed to lose himself in the dance until confronted by the images of his dancing partner and himself in a long scratched mirror hanging precariously behind the bar, genuinely shocked at the reflection of the hollow eyes, listless, painted Oriental girl in his arms. For a moment, it seemed impossible that the man holding the repulsive-looking creature was himself. Seized with an overpowering feeling of revulsion, he left his dancing companion in the center of the floor, returning to his table. Carr-Wilson and the other girl were nowhere to be seen. As he sat down, one of the waiters furtively slipped him a note from Monty, asking Mike to wait for his return. While waiting, Mike proceeded to get very drunk. One hour later, Monty returned just in time to prevent a fight between his friend and a huge bellicose American signals captain.

The following morning, Reardon, cursing his stupidity at "tying one on" the night before, learned that Dearing had left instructions for him to take the Deuce out on a long route march after climbing the towering hill adjacent to the camp. Mike was certain that the body-punishing day would never end; soon, every step became an agonized motion. Faced by the backbreaking task of climbing the hill at the conclusion of the long hike, he couldn't restrain himself from groaning aloud, "Of all the goddamn arms and services I could have joined, I had to choose the bloody infantry. What an idiot!"

Graves was in a reflective mood after his return from the brigade commander's orders group. The moment he had both dreaded and anticipated had finally come; his battalion was moving up to the front. Making a few notes, he sent for the key officers of his command. As the drenched officers moved into Graves's headquarters tent, shaking the monsoon rain out of their clothes, the CO's batman passed to each a cup of steaming hot coffee.

The battalion commander's orders were brief: the Royals would move up to their assembly area near Suwon in two columns, one by road and the other by rail; Graves and his headquarters staff leading the motorcade; the second in command of the companies, under the command of Major Harcourt, proceeding at once to the assembly area with an advance party to prepare the area for the arrival of the battalion. The bulk of the Royals' men were to be transported north by the unpredictable Korean railway system. Graves, finished presenting the details of the movement plan, terminated the meeting; the company commanders returned to their lines to pass on the orders to their subordinates. In addition to the welcome news that they were at last moving up to the line, the Royals received an even more pleasant surprise: the first mail from home had arrived.

Paul Anderson tore open the envelope with the Tacoma postmark and eagerly read the contents:

My Darling,

I have some news for you that is both wonderful and frightening. We're going to have a baby sometime in November. Although I suspected I was pregnant before you left, dearest, I didn't want to worry you in case my suspicions were unfounded and you would be needlessly worried at a time that was difficult for you at its best. I haven't told anyone yet, not even my sister. Please don't misunderstand me, Paul, darling, I want our baby very much, but I'm frightened. I don't know quite what to do. If only I could have you beside me, everything would be so much easier, but I realize that it is impossible. I'll have to tell Dad and Mother soon, it wouldn't be fair for me not to do so. I thought I'd wait to hear from you, my darling, before I did, and I do so very much want to hear from you . . .

When he finished reading Anne's pathetic letter, his eyes were filling with anguished tears. "My poor darling—I didn't know! Oh god! If only you had said something to me before I left."

Paul's mind was in a turmoil. At first unable to think out the situation, he sat hunched over on his cot, his face in his hands, trying desperately to think of a solution to help Anne.

"I wish that blasted rain would stop. It's driving me crazy!" Paul snapped at the ceaseless drumming on the tent roof. "There's only one thing for me to do, I'll have to talk with the padre." Putting on his poncho, he stepped out into the teeming rain.

Capt. Donald Royce, the Royals' padre, had joined the battalion in Fort Lewis. He was a very sincere man, unfortunately not too well versed in the realities and ruggedness of military life, the sometimes shocking problems of soldiers. He was more accustomed to the relatively gentle sin of the members of his parish in the small east coast town he had served prior to joining the Special Force. Initially, he was pleasantly excited when his bishop summoned him, asking him if he would be interested in looking after the spiritual welfare of Canadian soldiers destined for service in Korea. Unfortunately, soon after joining the Royals, he found the task of being an army padre often more difficult than rewarding. Padre Royce had made a questionable decision, not believing in war; he found it difficult to rationalize the actions and motives of men dedicated to war as a career.

Somewhat startled by Anderson's abrupt entrance into his tent, the padre didn't have to wait long for his visitor to speak or to realize the young officer was very upset. "Come in, young man, come in. You're Anderson, Paul Anderson, I believe. You must excuse my poor memory, but I don't believe that I've seen very much of you?"

"No, Padre, I haven't been a regular at your services, I must admit."

"Please sit down, Paul. Over here on my cot. I'll clear away some of my kit for you . . . Now, my son, what can I do for you?"

"Well . . . ah . . . it's a rather difficult problem, Padre," Paul began, telling him about Barbara and Anne, handing him Anne's letter.

Royce read the letter slowly. When he finished, he looked up into Anderson's expectant face, saying, "You do have an awkward situation confronting you, my boy. Do you have any idea what you intend to do about it?"

"No, Padre, I thought I'd discuss the matter with you first. I thought you might have some experience in these matters and could advise me. Surely my situation isn't unique? Padre, I love Anne very much and want to marry her. I realize what we did wasn't wise, and perhaps not even right, but we love each other sincerely."

"True, Paul," Royce replied, "your problem is not unique. In fact, I have had to deal with an alarming number of similar situations since joining the battalion. I suppose you realize there isn't a hope of your receiving permission to return home? The brigade commander has refused to approve repatriation for any sort of personal reasons, including death of next of kin."

"Yes, Padre, I realize that, but is there a way that I could start divorce proceedings against my wife? Some quick method through service channels? Then perhaps I could marry Anne by proxy. I just have to do something, Padre!"

"Now, now, Paul, calm down. It's not as easy as all that. I suggest you leave the situation in my hands for a little while and I'll see what I can do. I'll let you know as soon as I come up with something. In the meantime, I suggest that you write the young lady and perhaps also to her father, explaining the situation and informing him of the steps you're taking. By the time you receive a reply, I should have something concrete. Then perhaps it will be prudent for me to write to the young lady's father."

"Thanks, Padre, for everything. I'll write to Anne and her father immediately! Goodbye."

Paul returned to his tent and started writing to Anne Martin, trying desperately to express the right words and sentiments he hoped would comfort the girl he so completely loved. Writing to her father was a far more difficult task than he had anticipated. It was hampered by the realization that Mr. Martin barely knew him. Consequently, lacking any sort of personal foundation or relationship with Anne's father to act as a basis for his letter, he rewrote the letter to John Martin three times before being satisfied enough to seal and mail it.

Later that night, Anderson tossed restlessly in his narrow uncomfortable safari bed, unable to sleep because of the grim, foreboding thoughts torturing his mind. It was dawn before he finally fell into an exhausted slumber, his face contorted by nerve-racking dreams, his fists clenched beside his tense form.

CHAPTER 19

Move to the Front

There was relative quiet on the war front for nearly three weeks after the major Chinese attacks that took place late in April. The UN forces had dug in, waiting for the next communist attack. It came on May 16, not in the central front as expected but in the east. The UN high command was quietly building up for a large-scale counterattack at the time of the communist assault. After detaching a few units from the central front to reinforce the South Korean forces in the east, the Eighth Army commander continued to build his forces up for the planned attack on the west-central sector, this attack to commence as soon as the Chinese attacks in the east had ground to a halt. The communist offensive stopped on May 22, the Eighth Army launched a full-scale attack on May 24, the killer offensive coded as Operation Cobra had begun.

The object of the Eighth Army's advance north was to win and hold the dominating features in the area of the thirty-eighth parallel. During the first week, the First Corps—consisting of the First ROK Division in the west; the Twenty-Fifth U.S. Infantry Division, of which the Canadians formed a part, in the east-central; and the First Cavalry Division in the center—passed through Uijeongbu and Munsan.

The Chinese, their supply lines extended far beyond their means to maintain them, retreated quickly under the impact of a series of well-executed UN attacks. In the beginning, the Chinese offered only token resistance; in fact, it wasn't until the Eighth Army had crossed the thirty-eighth parallel and captured the key towns forming the points of the Iron Triangle—Pyongyang, Kum Hwa, and Chorwon—that the enemy's resistance stiffened enough to slow down the UN advance.

The men of the Royals, including Colonel Graves, were unaware of the real purpose of their hurried move to the battle line, Graves thinking the Canadians were merely destined to take over the defensive responsibility for the UN forces that had been pulled out of the central front and sent east, having no idea a general offensive by the Eighth Army was pending.

The motor trip along the erratically laid-out highway to the assembly area was hot, dusty, and nerve-racking. Besides looking out for the normal driving hazards, the Canadians in the motorcade had to keep careful watch for any suspicious civilian movement, indicating a possible attack by one of the many communist guerilla bands known to be hiding out in the hills bordering the north-south highway. The Royals' vehicles operating at a top speed of twenty-five miles per hour wended their way from Pusan to Taegu, from Taejon, famous for the stand made there by General Deane of the US Army, then to Taejon to Suwon, finally, to their assembly area.

During the course of the three-day trip, the surrounding landscape changed from the broad valleys covered with lush green subtropical vegetation, to a landscape common to the Gatineau Hills of Quebec, the countryside and verges of the roads showing evidence of heavy fighting, taking place the past months. Hundreds of trucks, dozens of burned-out tanks, both communist and American, lay twisted and rusted in the ditches, giving mute testimony of the violence and death occurring in the early days of the fighting, ragged women and children, hungry and homeless, begging for food, lined the roads passing through their smashed villages and towns. This human war debris bore no resemblance of the crafty youths and sullen heavily made-up women haunting the teeming streets in Pusan. Everywhere, groups of refugees could be seen carrying everything they possessed, moving north to the homes they had hastily vacated months before in the wake of the communist surge south.

The men in the Royals' motor column were a grotesque sight as they drove northward, covered with a thick layer of fine penetrating dust, irritating their eyes, noses, throats, and sweat-saturated skins, despite the precautions wearing berets, goggles, handkerchiefs over their faces, and full clothing. The Canadians found it difficult, becoming accustomed to the quick changes of climate consisting of cool mornings, blistering hot afternoons, and cold wet nights. After nearly three days on the road, approaching their destination, the motor convoy was met by a directing group from the advance party, leading them into the battalion assembly area. The following day, the main body of the Royals arrived by train; when all the components of the brigade finally arrived and were linked up, they moved into divisional reserve under the command of the commanding general of the U.S. Twenty-Fifth Infantry Division.

There was some indecision on the part of the divisional commander as to the role the Canadian brigade was to fill in the impending offensive. For a few days, it looked as if the Royals would be taking over from a Puerto Rican battalion; this was changed. The Royals were warned to be ready to relieve a battalion from the British twenty-eighth brigade; this order was also changed. The final decision, the Canadians would take over from the Turkish brigade and act as one of the spearheads of the massive offensive.

The divisional commander's plan of battle was a simple one, an American infantry tank battle group, completely mobile and in regimental strength, to advance with all possible speed, taking up a defensive position just north of the hotly disputed thirty-eighth parallel. The Twenty-Fifth Canadian Infantry Brigade group, flanked by a U.S. regimental combat team, was ordered to mop up any pockets of resistance bypassed by the battle group, relieving the mobile group as soon as possible.

CHAPTER 20

Operation Cobra

At 10am on the May 24, the Canadians moved over their start line as part of the Eighth Army's long-awaited counteroffensive. Four days later, the Canadian brigade culminated its rapid advance, relieving the American battle group holding the high ground at the junction of the Pochon and Yongpyong Rivers; the advance, successful far beyond their expectations, the main phase of Operation Cobra, was over.

On the night of May 23, the men of the Deuce were carefully checking their weapons and equipment under the watchful eye of Sergeant Cross, an air of tense excitement, a feeling of mounting anticipation was infecting every man. At long last, they were about to face the enemy, an enemy whose shadow they had so relentlessly pursued through six months of arduous training.

"Hey, Frome! Looks like you're going to get a chance to get some use out of your 'sweetheart' soon."

"Never mind, Balaski. You had the rest of the wise guys around here will be damn glad to have Freddie's chopper do your talking tomorrow, especially if some ugly little Chink decides to run his bayonet down your bloody throat," snapped Frome.

"Okay, okay, killer! But tell me, who's going to carry who? Are you going to carry that Bren or is it going to carry your—?" Blackie chaffed.

"You big guys give me a pain in the ass! Full of guts till the chips are down then you squeal a different tune," Frome sneered in a flat menacing voice standing up to face the taller heavier man. "You won't sound so big, loudmouth, with a Chink bullet in your belly."

Blackie was about to strike the slight wiry figure facing him defiantly when he felt his raised hand seized in a grip of steel.

"Save your fighting for tomorrow, you clowns, 'cause if I hear any more of this goddamn nonsense, I'll beat the living hell out of both of you. Understand?"

Blinded by anger, Blackie wrenched his arm out of big Jack Harvey's grip, raising his fist as if to strike the towering corporal; the other men became quiet as they waited expectantly. Harvey waited for Blackie's blow, a smile akin to a sneer on his ugly face, his ham-like fists clenched into two balls of punishing bone and muscle. The blow never came; Balaski turned away from the corporal, muttering to himself. The tension dissipated as the men resumed their work.

It was surprising to see so few men bothering to write home the night preceding the attack; most were content to lie back on their blankets, talking and smoking after finishing their preparations.

Bernie Viau, one of the few members of the Deuce who bothered to write, had a good reason. His wife, Dorothy, was pregnant. Her letter telling him the good news was a wonderful thing to read, so full of happiness and hope. A large lump formed in his throat as he read the part saying, "Please be careful, my darling, you have two of us to worry about now!"

The officers of the Royals were both busy and worried, busy going over their respective assignments in the battle plan for the following day, worried about their ability to do the jobs expected of them. The officers with Second World War battle experience found the war in Korea an unreal, eerie experience; all about them lay the signs of battle, the devastation of war, everything but the enemy. As they were driving their vehicles at will in No Man's Land, they were amazed by the careless way men and officers alike walked unconcernedly in the open sky lined on the ridges. The veteran officers were appalled because any one of these actions could result in disaster against the resolute German during the struggle for Europe.

This was a new war for these men, a conflict employing the principle of sacrificing space for time, a fluid type of war first introduced by the Russians.

Paul Anderson was writing a short letter to Anne Martin by the light of his flash light. He was devastated over Anne's awkward predicament of having to face her family and friends alone. Feeling useless, he was consumed by guilt and self-recrimination. Paul did the only thing left in his power, writing to Anne whenever having the opportunity, hoping his letters would help bolster her courage for the ordeal she would have to face alone. His mental state was further agitated by his fear of Anne's father's reaction to his letter. Each day became an agonizing wait for mail from Tacoma.

131

Early in the morning of May 24, the Royals were moved by an American transport group to their start line located across the front occupied by the Turks. After a two-hour delay, the U.S. mobile task force, bristling with tanks, rumbled through the Canadians' position. Finally, the Canadian brigade moved off on a two-battalion front, with the Royals responsible for the left flank. The anticipated advance soon proved to be a farce; the Royals were completely unopposed. The men carrying full equipment soon became burdened down by the weight of their weapons, digging tools, and packs and would have welcomed any sort of enemy opposition giving them a short breather. By the second day, the tempo of the rapid advance increased to that of a race, the strain on the men becoming so great they began ridding themselves of their surplus equipment whenever the opportunity arose, until the path of their advance was littered with large packs, shovels, picks, and bandoliers of ammunition.

Chuck Dearing, thoroughly disgusted with the ridiculous race being run by the other companies at the expense of their men, halted his company for a well-earned rest, having all his men remove their large packs, retaining only their battle order, loading them on the company vehicles under the supervision of big Red Nichols, the company quartermaster sergeant.

"The hell with the race! I'm not going to kill my men before they ever get a chance to fight!" Dearing roared into the intercom when ordered by Graves's battalion headquarters to explain the reason for his unscheduled halt.

In the course of their free-wheeling advance north on the road following the Pochan Valley, the tanks of the American battle group thoroughly shelled every possible enemy location. Unfortunately, many of their shells crashed into the small hillside villages bordering the road. The Royals, combing the hills for pockets of enemy resistance, did not encounter a single live Chinese soldier, instead were confronted by the devastation created by tank fire. Monty Carr-Wilson was led by a badly wounded Korean to a thatched-roof mud hut that had evidently been his home. Reluctantly entering the shattered dwelling, his nostrils were filled with a sickening stench. The source lay groaning on the dirt floor, a dying woman covered with hideous fly-infested wounds, instinctively trying to nurse a dead baby at her swollen purple breasts. Approaching closer, trying desperately to control his nausea, an angrily buzzing cloud of blue flies rose from her open festering wounds. Carr-Wilson, unable to stand the sight and smell of the broken body any longer, reeled out of the hut vomiting violently.

When he recovered, he called out, "Preston, come over here. Double back to battalion headquarters and try to locate the medical officer. If he's not too busy, bring him back here as quickly as possible," he commanded.

As he waited, Monty watched a small column of women and old men dressed completely in white cotton moving up the side of the hill, carrying tightly bound bodies of their dead, the sound of their tragic chanting carried by the wind to the valley below. Soon after this, a Canadian news correspondent assigned to write up the "Royals' attack" came upon a wrinkled old Korean listlessly poking at the smoldering ruins of his former home. Using his young Korean interpreter, the newspaperman spoke to him.

"You must be very happy to have been freed of the domination of the communists once again. Tell me, in your opinion, how do the United Nations forces compare to the Chinese in regards to their treatment of your people?"

The Korean patriarch looked quizzical for a moment then turned around slowly as he examined the shattered remains of his village, his face etched deeply with the unmistakable lines of age and suffering. He thoughtfully replied with a quiet dignity, "Papa-san says, does it matter to the grass what breed of bull that tramples it?" the interpreter replied.

The battle line was changing so rapidly Colonel Graves was having difficulty keeping in contact with his far-flung companies. Normal tactics and battle formations were completely ignored as whole units were leapfrogged over one another by transport to allow the attacking forces to keep pace with the rapidly retreating Chinese and North Koreans. Officers and men, laughing, confident, glorying in the chase, were straining at an invisible leash in a frantic effort to close with the elusive enemy. When small pockets of enemy were encountered, the company commanders vied with one another for the privilege of pressing home the attack. Perfectly coordinated attacks—consisting of air strikes, artillery and mortar bombardment, followed by aggressive infantry tank assaults—quickly cleared the hills of the enemy rearguard. The Royals seized all their objectives in remarkably short order, with surprisingly light casualties to themselves.

One objective was seized in a textbook-like operation. Buck Carson, D Company commander, sent Red Saunders's platoon into a cluster of huts at the base of his objective to draw the enemy's fire. As soon as he had spotted the Chinese positions on the hill, he ordered the tank troop supporting him to bring their accurate fire to bear on the enemy. He lead his remaining two platoons in an assault up the hill under the cover of a heavy barrage laid down by the Royals' mortars, supporting artillery, supporting tanks and heavy machine guns. By the time Carson reached the top of the enemy-held hill, the Chinese had fled, leaving behind their dead.

The Royals, led by C Company, reached the parallel, relieved the American battle group, rested for a day on the invisible boundary, hurtling into North Korea.

CHAPTER 21

The First Battle

The Canadians had advanced six miles into North Korea completely unopposed. Before the brigade commander learned that the advance of the American regimental combat team on his right flank had been checked by strong determined enemy resistance two miles in the rear, the Canadian brigade was virtually alone. Toward noon, the Royals' advance guard was confronted by the rotting, stinking remains of a Chinese mule supply train, the bloated, fly-infested corpses of both animals and men lying strung out on both sides of the road, victims of a well-executed air strike. The stomach-retching stench filling the entire valley in this choice setting, the brigade commander decided to halt the Royals. Suddenly, a long series of loud "pops" sounded, originating from a series of saw-toothed ridges lying directly to the Canadians' front. The brigade, being fired on by a battery of Chinese mortars, began scattering at the sound of the terrifying whirr of the falling mortar bombs, followed by loud booming explosions as the bombs struck. The mortar fire was now supplemented by the staccato chatter of heavy machine guns. They had at last found the enemy and in strength.

The brigade commander decided to launch a battalion strength, attack at dawn the following morning, the Royals given the job. As he made his appreciation of the situation, conflicting intelligence reports were trickling down to him from divisional headquarters; the only substantial report received reported a great number of Chinese troops moving south from the vicinity of Chorwon, heading in the general direction of the area occupied by the Canadian brigade. The brigadier called his battalion commanders to attend his orders group, presenting the situation to them as best he could, instructing Graves to seize and hold a series of three hills lying to the front, with special emphasis given to capturing the dominant hill in the area, a high steep-faced feature, known simply as hill 468 on their maps. The Canadian commanders refused to put any serious stock in the intelligence reports indicating a strong Chinese buildup, having received similar reports during their rapid advance, launching carefully executed attacks, only to find the enemy had either fled or had never been in the indicated location in the first place.

As the brigade commander arranged for the Royals' support, which was to consist of artillery, tank, mortar, and air strikes, Colonel Graves conducted his own reconnaissance, calling his company commanders together, issuing his orders.

"Gentlemen, the intelligence officer has marked on your maps all the information about the enemy that he has. You've had a chance to see the ground ahead, and I only wish we could have a look at what lies behind. We are not certain as to the actual strength of the enemy, but the brigadier believes that their main line of defense lies some ten miles north of us, near Chorwon. We are faced at the moment by a relatively light enemy screen, seemingly well supplied with light mortars and machine guns. We believe that they are quite thin on the ground. At present, we are quite alone, the Americans on our right hard pressed. The Americans on our left are hard pressed some two miles behind us, so we can't count on any help from them. We're going to receive all the support available, which, as you know, includes the tank squadron, regiment of artillery and mortars, from both battalions. I'll give you their tasks later on. The intention is that the Royals will seize and hold the objectives allocated.

"Now as to the method, Chuck, I'm sending your company at 0600 to take the village of Chail-Li. It is about two miles up the road. Don't look so startled, your boys will be transported by the half-tracks from the mortar platoon. You can also have the flamethrowers to help clear the village. I'm hoping your move will distract the Chinese long enough to permit us to gain a good foothold on the main objectives, especially 468.

"Jack, I want you to take the ridge marked 'Pear' on your map. Your job is to act as a firm base for Chuck's attack and to support him if necessary. As soon as Chuck is firmly on his objective, I'll move you up.

"Vince, when Chuck has signaled his success, I want you to attack the hill. Here it is—hill 345, just to the southeast of the village. From there, you should be able to give Chuck some support and, at the same time, protect Jack's move forward from his holding position.

"Buck, I'm giving your boys the big one—468. If the other companies are successful, you shouldn't have too much trouble, but we must capture that feature. Otherwise, all the rest of the effort will be useless. The brigade commander has ordered an air strike from the USAF tactical air support group to clear off the top for you. Tanks! I want you to shoot A Company unto its objective and to stay in the vicinity of the village until I give your orders to the contrary. Mortars . . ."

Colonel Graves continued giving the rest of the details of his orders, including the administration procedures that would be followed, the intercommunication network, relative code signs, and times that were to be used during the attack. At the conclusion of his orders, he asked for questions.

Dearing was the only one to speak up. "Sir, it strikes me we're going to be spread pretty thin by the time we reach our objectives. Frankly, I'm a little doubtful we'll be able to give each other much support if the situation suddenly gets dirty. There'll be just too much distance between us."

"I wouldn't worry about it, Major Dearing. I don't think this should present a serious problem. In fact, I'm sure as soon as the Chinese determine the scale of our attack, they'll withdraw to their main line of defense. Any other questions, gentlemen? No? Very well. Synchronize your watches."

Graves, looking directly into the faces of his company commanders, in turn said quietly, "Tomorrow may be our big moment, gentlemen. I know you won't let the Royals down! Good luck."

Later that evening, it began to rain, the air becoming uncomfortably chilly, the moonless night, the persistent drizzle having a depressing effect on many of the Royals. The usual camp sounds of laughter and joking subsided to a low unintelligible murmuring, seeming the men becoming aware this time death awaited them in the hills beyond. Many of the Royals had trouble sleeping through the night, the sentries on watch often startled by someone crying out in his sleep.

The men of the Deuce had taken up a position in a barren orchard. Those who could not sleep were sitting, huddled in their ponchos, quietly talking.

"Don't forget, Blackie, you promised me. If anything happens to me, you'll write Dorothy," Bernie whispered huskily to his poncho-shrouded friend.

"Don't be a damn fool, Bernie," Blackie grumbled. "Nothing is going to happen to you, not with Old Blackie around. You just wait and see—it'll be a piece of cake."

"I'm not so sure. I have a funny feeling in my chest—there's going to be trouble."

"Everybody feels that way, kid, the first time. I was scared crap less the night before I went in on my first attack. Believes me, the bloody Jerries were a hell of a lot tougher than these bastards. Look, Bernie, try and get some sleep and stop worrying."

Paul Anderson couldn't sleep, it was not the impending attack preventing him. He still had not heard from either Anne or her father. Puzzled and concerned at not receiving a single letter from Anne in nearly a month, he was convinced something serious had happened in Tacoma; it was not the mail. Many of his men continued to receive letters in spite of the constant movement of the battalion.

"If there was only something I could do! I feel so damn helpless," he cried aloud.

Don Standish, commander of D Company's tenth platoon, was frightened. It was not the first time he had felt this way. His fear of death started soon after the Royals commenced their initial advance, but now it was becoming overwhelming. During the orders group given by Buck Carson, he tried to work up enough nerve to tell Carson how he felt, but he was unable to do so. He tried, believing that the other platoon commanders feeling the same way but wouldn't admit it, knowing this wasn't true. Red Saunders, commander of the twelfth platoon, wasn't afraid of anything, his men openly admiring his courage. Standish, realizing that some of his NCOs sensed their officer's fear, managed to keep up a front. He wasn't sure how much longer it would work, shamefully recalling his bragging at Fort Lewis that he was going to win a decoration for gallantry when he saw action, remembering vividly his bravado in leading attacks against a mock enemy during the training phases in the States. He had been so aggressive; some of the other officers concluded that if anyone in the battalion won a medal, it would probably be Standish. He wasn't thinking of winning any medals at this moment.

Mike Reardon fell into a deep sleep after splitting a bottle of rum with Carr-Wilson. Relieving the tension in the Deuce, he organized a pool among its members, the proceeds to go to the first man in the platoon to be wounded. When he finished collecting, he said, grinning, "Serve you bastards right if I cop the first one."

Ed Banks countered right back, "From what I hear about casualties in platoon commanders, you got a good chance, boss!"

Cpl. Jack Harvey had just fallen asleep when Frome's loud coughing awakened him. "What in hell do you think you're doing, Frome? Keerist, I'll never get back to sleep now!"

"I'm sending coded messages through my bloody nose to the Chinaman," Fred snapped back, starting another fit of coughing.

Sergeant Cross, rolling partly out of his soggy blankets, snarled, "Shut up, you assholes, and get some sleep"

At four in the morning, Dearing's company sergeant major, assisted by the sentries on guard, commenced shaking the men of the company, almost welcoming the morning after spending most of the wet, miserable night lying on the soggy ground. The company cooks miraculously managed to cook up a breakfast for the men. The sausages were cold, the eggs were tasteless, but the coffee was steaming hot. By four thirty, the entire battalion was up and about. At five thirty, in the misty morning light, Dearing's company was loaded on the half-tracks, ready to move off at six.

Graves looked apprehensively at the rain-filled sky, realizing unless the weather cleared soon, the air strike against 468 could be called off. "Probably won't affect the situation very much whether they show or not," he rationalized.

Precisely at six o'clock, four white half-tracks were loaded to capacity with the men of A Company, three tracked flamethrowers, and the tank squadron started rumbling northward, heading for Chail-Li, soon disappearing from view. As the Royals' battle group moved off, its supporting artillery began laying a heavy barrage of shells on the village objective. Colonel Graves, watching the column from his armored car until the last vehicle disappeared into the wet mist that was blanketing the valley, decided to utilize a mobile command post, enabling to move around the battle area, observing at close range the progress of his companies' attacks. Shortly after, following the initial departure, B, C, and D Companies moved off on foot toward their objectives. Although hearing tank and machine-gun fire in the distance, Graves still had no word from Dearing regarding his company's situation. Unable to wait any longer, he had his radio operator call A Company to obtain a situation report.

"Hello, Able 1, hello, Able 1, sit rep. I say again, sit rep. Over."

After a delay of a few minutes, Dearing's voice crackled in the CO's earphones. "Hello, Able 1. Am reorganizing on objective. Am being engaged by light machine-gun and mortar fire from hill northeast of village. Tin cans are presently engaging enemy there. Out."

At six forty-five, the Royals' commander received a situation report from B Company commander, Black Jack Wilson, to the effect he had reached his objective without opposition.

Graves heard his signaler call him over the intercom. "Big Sunray wants a situation report, sir."

He was about to give a report to the brigade commander when Major Logan's big voice boomed into Graves' earphones. "Hello. Charlie 1. Have reorganized on objective. Can see strong enemy force, approximately two hundred, moving down ridge toward Chail-Li. Over."

"Hello, Charlie 1. Sunray speaking. Can you give support to friends on your left by engaging enemy? Over."

"Hello. Charlie 1. No . . . range is too great. Over."

"Hello, Charlie 1. Roger . . . Out."

Graves was trying to contact Dearing, warning him of the new enemy threat, but was unable to do so. He directed his signaler to contact D Company.

"Hello. Dog 1, fetch Sunray . . . Over."

"Hello, Dog 1, Sunray speaking," Buck Carson replied.

"Hello, Dog 1, sit rep . . . Over."

Carson informed Graves that he was advancing steadily but being harassed by light machine-gun and mortar fire. Graves was then called by Logan again.

Hello, Charlie 1. Can you engage? Over."

"Hello, Charlie 1. Range too great for effective results but will try . . . Out."

"Hello, Dog 1. Proceed with all possible speed to your final objective. Enemy force, estimated three hundred, advancing to the top from the north side of objective . . . Over."

There was no answer from Carson, Graves having lost contact with D Company.

"Damn these bloody hills!" he cursed vehemently.

"Sir, Big Sunray demands a sit rep," his signaler called.

"Keerist! Why in hell doesn't he let me alone for a few bloody minutes so I can fight this goddamn battle!" Graves growled.

"Hello, Charlie 1. Friends in village now being heavily engaged from the north and northeast. Tin cans running short of ammo. Sunray of friends request I act as control relay as he cannot contact you . . . Over," Logan radioed.

Graves thought for a moment then replied, "Hello, Charlie 1. Instruct Sunray re tin cans to start sending them back in shifts to re-ammunition. Will use you as relay for friends . . . Out."

Graves was now genuinely worried. His tanks were running short of ammunition, out of direct communication with two of his companies.

Dearing's position is becoming precarious. I'd better send Baker Company up to give him a hand, he decided.

"Hello, Baker 1. Prepare to move to secondary objective . . . Over."

"Hello. Baker 1. Roger . . . Out," Wilson promptly replied.

"Big Sunray wants another sit rep, sir!"

"Well, you just tell Big Sunray that I'm too goddamn busy—no, never mind, I'll speak to him," Graves snapped, annoyed by the brigade commander's constant request for situation reports and thereby cutting in on the battalion's communication's net.

Graves watched Wilson's company move off their ridge, stringing along a track running at right angles to the main road. He had a strange premonition of disaster watching B Company form up along their start line. The thought no sooner entered Graves's mind when he heard the unmistakable whirr of falling mortar bombs; a clump fell into the center of the platoon on Wilson's right flank. After few terrifying seconds, the fifth platoon of Baker Company ceased to exist.

To permit Major Wilson time to evacuate his many casualties and reform his company, Graves called off B Company's attack, ordering Wilson to take up his former position.

Two Sherman tanks detached from the squadron at Chail-Li to re-ammunition lumbered into Graves's view. He had his driver move his armored car out to the edge of the road, flagging them down.

"How is everything up there?" he anxiously asked the black-bereted young troop commander.

"Not too well, sir. We're holding out okay right now, but the Chink fire is getting heavier all the time. I don't know what will happen if they decide to attack. God knows there are enough of them out there."

"Ah . . . Thanks for the information. I guess you'd better be getting on your way."

Dearing had positioned his company in a circle on the fringes of the small village. The chattering of the Canadian Bren guns and rifles was being drowned out by the intense Chinese fire originating from the barren hills bordering the village.

During a lull in the firefight, Reardon ran zigzag to a pile of rubble sheltering Jack Harvey.

"Any signs of a buildup, Jack?" he asked. "The boss seems to think that the Chinos may be getting ready to give us the bum's rush any time now."

"Not in front of us, sir, but I saw a horde of the little bastards heading toward one platoon. Frome got a couple of them, but that didn't stop them at all."

"Corporal! Corporal! I think I can see some Americans setting up a machine gun about three hundred yards over to our right."

"Where on the right, Viau?"

"Over by that hut on the ridge."

Reardon and Harvey looked over at the place indicated by Bernie. At first, the poncho-clad figures appeared to be Yanks. When Mike observed them through his binoculars, he quickly recognized the Chinese soldiers clothed in captured American equipment setting up a heavy Browning machine gun.

"I'd better get to hell back to my wireless set and pass the good news on to the major," he worried. "Christ! When the little bastards open up with that goddamn thing they'll really give us hell!"

"Maybe I'll be able to save you a little trouble, boss. Balaski is a pretty good shot. Hey, Blackie! I got five bucks that says you can't hit the Chinks setting up the machine gun on our right," Harvey challenged.

"You're on, Corp. You just lost yourself five bucks."

Taking careful aim, Blackie fired at the Chinese gunner who was taking up his position behind the gun. His body jerked under the impact of the Canadian's .303 slug. A second Chinese soldier tried to take his comrade's place, only to meet the same fate. Fire more times, the Chinese tried to get the machine gun into operation, and five more times, Blackie's uncanny accuracy took its toll. Finally, they gave up the attempt. In the meantime, Frome and Harvey brought a combined burst of Bren and Sten machine-gun fire on a group of fifteen or so enemy trying to sneak up on Harvey's besieged section. Seven Chinese fell, and the remainder scurried back to a group of boulders at the base of the hill.

As Reardon ran back to where Kalamazoo, his signaler, was positioned, a Chinese machine gunner zeroed in on him. Small puffs of sand kicked up around his running feet, the first indication he was being shot at. Reardon dove for the cover of the shattered wall falling on top of his signaler.

"You hit, boss?" Kal questioned anxiously.

Mike felt himself all over, his brow covered with a cold sweat. "Nope! The little bastards missed me this time, though I'll never know how. Any more scoop from the company commander?"

"Nothing, sir, except we're still out of contact with battalion HQ, and there ain't no sign of B Company on our left."

"Something must have buggered up someplace. Baker Company was supposed to move up and take care of the left flank as soon as we gave the success signal for taking this stinking place."

Mike scanned the area being covered by Paul Anderson, the situation seeming relatively quiet on his front at the moment. A short while earlier, Paul's platoon had suffered a number of serious casualties, a result of a pinpoint mortar bombardment.

"Hey, Johnson, don't let your section bunch up so much. Spread them out! One bloody bomb and your whole goddamn section will be blown to hell," Mike yelled above the battle din.

During the initial stages of the fight for the village, Anderson felt more like a spectator than a participant, finding it hard to believe that the fire being directed against his men and himself was intended to kill them. He was holding this peculiar attitude until a well-directed cluster of mortar bombs completely decimated one of his sections, not realizing that his men were bunched up, presenting an excellent target for the enemy. He foolishly believed it really didn't matter—no one was going to get hurt. Everything seemed so unreal, a bad, exciting dream; his dreamlike state was shattered by the flattened bodies of his dead, the whimpering, screaming torn bodies of the wounded. His own problems seemed insignificant in the face of the stark drama of life and violent death enacted before his shocked eyes. Paul had received his baptism of fire.

Monty had been wounded, not seriously but just enough to allow him to wear a field dressing on his head, striking the dramatic pose of the proud wounded warrior, bent but unbowed. A piece of singing shrapnel laying open his scalp cleanly, momentarily stunning him, outside of causing heavy bleeding did no serious damage. His platoon was holding the most precarious position in the company area, precarious because the Chinese, for reasons known only to themselves, decided to concentrate the bulk of their small arms fire against the Canadian defenders in that spot, any movement of his men drawing wild bursts of fire from the enemy. In spite of this, the casualties suffered by one platoon had been light. Carr-Wilson, scanning hillsides and ridges that walled the village, saw them swarming with Chinese moving boldly in full view of the Canadians. Wistfully looking down the road leading to the brigade area and safety, a persistent, plaguing thought buzzed in his head, *I wonder if we're going to get out of this bloody mess.*

The relentless spring monsoon rains, changing the steep slopes of hill 468 into a slippery quagmire, made D Company's task of ascending the feature not only difficult but also dangerous. Buck Carson decided to leapfrog his platoons up the hill until approaching close enough to the summit to launch a coordinated company-strength assault. The ascent by his company was unopposed until its forward elements reached a point fifty yards from the top, at which point they were engaged by heavy enemy machine-gun and mortar fire.

Cpl. Harry Neilson, commander of the second section of the tenth platoon, was leading Dog Company's snakelike advance up the southern slopes of 468. His main function, besides watching out for enemy activity, was to scout out a suitable route for the remainder of the company to follow, Standish coming twenty yards behind with the remainder of his platoon. Slipping, sliding, pulling one another up using their rifles for support, he approached the top, Neilson finally reaching the base of a smooth, steep ledge too high for a man to negotiate alone, low enough for a man to manage if given a hand.

The corporal called to the man covering him, "Hey, Bill! Come up here and give me a boost. Once we get on that ledge, I think we'll be in the clear.

Steady now. Don't lift me until I give you the word. Otherwise, we'll both go over ass over teakettle. Okay. Now!"

The last thing Neilson saw in this world was the crouching figure of a Chinese soldier holding a submachine gun pointing at the center of his astonished face. The burst of machine-gun fire from a close but unseen enemy shocked Carson, ordering Standish to clear out the enemy pocket and Red Saunders to make a dash for the summit around Standish's right flank. In a surprisingly short time, Saunders radioed back to Carson that he had reached the top, taking up a defensive position facing the enemy front. Buck then ordered Standish to proceed with all possible haste to link up with Saunders.

Standish's frightened voice shouted into Carson's earphones, "We can't move any further. We're pinned down up here!"

"What do you mean pinned down? I can hear only one Chink machine gun from down here. Now clear the goddamn thing out and get on with the bloody war!"

Carson then called Brock, eleventh platoon commander, to move his platoon around Carson's headquarters.

"Hello, One Dog. For Christ's sake, boss, tell Standish to get the lead out of his ass. There's a hell of a pile of Chinks heading this way. I'd say a couple of hundred anyways. They're about three hundred yards away but moving fast!"

"Hold your fire until they get within range. I'll get the tenth platoon up there as soon as possible. Out to you. What's holding you up, Don? No, I want to speak to Sunray, over."

Carson was waiting for Standish to reply when a solitary Chinese mortar bomb fell directly in the center of Carson's headquarters, not realizing he had been hit until he tried to struggle to his feet, only to collapse in a helpless heap, his left leg torn and shattered by a large mortar fragment.

When Standish witnessed Neilson's body tumbling helplessly down the side of the hill to stop just short of where he crouched, something inside him snapped, unable to move or think, staring at Neilson's faceless body, horrified. His signaler called him. When Standish failed to answer, he came over to shake his shuddering platoon commander. "Sir! Sir! Major Carson wants to speak to you right away."

"Go away! Go away, goddamn you, and leave me alone!" Standish shrieked at his startled signaler.

"Look out, sir! A Chink!" the signaler shouted as he brought up his rifle to fire. He was too late. He was killed by a burst of machine-gun fire.

Standish fell to the ground, shaking violently. He was eventually sent back to Canada a broken man.

Encouraged by his success, the lone enemy machine gunner crept to the edge of the ledge and riddled three more men of Neilson's section. Undecided as to what they should do after their section commander had been shot, they stayed in their positions which, unfortunately for them, were in full view of the Chinese soldier occupying the ledge. Hearing the screams of the men ahead of him for fire support, Corporal Parker moved up to find out what was holding them up. He stared unbelievingly at the dead and dying Canadians strewn around the base of the ledge.

"The rotten little bastards! The dirty rotten bastards!" he grated. "Come on, you guys! Let's get that son of a bitch up there."

Parker led the unexpected rush, having the personal satisfaction of killing the gunner but not before the Chinese had managed to wound two more Canadians.

Saunders's position at the top of the hill soon became untenable, deciding to make a desperate bid to keep the Chinese away from the summit on learning of Carson's wounding and the heavy casualties suffered by the tenth platoon. Knowing his situation was desperate, he could not possibly hold off the Chinese for any length of time without support. Reluctantly, Saunders gave the order to withdraw.

In the valley below, Graves, unable to contact Dog Company since morning, was depending heavily on Carson to capture and hold his key objective, knowing if he could manage to hang on to and reinforce 468, it would dominate the surrounding features and valleys, which in turn would force the Chinese to withdraw northward. The Chinese, realizing this, were doing everything in their power to drive the Canadians off the hotly contested hill. A report of D Company's progress finally came through via Major Wilson, assuming wireless control, whose report was discouraging, to say the least, stating that Carson was dead, his company now hopelessly cut off. In addition to this piece of bad news, Graves was informed by Logan that he had received a report from A Company stating that Dearing was wounded and his company being cut to pieces. In the face of these reports, both of which proved later to be exaggerated, the brigade commander decided to withdraw the Royals to a position behind his other battalion and ordering Graves to commence with withdrawal. John Graves was a crestfallen, disappointed man. This was the first time he had ever been forced to retreat. He found the experience the bitterest of his life.

Reardon's platoon, supported by the tanks, was given the task of fighting the rearguard action as Dearing ordered the rest of his company to break contact with the Chinese commenced withdrawing southward. A withering hail of deadly fire from the tanks and the Deuce discouraged any attempts on the part of the communists to follow the retreating Canadians.

It was now late afternoon, heavy mist returning to the war torn valley. Graves had moved his armored car dangerously close to the approaches of the village to personally supervise Dearing's withdrawal. Out of the thick mist, a ghostly column appeared—the men of Dearing's company. Some were laughing and joking, a few were crying tears of relief, many looked grim; but all were thoroughly frightened, and no wonder, they had experienced a very close call, managing to get out by the skin of their teeth.

Adding to his already formidable collection of troubles, Graves learned two tanks of the rearguard party were stuck in the soft earth of a rice paddy, lying on the east side of the road. Graves spent a very anxious half hour waiting for the tank recovery vehicle to extricate the bogged down Shermans.

While the CO had been occupied with Dearing's company, Major Wilson had "talked down" the disorganized remnants of D Company from their precarious position on 468. On reaching the valley floor, he directed them to the rear, waiting with his company to protect the withdrawal of Dearing and Logan.

Colonel Graves, still in his armored car, was the last man to leave the beleaguered area; the battle was over.

The exhausted Royals did not sleep that night; rumors of a strong Chinese attack, following up their successful defense against the Canadians, kept every officer and man alert. It was not until the following morning that the Royals were able to take stock of themselves. The primary reason for the failure of the attack was obvious: it had been too ambitious, too much for a single battalion to contend with. Dearing had been right.

As Paul Anderson gazed at the peaceful, inscrutable hills to the north, the scene of death and violence the day before, he couldn't help wondering at the number of times through the centuries these same hills had been contested by foreign invaders. In the ensuing years of war and pestilence since the first marauder had set foot on Korean shores, only one thing had remained unchanged, the hill, which, like a perfidious mistress, readily submitted to the strong but belonged to no one for very long. Now it belonged to the victorious Chinese and the Canadian dead.

Two days later, an American regimental combat team relieved the brigade, which was placed in divisional reserve to "lick its wounds."

CHAPTER 22

The Ambush

The conclusion of the Canadian brigade's first major engagement coincided with radical change in the political scene; the United Nations was trying hard to arrange a cease fire between the belligerents as a prelude to conducting truce talks. The impact of the negotiations on the war was a general decrease of military activity on all fronts; patrol bases were established at key points along the line, limiting the fighting by both sides to patrol actions.

After a short breather in reserve, the Canadian brigade was placed under command of the First Cavalry Division directed to establish a patrol base north of the junction of the Imjin-Hantung Rivers, the Canadians responsible for a five-mile front anchoring the southwest corner of the Iron Triangle.

The three battalions of the brigade occupied the line of sunbaked, barren hills bordering the southern extremities of a once proud progressive industrial city, Chorwon, the war reducing this center to a grotesque, twisted and pock-marked, rat-infested shambles. Each battalion patrolled the shattered remnants of the city in turn, collecting seemingly endless droves of southbound refugees for screening in an attempt to uncover communist soldiers infiltrating the UN lines disguised as civilians.

Hungry refugees could be seen poking listlessly among the fetid, putrid-smelling ruins, searching for anything of value that could be bartered for food. Bronze-colored women, their bodies lean, their eyes bright from starvation, tried to suckle their hunger-bloated offspring at their shrunken breasts in a desperate, often futile effort to keep their babies alive. The men, backs bent by the awesome loads they carried on A-shaped pack boards, leaned heavily on walking sticks, trickling rivulets of perspiration following the deeply etched lines of their prematurely aged mahogany-colored faces. The unmistakable marks of war's suffering and bewilderment had been deeply inscribed on the normally cheerful faces of both adults and children. At times these unfortunate people seemed completely oblivious of the war, and the sweat-drenched Canadians herded them to the refugee collecting points, which were administered by the Republic of Korea soldiers.

Chuck Dearing's company had taken up a defensive position on a rounded shallow-sloped hill that formed the extreme right flank of the Canadian brigade. On his right, across the main highway running through the city, the left-hand company of a Puerto Rican battalion was established on a hill very similar to that occupied by A Company. Behind him, in the valley, lay the battalion HQ; on his left, on a somewhat higher and steeper hill, was Vince Logan's C Company; directly to his front, starting at the base of his hill position, the southern extremity of the bombed city. Inside his company perimeter, his men were playing Korean records on an ancient phonograph they had scrounged.

In the north beyond the city, Dearing could see a hazy line of hills constituting the communist main line of defense. Standing in front of his command post, looking over the city and its adjacent reservoir, he wondered how Mike Reardon was getting on in Seoul on his short leave.

Hope he doesn't get in too much trouble. A couple of drinks and he's liable to make a damn fool of himself, he thought worriedly.

The Deuce, commanded by Sergeant Cross in Reardon's absence, had finished digging and wiring the position, most of the men either sleeping, talking, or sunning themselves. Cpl. Gus Johnson, his brother Al, and Ed Banks were casually examining the hazy line of commie hills lying to the north of the rubble-filled city.

"I wonder if the Chinks are sitting back there looking at us the same as we're looking at them?" Ed remarked to his two companions.

"Sure they are, Ed. Why, Al and me was saying just a while ago that the Chinos are probably watching us now, hoping the same as us that the Kaesong peace talks will work out so that we can get the hell out of this flea-bitten gook paradise and go home."

"Go home? Why, we just got here! The poor old Chinamen would be hurt if we took off before we got a chance to know them."

"Very funny, Banks, very funny. I thought you had enough of the Chinks at Chail-Li to do you for the rest of your life."

"That was different, Gus. I'd sure as hell hate to leave and have the Chinks think they could lick us, that's all."

"I know one guy who isn't worried about the peace talks right now," Al Johnson commented with a leer.

"Who?" his friends chorused.

"The boss. He's probably setting up his own peace talks in Seoul right now, the lucky bastard. As I've always said, the bloody officers get all the luck." He sighed, leaning back against a large rock, at the same time trying to brush away a cloud of wasps persistently attacking the jam on his hardtack biscuit.

"Hell, Al, it wouldn't be so bad here if it wasn't for the god-awful heat and all the queer bugs—damn! One of the little SOB's stung me!"

"Relax, Al." Ed laughed. "He can't needle you again."

"Big joke, big joke," Al replied angrily. "Probably a 'presento' from the damn Chinamen," he continued ruefully, watching an inflamed red bump growing on his forearm.

The attention of the three soldiers diverted to a long train of weary Korean men and women moving steadily along one of the main thoroughfares of the city below.

Wiping the sweat off his face with his rolled shirt sleeve, Al commented, "Look at them all, Gus. You wouldn't think we'd cleared all the gooks out of that stinking city yesterday. I wonder where in the hell they all come from?"

Ignoring his brother's question, Gus remarked, "You know, the Chinos have passed a lot of their characters through our lines disguised as civvies. Put Koreans, Japs, and Chinamen in those baggy white suits and they all look the same."

"Sure thing." Ed laughed. "Complete with bugles and whistles, a Chink version of Guy Lumbago and his Royal Comedians."

"I think both you 'Gibonis' are nuts," snorted Al.

"'Giboni'?" queried Ed. "What in hell is a 'Giboni'?"

"A yo-yo without a string," answered Al, laughing loudly. "And what could be more useless than a yo-yo without a string?"

"It's a damn good thing both you third-rate clowns are in the army," Gus interjected good-naturedly. "Otherwise, you'd starve to death."

"Never happen," Ed asserted. "I was making nearly a hundred bucks a week before I joined up."

"You young guys are all the same," Gus answered. "All of you were in the big time joining up for the adventure. I'll bet a month's pay you weren't even making a hundred a month."

"That's all you know, Gus," Ed heatedly replied.

"I don't like to change the subject, but have either of you money experts got any water?" queried Al. "I'm dry as hell."

"Didn't you fill your water bottle this morning?" Gus inquired.

"No, I forgot," Al replied indifferently.

"Damn it all, Al, will you never do what you're told? You knew blasted well what the sergeant's orders were. I ought to put you on charge."

"Okay, okay, Corporal!" Al retorted sarcastically.

"Don't get smart, Al," Gus angrily warned his brother. "I can still beat hell out of you."

"It's too damn hot to go up and down this SOB of a hill just to fill up blasted water bottle, and as for beating the hell—"

Ed suddenly interrupted the heated argument, saying, "Hey, you guys, cut it out. The sergeant's coming."

Determined to get in the last word, Gus threatened angrily, "Look, Al, I'll give the orders to this section, and you'll damn well carry them out, or else, I'll have your—"

"What's the beef, Gus?" Sergeant Cross inquired good-naturedly. "Sounds like you guys are having a slight difference of opinion."

"Not really, Sarge," Gus answered, his face flushed with embarrassment. "I was just straightening out a few things."

While standing there looking at the three friends together, Cross could not help marveling at the peculiar faculty, possessed by most Canadians and Americans, for forming very efficient teams out of individuals having little, if any, common characteristics. The sergeant, squatting on his haunches Korean style beside Gus, said, "Got a job for you tomorrow, Gus."

"What's the deal, Sarge?" Gus quietly asked.

"Security patrol," replied Cross. "You're to take a couple of your guys and check the Chorwon riverbank for gook civvies. I'll give you the rest of the info at tonight's orders group."

The river Cross referred to was actually a wide shallow stream flowing through the center of the city, supplying water to a large reservoir forming Chorwon's eastern limit, the river forming a convenient line of demarcation between the Canadian and the communist defense localities, also serving as the patrol boundary for the Canadians by day, for the commies by night.

Gus, absentmindedly scratching at the sweat-soaked matted hair covering his chest, suggested, "Three should be enough for the job, Sarge," after a few moments' reflection.

"Yes," Cross agreed, "three should be plenty. Things have been unusually quiet around here the past two weeks," he added regretfully. "So there shouldn't be any trouble." Cross straightened up from his cramped position, saying, "I've got to take off for company HQ, Gus, the major is having an orders group. Take over the platoon until I get back." The sergeant switched his attention from Gus to the other two. "So long, guys, see you later."

"So long, Sarge," replied the three men in unison.

"Well, Gus!" Al exclaimed cheerfully. "That means Ed, you, and me."

"Like hell it does," retorted Gus. "You're staying this trip."

"Don't be foolish," Al argued heatedly. "We've always gone on patrol together. You heard the sergeant say it was just a routine job. Besides, I'm pissed off sitting in the same bloody hot hole on this damn hill day after day!"

"Look, Al, stop bugging me," Gus warned. "How many times do I have to tell you I'll make the decisions in this section? You're not going, and that's all there is to it."

That evening, after the sergeant's orders group, Gus led Ed and the very persuasive Al to the summit of the hill. Arriving at the top utilizing the maplike panorama of the city below to point out the route and objectives of the patrol to his companions, he carefully outlined in detail the plan they would follow, answered their questions. After reviewing the plan carefully, he led his small party back to their position.

Returning to the area, Gus was handed a small packet of letters by one of the other members of his section. Ed was the fortunate member of the trio receiving no less than three letters, while his two friends received one each. Ed couldn't restrain himself from jeering at the brothers. "I guess we know who the popular guy around here is. *Cherchez la femme*," he crowed, kissing a letter from his girlfriend.

"Aw, knock it off, Ed," interrupted Al. "I'd hate to have to promise to marry a dame just to get a lousy letter."

Finally, Gus demanded of his two companions, "How about reading your mail instead of yacking about it!"

Following this remark, the three men settled themselves opening their letters.

Al's letter was from his mother. Mrs. Johnson made a point of writing both her sons at least once a week, outlining the neighborhood events and gossip she knew would be of interest to them. In her letter to Al, she described the sad state of the garden flowers and the unexpected marriage between Harry Maxwell, Al's best friend, and Veronica Pearce. Al stopped reading at this point and laughingly interrupted his brother by saying, "Hey, Gus, it looks like Harry finally got Veronica in the family way!"

"Small wonder," Gus answered briefly, remembering an incident. He accidentally stumbled on them making love on the Maxwell living room floor while paying Harry a surprise visit on his last day of embarkation leave.

Mrs. Johnson concluded her letter by asking her youngest boy to take very good care of himself and to listen to his elder brother.

Gus knew, from the handwriting on the envelope, that his letter was from his estranged wife Betty, the first letter he had received from her in over a month. Before opening it, Gus lit a cigarette, moving into the shade of an overhanging rock to shield his eyes from the bright rays of the setting sun. Gus needed only to read a few lines to understand the meaning of his wife's letter. Betty, having met someone else, wanted a divorce. She explained the man in question had a good job, could be depended upon to stay home to look after his responsibilities, and would make a good father for Debbie, Gus and Betty's four-year-old daughter. Then she finished, writing he had no business going to Korea against her wishes. There was no use trying to get her to change her mind.

When Gus finished his wife's Dear John, he was so preoccupied with his thoughts, completely forgetting the cigarette he was holding until it began burning his fingers. Cursing at the searing pain, he shook the cigarette from his fingers, making his way to his bunker. Standing guard later that night, Gus decided he would write to his wife after he returned from patrol, asking her to hold off making a final decision until he returned home.

The sentry detailed to awaken Gus at five o'clock on the morning of the patrol was surprised to find his section commander wide awake, sitting upright, smoking a cigarette, enjoying the refreshing coolness of the early morning. He mumbled a hoarse thanks to the sentry. Instructing him to awaken Ed and his brother, he commenced pulling on his heavy high-topped black boots. Minutes later, while cleaning his machine carbine, he heard the loud voices of his brother and Ed.

"Pipe down, you guys," he ordered, "the rest of the section is trying to sleep."

As Gus left the shelter of his bunker to meet his two comrades, the bright horizontal rays of the rapidly rising sun blinded him, forcing him to wrinkle up his face like a disgruntled ancient monkey.

"Looks like another scorcher," Al remarked to his brother.

"It'll be hot as hell in the city by the time we get there," Ed added.

"By the way, Al," Gus directed, "you'd better make sure you fill your water bottle when we get to the bottom of this hill. I don't want any more of yesterday's nonsense."

"Yeah, yeah," his brother replied impatiently. "I'm not that damn stupid."

"Sometimes I wonder." Gus smiled, stretching his lanky frame. Yawning prodigiously, he addressed Ed, "You all set, Ed?"

"Yep," Ed replied still half asleep. "I'm all hot to trot. In fact, if it gets much hotter, I'll have the 'trots.'"

"Might be a good thing," Al answered sarcastically. "A little diarrhea might clean some of those lousy puns out of your system."

Ed ignored Al's remarks, pulling his third letter from his shirt pocket, reading it aloud. "Dear Sir: I have been instructed to inform you that unless you settle the balance of your account with the Hotchkiss Men's Clothiers, we will be forced to take drastic action to collect same. Signed, J. P. Willoughby, Manager, Acme Collecting Agency."

"Well, I'll be damned!" Gus exclaimed.

"How do you like 'those apples'?" remarked Ed. "Maybe they'll hire a couple of Chinks to collect it from me. Can you imagine a Chingook sneaking up to my bunker in the middle of the night, tapping me on the shoulder with his burp gun saying, 'So solly, please, but you hubba hubba pay, honorrable mista. Willoughby two t'ousand yen, else you go meet honorable ancestors'?"

Sergeant Cross was waiting for the members of the patrol at the base of the hill, had thoughtfully brewed a pot of hot coffee for Gus and his two companions, telling them to fill their mugs. "By the way, Gus," he remarked, "there's going to be a Yank engineer recce patrol checking the streambed, so keep your eyes peeled for them. If you keep moving, you should be back by noon. Don't bring a lot of civvies back with you. We'll get the field security boys to do that. Any questions, Gus?"

"No, I don't think so," the corporal replied. "The boys and I got the picture. Hey, you guys, finish you coffee, it's almost seven."

Al momentarily ignored his brother's command and continued talking to one of his friends from the platoon headquarters.

"Didn't you hear me tell you to get a move on, Al?" Gus directed.

"I'm coming, I'm coming," Al answered, gulping down his coffee. "Keep your shirt on!"

As they approached the edge of the city, the members of the small patrol fanned out, with Gus covering the right-hand side of their route, Al the left, and Ed following about ten yards to the rear. The heavy stench of the city increased with each step until, finally, Ed was forced to tie a dirty handkerchief over the lower half of his face to prevent the indescribable stink from turning his stomach. A short time later, they spotted a long straggling line of Korean refugees moving toward the patrol.

"Shall we let them through?" Al asked his brother.

"Yes, we might as well. Check each one of them over carefully and make sure they are not carrying anything that even looks like a weapon."

Gus then turned his attention to Ed. "Keep a close watch on these characters after we pass them through, Ed," he commanded. "If any one of them makes a suspicious move, let him have it!"

"Okay, Gus," Ed replied obediently.

The withering heat of the mid-morning sun was making the three Canadians sweat profusely. The closer they got to the center of the city, the hotter it seemed to get. They were meeting fewer civilians now; consequently, they were more at ease. Ed was decreasing the distance between himself and Al until he was almost shoulder to shoulder with his friend.

Suddenly, Gus noticed this, shouting, "Damn it to hell, Ed! I told you to stay ten yards in the rear to cover our backs. If you want to live to sleep with that flaming girl of yours again, you had better do what you're bloody well told!"

Gus's last remark made Ed flush with anger. He was about to tell Gus to mind his own business when Al cut him off, saying, "Can it, Ed. Gus is right. You better get back to your slot pronto."

Finally, they reached the bank of the river. Gus had spotted a group of huts near the riverbank, hoping as soon as his patrol reached them, he would let his boys have a smoke and water break. As they approached, they spotted a lone Korean male sitting in the shade of the hut nearest the river; Gus grew cautious as he neared the man, noting the stranger was young, an unusual sight in manpower-drained North Korea, clean shaven with closely cropped hair. Highly suspicious of the Korean's military appearance, Gus decided to search both the Korean and the surrounding area very carefully.

Standing directly in front of the stranger, Gus motioned him to his feet. "Ed, you cover me while I search this character. Al, you check inside and around these stinking huts."

Gus searched the Korean thoroughly while the stranger jabbered incoherently in his native tongue, at the same time pointing to himself and in the general direction of the United Nations' lines.

"My god!" Al commented, "this character has enough room in those baggy pants to store an antitank gun."

"Maybe," replied Gus, "but he isn't carrying one in them today. Say, Ed, you had better give Al a hand checking the huts. I'll take care of our gook friend."

Ten minutes later, the two men returned to the place where Gus was standing guard over the Korean.

"Everything okay?" Gus asked.

"Yeah," Al answered readily. "The other huts are clean. The one behind us has a few beat-up rice mats on the floor and a bag full of junk, probably belonging to this guy."

"Did you check the gear?" Gus questioned.

"Naturally," replied Al in a pained voice.

"I don't like the looks of this bird," Gus remarked. "As soon as we've had a smoke, I'm going to take him back with us. We can see all we need of the riverbed from here."

When Gus finished speaking, the Korean made signs wanting to pick up his gear in the hut Al had inspected. Wiping perspiration from his face, Gus waved to the man to go ahead, the Korean smiled slightly, made a short bow, disappearing into the dark smelly confines of the thatched mud dwelling.

"Who's got some smokes?" Ed demanded.

"When will you start carrying your own weeds?" Al countered. "You're always bumming cigarettes." Suddenly changing the subject, he asked, "Shall I keep an eye on the gook, Gus?"

"No, don't bother," Gus replied, "I'll do that."

He pulled out of his shirt pocket a sweat-soaked but still serviceable pack of American cigarettes, offering them to his friends.

Meanwhile, inside the hut, the crafty Korean quickly unrolled a loosely rolled rice mat lying unnoticed beneath a latticed window located beside the door, the unrolled mat revealing a short-barreled Russian submachine gun. Crouching low on the floor, he stealthily poked the ugly black barrel of the weapon through the lower slats of the window. Slowly raising himself to his knees, he took a careful aim at the three Canadians standing barely ten feet away.

Al and Ed were facing Gus with their backs toward the latticed window. Al was in the process of lighting his brother's cigarette when Gus spotted the snout of the machine gun poking through the window. He tried to scream out a warning before a white hot steel first smashed his lungs, exploding in his brain.

The Korean momentarily observed the three motionless bodies sprawled together in the blood-splotched dust of the courtyard, quickly moving out the rear of the hut, running toward the river.

CHAPTER 23

The Chase

The UN forces began to step up their patrol activity along the entire Eighth Army front as a result of a stalemate in the Kaesong peace talks. The Canadian brigade ordered to send large tank-supported patrols up the broad valley linking the city with Pyongyang. The purpose of these patrols was to keep in contact with the enemy, at the same time dominate the city and adjacent reservoir.

Late in June, three companies of Royals, supported by tanks and artillery, carried out a very ambitious fighting patrol designed to capture the dominant feature north of the city, hill 730, Old Hooknose. Colonel Graves's plan was quite simple: establish a firm base on a ridge north of the reservoir with D Company, now commanded by Jungle Jim Phillips, pass through A and C Companies in a series of leapfrog moves to take them to a ridge leading to the summit of the formidable objective. The final assault to the top was to be made by Vince Logan's company, with Dearing providing support, and a platoon acting as a cutoff working behind the hill firing on any enemy trying to withdraw. According to American intelligence, the hill was supposedly lightly held. The plan was excellent, except for one flaw: unknown to the Canadians, the Chinese had quietly occupied Old Hooknose in strength, anticipating the Canadians might try to take it.

Mike Reardon's return from his four-day leave coincided with Monty Carr-Wilson's return from the military hospital in Seoul, the two friends spending their last night in Seoul together, first getting loaded in a U.S. Army signals officers' mess, picking up two nurses Monty had become well acquainted with during his short sojourn in the hospital, spending the night "on the tiles" with their attractive companions.

Chuck Dearing, very happy to see them, was uneasy about his taciturn commander of the third platoon, very uncommunicative since the battle at Chail-Li. At first, Dearing thought Anderson's nerve was going, changing his opinion when he talked with the battalion padre who told him, without the details, Paul had a serious problem. Dearing tried to speak to Paul about his trouble without success. Now that Monty was back, Chuck was hoping Anderson might cheer up a little, or at least relax.

Paul, giving up hope of hearing from Anne, asked the padre to write to her father, thinking that a letter from a third party might prompt either Anne or her father to send him some word. The answer came to him via the padre in the form of a small cardboard box containing a few personal belongings he had left with the Tacoma girl: a pipe, his signet ring, and his crumpled photograph— nothing else, not a word. He couldn't understand why Anne hadn't written, feeling certain she loved and trusted him, but not she not writing made him suffer; it was not in keeping with her sensitive nature. He concluding bitterly her parents had managed to turn her against him. Now everything was lost: his wife, his sweetheart, the unborn baby he would never see.

Anderson, looking up into the star-filled heavens, shook his fist at the silent sky. "Damn you up there, whoever you are! How can you make a mockery out of life if you are God!" He cursed savagely.

Reardon listened quietly as Sergeant Cross related the details of the ambush of the Johnson brothers and Ed Banks. Cross finished the tale by saying, "I put Balaski in charge of Gus's section because he's had the experience and, more important, the men trust him."

"Yeah, that's fine. He should do a good job. Any word on reinforcements? We're getting pretty thin, and twenty-eight men aren't enough to do a forty-man job."

"I asked the major about replacements, and he said he'd look into it next time he saw the CO. The lads are still pretty sore about the Johnson boys and Banks, they may be hard to control next time we go on patrol. They've got it in for the civvies."

"Get the Deuce together, Eric. I want to talk to them."

"I think that would be a hell of a good idea, sir."

The Deuce's commander addressed his men sitting before him in an irregular semicircle. "Sergeant Cross had just given me the gen about Gus, Al, and Ed. It looks to me like they were cut down by a gook soldier disguised as a civilian, for a Chino soldier could never have gotten that close in broad daylight. Things have become pretty slack since the peace talks started. Consequently, we've become damn slack too! It just cost us three bloody good men. If the little brown bastards want to play rough, it's okay by me. From now on, I want you to remember we're in North Korea, and that every one of these slant-eyed heathen's a potential enemy. If every any one of you see a gook behaving in a suspicious manner, no questions, blast the bugger before he blasts you. Is that clearly understood? Okay, then act accordingly."

Reardon's orders regarding civilians lifted the men's spirits; now they could fight back instead of just providing convenient targets for some ambitious young commie set on establishing a reputation for himself.

On their way back to the line from Seoul, Mike told Monty about the sudden and dramatic changes taking place in Anderson during the weeks following the aborted battalion attack, Monty finding his friend's words difficult to believe.

"I don't blame you for looking so doubtful, Monty. I wouldn't have believed it if I hadn't seen it myself. I've got a goddamn good idea what's eating Paul. I'm certain something has fouled up in the Tacoma deal. I tried to talk to him once about it, but he gave me the brush, so I never mentioned it again. I know he hasn't received a letter from her since Pusan, which struck me as being strange, considering how thick he and Anne had become before we sailed. I figured at first that maybe his wife was giving him a hard time."

"No, Mike, I hardly think so. In fact, he'd gotten over that unpleasant mess quite well before we left the American side. I agree, it must be the girl in Tacoma, something serious. Paul isn't the type to bother himself over inconsequential matters, he takes life far too seriously for that."

"Well, as I was saying, I didn't pay too much attention to his moods until we went out on a company patrol to contact the Chinks north of the reservoir. Dearing told us to take it easy and not to get involved, wanting to avoid any useless casualties. All we had to do was find out where the Chinos had set up their outposts by drawing their fire, shoot back at them then withdraw. No sweat there at all.

"Everything went fine until the Chinks opened up from about eight hundred yards. Nobody got hit, everything was clicking. I started to fire back as per syllabus. Dearing ordered Anderson to move his platoon around to the flank of the Chink hill in case they should pull off, but do you know what the silly bastard did?

"He not only moved around the flank, but he also assaulted the bloody hill damn near ran into my fire! On top of that, the clot stood up all through the firefight! I thought he'd had his chips at least three times, but the harder the Chinos tried to hit him, the more they seemed to miss. When he finally charged the ridge, he must have been at least twenty yards ahead of his lead section. Monty, if I didn't know that guy as well as I do, I could have sworn he wanted to get killed, no kidding!"

"Maybe he did, Mike, maybe he did," Carr-Wilson quietly replied.

"One thing for sure—Dearing was as mad as hell. He really blasted Paul for needlessly risking his men's lives, telling him he was bloody lucky the Chinks decided not to put up a scrap and took off. Otherwise, he'd probably have got his. Do you know what he said? 'I couldn't care less!'"

"I'll have a talk with him when we get there. Maybe he'll unburden himself to me."

"I don't think so, Monty. The padre came up to see him the day before I left. He gave Anderson a package of some kind. Whatever it was sure didn't help any. He looked even worse after the padre left."

As soon as Carr-Wilson reported in to his company commander, subsequently taking over his platoon from his sergeant, he sought out his friend Paul. When they met, he was shocked by Anderson's appearance. Paul was becoming much thinner, his face drawn, his eyes ringed with dark shadows, his colorless lips twitching, his hands trembling when he greeted his friend. "Good to see you back, Monty. We missed you around here. How was the hospital? Must have been a nice change to sleep between sheets instead of a dirty hole in the ground."

Monty made up his mind to approach the matter directly. "How is everything in Tacoma, Paul? Have you heard from Anne lately?"

"None of your damn business! You're just as bad as the rest, always snooping into other people's affairs," he snapped, turning to leave.

"Now just hold on for a moment, old man!" said Monty sternly. "I certainly didn't intend to pry. I merely asked a civil question, and from you, at least, I expected a civil answer."

Paul hesitated, "Sorry, Monty. I didn't mean to behave like a boor. I've had a lot of things on my mind lately and—"

"Would you like to tell me about it, Paul?" Monty asked gently.

"No . . . I'd rather not . . . Thanks anyway. Well, I'd better go back to business, so if you'll excuse me—"

"Before you go, I thought you might like to know I received a letter from Anne's sister while I was in the hospital."

Anderson looked as if he had been slapped, leaping toward Monty, grabbing him by the front of his shirt. "What did she say? For god's sake, man, just don't stand there. What did she say?"

"What did she say about what, Paul? For heaven's sake, take it easy, will you? You don't have to strangle me."

"I'm sorry. What did she have to say about Anne? It's very important to me that I know."

"Obviously," Carr-Wilson replied dryly. "To be perfectly honest with you, old man, she scarcely said a thing about Anne, except that she was visiting some relatives in Saint Paul, Minnesota."

So that's where they sent her, Paul thought excitedly. *That's right! I remember now. She has an uncle living in Saint Paul, and he and his wife have been unable to have a family.*

Then he spoke aloud, "Monty, would you do me a great favor and write Margaret, asking her to give you Anne's address? I wrote to her once but didn't get an answer."

"Why, of course, Paul. In the meantime, keed, take it easy. You're pushing yourself too hard. I don't know what's wrong, and apparently, you don't want to tell me, but believe me, it isn't worth destroying yourself for."

Dearing was relieved to have his three platoon commanders together again. He was pleased by the agreeable effect Carr-Wilson's return had on Anderson. He read over carefully the notes he had made during Graves's orders group, made a few more, then called for his platoon commanders. They arrived a short time later, with the other members of the company O group which included, besides the three platoon commanders, a representative from the tanks, his mortar representative, and the leader of the section of medium machine guns being assigned to him for the operation against hill 730.

"Well, Monty, it looks like you arrived back just in time to take part in our biggest operation since Chail-Li."

"Yes, sir. I suppose you could say that I'm just naturally lucky," Monty replied jokingly.

Dearing presented his orders quickly and efficiently until he came to the difficult question of designating the platoon that was to have the tricky responsibility of acting as the ambush force. He looked briefly at the three expectant faces of his platoon officers, deciding not to use Carr-Wilson because of his recent return from the hospital. He felt Anderson was too unpredictable at the present time, leaving him with Reardon.

"I think I'll give that little gem to the Deuce, Mike."

"That's fine, sir, but I'm shorthanded. Any chance of our getting a few more bods for the job?"

"No, I'm afraid not. We're due to get some reinforcements, but they won't arrive till next week."

As soon as Dearing concluded his orders, the platoon commanders returned to their areas to brief the NCOs on the details of the operation against Old Hooknose. The Deuce received with mixed emotions the information about their hazardous part in the operation.

"I'll bet you anything he volunteered for the job," one of George Whitefoot's men complained bitterly. "He's probably trying to win a bloody medal for himself."

"Aw, shut your trap, Dennison. You talk too much," the big Indian ordered menacingly.

"What's the matter, Dennison? Turning chicken?" Frome called over from Jack Harvey's section area, clucking like a hen to add emphasis to his remark.

"Hey, Blackie, George—come over here for a minute, will you? I want to talk to you," Jack Harvey requested. When they arrived at his pup tent, he continued, saying, "I just heard a rumor from one of the guys at company headquarters that Cross is being promoted to staff sergeant and is going to support company. No kidding, guys, he's supposed to leave tomorrow morning."

"Keerist! That means we'll be at the mercy of Rover Boy then!" Blackie exclaimed worriedly.

"Aw, he ain't so bad. I seen a lot worse than him during the last war. At least he ain't chicken," Whitefoot commented.

"Sometimes I wish he was a little chicken. He treats the bloody war like a football game," Big Jack interjected feelingly. "But I agree with you—I've seen a hell of a lot worse and some of them in this battalion too."

"Well, we'll never have to worry about Reardon running out on us," the Indian corporal stated.

"That's for sure! In fact, he keeps us busy keeping up to him. Say, I wonder what's been eating the professor lately."

"Damn if I know, Jack," Blackie replied in a puzzled tone. "All I know is that he scared the living hell out of the boys in the third platoon the last time out." Then lowering his voice, he continued, "I heard from one of Anderson's gang that he's got some sort of woman trouble."

"Who hasn't?" Harvey retorted sarcastically. "Well, I'm going to turn in. I got a feeling tomorrow is going to be a long day. Good night, guys."

Immediately after dawn the following morning, D Company was loaded onto half-tracks and transported to the ridge that was to serve as the firm base for the assault forces. They drove slowly through the rubble-strewn main street, the tracks of their vehicles kicking up a huge cloud of stifling dust visible for miles. They drove by the cool inviting waters of the reservoir, checked with the Royals' outpost position then proceeded to a low ridge that lay directly ahead.

A half hour later, two troops of tanks and a battery of artillery began to rumble down the road previously covered by Dog Company; their mission was to support the movement of the patrol up the valley and on to its objective. The artillery battery was going to be established behind D Company's position, while the tanks were designated to accompany the assault forces up the valley. A and C Companies moved on foot behind the vehicle column. Although still early morning, the combination of the blinding dust kicked up by the support convoy and the hot rays of the early sun made the men in the marching column very uncomfortable, cursing bitterly at their more fortunate motorized brethren, not only for the discomfort they were causing but also for advertising to every Chinaman in the upper valley the Canadians were coming.

The sections of the Deuce moved along the sides of the main road in single file. Harvey's section was leading, followed by Reardon and his headquarters. Whitefoot's and Balaski's sections were spaced out behind headquarters on opposite sides of the road. As soon as Dearing's company reached D Company's position, Reardon's platoon split off to the right, while the rest of the company followed C Company up the left-hand side of the broad sunbaked valley. Graves was hoping the movement of the assault column would distract the attention of the enemy in the area away from Reardon's vulnerable platoon.

When the Deuce had arrived midway to the final objective, they encountered their first obstacle, a deeply eroded riverbed containing a small trickle of water. Beyond the riverbank lay a large collection of black volcanic rocks at the base of a bomb-blasted hill. According to American intelligence reports, the rounded sand-covered feature was supposedly occupied by a strong U.S. Army outpost. As Mike scanned the shell-pocked slopes, he was unable to detect any defenders. He handed his binoculars to Jack Harvey who was lying beside him on the riverbank.

"Can you see any signs of the Yanks on that brown sandy hill to our right, Jack? I can't see a goddamn thing! This bloody sweat keeps running into my eyes and fogs up the eyepieces."

Harvey slowly scanned the scarred slopes of the low-lying hill. "I don't see a damn thing on there either, sir. Somebody must have gotten some duff gen."

"Well, we can't stay here any longer. We'll have to get by those damn rocks somehow . . . Hey, Blackie, George! Come over here!"

Reardon outlined his plan of movement for the next leg of their patrol. "Tell your guys to keep a sharp lookout from here on in. There'll be hell to pay if the little bastards have spotted us and try to cut us off."

Mike gave one more order to his corporals before they returned to their sections. "The men are drinking too damn much water! From here on, we'll only drink when I say so . . . Okay, let's get the show on the road!"

As the men of the Deuce were gingerly picking their way through the sharp-edged volcanic deposits, some of them were cursing, muttering to themselves. Dennison, a recent arrival to the Deuce and a Second World War veteran, was cursing more loudly than the others.

"What a stupid place to take us," he complained. "If the goddamn Chinks start mortaring us in these bloody rocks, the bloody rock splinters will kill us if the shrapnel doesn't."

"If you don't shut your loud mouth, Dennison, I'll shut it for you!" Whitefoot warned.

"Mr. Reardon, I'm out of contact with Dog Company!" Kalamazoo reported.

"Try to contact Able or Charlie then."

"Right, sir," Kal replied. "Hello, One Able. Hello, One Able! Message for you from Noodnick. Over." Mike's signaler futilely tried to raise both A and C Companies.

"Damn it to hell! That tears it," Mike cursed to himself.

The Deuce moved stealthily through a deserted collection of Korean huts, now less than a mile now from their objective. Reardon held a hurried consultation with his section commanders.

"This is the situation, we're out of contact with the rest of the battalion. Kal hasn't been able to raise anyone."

"Don't you think we'd better move back some until we can make contact to find out the score? I'll be quite honest, boss, I don't like the look of things," Jack Harvey stated.

"Goddamn it, George, I thought I told you no one was to drink until I gave the order," Mike said irritably.

"That's right, sir. I passed it on to my men," Whitefoot answered.

"Then what the hell is Dennison doing draining his water bottle?" he snapped at his startled corporal. "No, I think we'll press on, Jack. We might be able to reestablish radio contact when we get a little higher. Okay, Jack, get your scouts moving."

Reardon's platoon continued its laborious advance toward the base of 730, becoming worried not seeing any sign of movement on the opposite side of the vast valley.

"Sir! Sir! I just picked up a message from Charlie Company. They've reached their final objective."

"That's impossible! Give me that goddamn thing," he replied, grabbing the earphones out of Kal's hands.

"My god, you're right! Phillips has reported he's on his objective, this is the ruddy objective, and there sure as hell hasn't been an assault up this bloody brute of a hill!"

"I think we had better get the hell out of here. The whole thing stinks," Harvey cut in anxiously.

"We'll stay here until I'm damn good and ready to move out, Corporal." Mike roared. "Keep a sharp lookout and leave the decisions to me."

"But, sir—"

"Goddamn it, man, do what you're told!"

High overhead, four jet aircraft were flying in lazy circles as a lone spotter aircraft fired a pair of white phosphorus rockets at the summit of the hill looming directly above the Canadians. With a graceful sweeping maneuver, the jets broke out of their formation and began screaming down to engage the objective. Suddenly, there were large black clouds of burning napalm smoke and the sharp clap of explosive rockets reverberated through the air.

"Mr. Reardon, I just got a message from Able Company. The objective was changed. This hill is loaded with Chinks!" Kal shouted to his commander.

Mike picked up the earphones and listened. He was relieved to hear Dearing's voice.

"Hello, One Able, message for Noodnick and his merry men . . . Get the hell out of there! The objective was changed, 730 is loaded with Chinks!"

Mike had heard enough and was turning to call his corporals when he saw Jack Harvey running toward him.

"Hey, boss! Take a look at that sandy-topped hill we looked at on our way up. I think I spotted some movement on it."

Reardon hurriedly put his binoculars to his eyes and scanned the slopes of the hill indicated by the corporal. Feeling his breath catch in his throat, his heart pounded furiously. Moving down the side of the hill was a swarm of Chinese, at least a hundred in number. Mike didn't try to kid himself; he knew what they were after. They had spotted the Deuce. "Unless . . . maybe they're after Able and Charlie," he said none too hopefully to himself. He called an O group of his corporals.

I'll have to make this fast. Our only chance is to try and link up with Able and Charlie Companies before the Chinks seal us off. I don't think they're quite sure where we are, but it's obvious we were spotted sometime during our move.

Mike pointed out their route then concluded his briefing, saying, "This is one time you won't mind running with Reardon. Let's go, you guys! Time's a-wasting."

The Deuce moved out of their position by sections in single file, Reardon detailing Jack Harvey's section to the responsible job of covering the withdrawal of the rest of the platoon and to protect the rear. Trusting to George Whitefoot's instinctive knowledge of terrain and his excellent sense of direction, Mike had him lead the platoon in its race out of the pocket, while he supervised the rearguard action. As they began dogtrotting diagonally across the valley, their equipment rattling with every step, they could see other groups of Chinese moving down the forward slopes of 730, obviously in pursuit of the rapidly retreating Canadian platoon.

"Never mind the bloody Chinks—keep moving!" Reardon shouted. "Come on, Balaski. Get the lead out of your ass!"

A half hour at a steady trot and the men were covered with sweat, their breath coming in short, hard gasps, fear clearly etched in their faces.

The forward elements of the pursuing Chinese began firing at the running Canadians. Fortunately, the range was too great for it to be effective. Some of the men threw themselves on the ground when they heard the Chinese bullets snapping over their heads.

"Get up, you stupid bastards! This is no place to stop! Come on, get moving. You won't get hit at this range."

"Shall I have Frome open up, sir?" Harvey panted.

"No, Jack, keep the boys going—the more distance we can put between the Chinks and ourselves, the better chance we have of getting out." Mike himself panted in short, painful gasps.

The killing pace began to tell on the exhausted Canadians, the better-conditioned and lighter-equipped Chinese overtaking them.

"Our guys can't keep this up much longer, boss," Blackie gasped.

"Get to the riverbed, get to the riverbed!" Mike panted. "Keep going, lads, only a hundred yards to go. George! Blackie! Drop your Bren gunners off on this side and get the rest of your men over on the other bank. Keep going! Don't stop now!"

The Chinese had closed in on the Deuce and were within three hundred yards of the stumbling Canadians, shooting wildly at their human quarry. One of Whitefoot's men staggered and fell heavily to the ground, his body arching itself backward into a bow, snapped forward again then lay still. Reardon paused briefly, falling to one knee beside the prostrate form; it was Dennison, dead, shot through the back of the neck.

Blackie's section, closely followed by Whitefoot's men, reached the edge of the riverbed, the same riverbed the Deuce had passed over earlier in the day. They stumbled, rolled, slid down its steep banks then scrambled desperately up the far side. George and Blackie coaxed, cursed, and kicked their men into a position from which they would be able to fire at the Chinese, whose forward elements were now only two hundred yards from the riverbed. In the meantime Reardon, along with Jack Harvey's section, had reached the cover of the riverbank. Mike quickly positioned his Brens where they had a maximum field of fire and waited.

The Canadians did not have to wait very long; the leading elements of their pursuers were now less than a hundred yards away but proceeding with more caution. He ordered his men to keep their heads down and to hold their fire until he gave the word. Closer, the Chinese advance guard came, now reinforced by their comrades who had caught up with them. Frame's finger instinctively began to squeeze the trigger of his Bren as the Chinese loomed larger and larger.

"Fire! Give the bastards hell!" Reardon yelled.

The deadly point-blank hail of machine-gun and rifle bullets cut down the first twenty Chinese who were running up the slope heading into the Canadians' position. The commie soldiers following behind quickly darted back to the safety of the covered ground to their rear not before another ten of their number had been dropped by the Deuce's machine guns.

Taking advantage of the lull, Mike ordered Jack's section and the Bren gunners to the far side of the riverbed while George's and Blackie's men covered them with a heavy rifle fire directed in the general direction of the Chinese. Looking through his binoculars, Mike could see the main body of the Chinese force arriving; he knew they would send some of their forces across the river both above and below his platoon position. For a moment, he considered ordering his men to make a run for it. Looking at their exhausted, pain-racked bodies, he realized they would never make it.

"No point in getting shot like fish in a barrel . . . Might as well make our stand right here," he deliberated quickly.

"Hey, boss! There's a bunch of Chinks moving up on us from the rear. Over on the left flank."

"Where, Jack? I can't see them. That's impossible!"

"Over there, sir. I can see them as plain as day!"

A fist of cold fear squeezed Reardon's guts as he raised his binoculars, his hands trembling to see the new threat. He'd almost convinced himself that the men approaching rapidly from the rear were indeed Chinese when his numbed senses started reacting normally. First, he recognized the formation they were moving in, good old arrowhead formation, then their broad peaked caps, khaki cotton shirts and drill trousers, and the unmistakable towering figure of Carr-Wilson striding ahead of the lead platoon.

"Hey, you bastards . . . They're Canadians! It's Able Company!" he whooped hysterically.

"Keerist, just like a movie! Here comes the bloody cavalry boys!" Blackie yelled, tears of relief streaming down his dirt-caked face.

The Chinese had no desire to continue their pursuit in the face of the substantially increased force of determined Royals and quickly withdrew, dragging their dead and wounded with them. When Dearing was sure that the enemy had cleared from the area, he allowed Mike and the Deuce to return to the other side of the riverbed to recover Dennison's body.

CHAPTER 24

On the Imjin River

The Canadian brigade had been carrying out its hit-and-run patrol tactics for over a month when, in mid-July, it was relieved by the Turkish brigade and, once again, placed under command of the U.S. Twenty-Fifth Division. The Canadians were now assigned a key defensive position at a ferry crossing on the Imjin River, the Royals establishing a two-company bridgehead fronted by a small but well concealed listening post across the swollen, rapidly rising river. The listening post, almost a mile in advance of the forward defended locations, had a dual purpose; its primary function was to give warning of the buildup of an expected large-scale enemy attack, its secondary purpose to relay information back to the defensive positions of any enemy patrol activity in their locality.

During the third week in July, strong enemy fighting patrols attempted to probe and penetrate the Royals' defenses but without success, thanks to the advance warning given by the Royals' cleverly hidden listening post. A protracted period of heavy rainfall had swollen the Imjin to alarming proportions. The ferry was washed away, line communications broken, and low-lying areas, including the headquarters area, were flooded. Had the Chinese launched an attack at this time, the situation of the isolated companies on the north side of the river could have been desperate. Fortunately, the Chinese were either unaware of the Canadians' problem or else were unable to do anything about it; in any case, the expected attack never came.

Early in August, the Canadian brigade was withdrawn from its river position and placed in divisional reserve. The Royals were relieved of their positions on both sides of the river by a battalion of Americans from the Twenty-Fifth Division. The Wolfhounds, as they were nicknamed, moved quickly and expertly into the Royals' positions, their last act of the changeover was to relieve the Canadians occupying the listening post situated on a high dominant feature well in front of the defensive locality.

Sergeant Ball, scout and sniper platoon sergeant, gaped in amazement at the cloud of dust kicked up by the platoon of Americans being sent out to relieve his five-man listening post.

"I'll be goddamned!" he exploded to his men. "That tears it, every Chink in North Korea will have this position taped now. Thank God we're getting the hell out of here!"

Slowly, the Wolfhound platoon made their way up the steep side of the hill led by one of Ball's men. When they arrived at the top where the sergeant awaited them, the American platoon commander, a startlingly young second lieutenant, shook his head in disbelief at the small group of Canadians facing him, asking in a rich Southern drawl, "Wheah are the rest of youah boys, Sergeant?"

"There aren't any more, sir. This is it."

"Why, man, you can't expect to hold this heah hill with five men! Why, the Chinks would gobble you up just like that," he replied, laughing and snapping his fingers to emphasize his last remark.

"We didn't intend to put up a fight, sir. Our job was to spot enemy movement and relay the information back to HQ. We've been bloody careful to keep the Chinos from knowing we were here."

"Well, ah'll be! Do you mean to tell me you just sat heah day and night peeking at the Chinese? Don't sound proper to me." He grinned, pleased with himself, as his men laughed.

"Regardless of how the job should be done, sir, one thing is certain, the Chinese sure as hell know the position is occupied now," Ball retorted, his neck flushed a deep red from the American officer's inferences.

"Now, man, don't you go worrying about little ole us. You bettah go with youah boys before they leave without you, we'll take good care of this little ole hill for you," the American continued patronizingly.

Ball shrugged his shoulders resignedly. "Well, I tried!" he muttered to himself as he looked at the forty odd young Americans grouped eagerly around their commander. The sergeant, his senses conditioned by years of experience, could not shake off his premonition of impending disaster.

"Well, sir, if there isn't anything else, we'll go now. Come on, guys, saddle up!" he shouted at his men then turned to face the smiling platoon officer, saluted smartly, and led his men down the hill.

Two days later, the American battalion, taking over the Royals' position, was hit hard by a determined Chinese attack, their two company positions

CHAPTER 25

Five Days in Tokyo

Late in August, the long-awaited five-day rest and recuperation leave in Japan was inaugurated in the Canadian contingent. Each leave party was to consist of one officer, one senior NCO, and fifteen men from the infantry battalions. The officers drew lots to determine their leave order, the senior noncoms were selected individually, and the men of the platoons were determined by quota. When the fortunate members of the leave party were selected, they were interviewed by their battalion medical officer, warning them of the dangers of sleeping with the multitude of available Japanese prostitutes operating in Tokyo. Finally, after completing a long complex process in preparation for the leave, they were transported to Kimpo airfield located on the outskirts of the South Korean capital to await their turn, along with Americans, Turks, Filipinos, Greeks, and other members of the UN forces, to be loaded on one of the Dakota aircraft shuttling back and forth between Korea and Japan, carrying men and equipment.

After a five-hour flight, the happy travelers landed in Tokyo at Takachawa airport, met by special buses which drove them to the Australian leave center at Ebisu situated on the outskirts of Tokyo. From there, the men were given the option of sleeping in camp or proceeding downtown. The officers were driven by special car to the luxurious Marunouchi Hotel, where rooms had been reserved for them. After spending five full days in the exciting Japanese capital, the leave parties were again assembled at Ebisu camp and, from there, retraced their journey back to their units in Korea.

Colonel Graves held the leave draw for his officers in his headquarters tent, asking an impartial visiting officer from brigade headquarters to select names from a hat. Shaking the hat thoroughly, he drew out the first slip of paper, reading it aloud, "Lt. Michael Reardon."

When Mike heard the news, feeling as if he'd had won the Irish sweepstakes, he let out a wild yell, hugging a very surprised Corporal Harvey.

Mike was dubious that the USAF pilot would be able to take his overloaded Dakota off the ground. It was bulging with troops, had a full load of gas, and to make matters worse, a heavy cargo was lashed to the deck directly over the wings. He couldn't help feeling uneasy as the aircraft slowly gained momentum down the runway, its engines roaring, the fuselage shaking in an alarming fashion, finally lurching into the air with a sickening shudder. Heaving a sigh of relief, Mike watched the rugged Korean countryside passing below until reaching the sharply peaked mountains and sawtooth ridges of East Korea. Soon, they were winging over the Sea of Japan, heading for the Japanese mainland. Reardon fell into a sound sleep, the excitement of the previous three days catching up to the exhausted Canadian slept through the remainder of the flight.

When Mike and his companion, a New Zealand artillery lieutenant he had met at Ebisu, arrived in front of the impressive façade of the modern Marunouchi Hotel, they were speechless, having spent the past four months living in the filth of Korea, feeling they were about to enter the Taj Mahal. The two young officers wasted no time, quickly checking in, turning their valises over to a bellhop who led them to their comfortable rooms. They quickly retraced their steps to the lobby, entering the main lounge, an eye-appealing richly furnished setting appropriately called the Gold Room.

Mike was sitting in a deep comfortable chair in the lounge, sipping his fourth rye on the rocks, a warm glow of sensuous pleasure filling every pore, still finding it hard to believe he was actually enjoying the luxury of civilized living. The painful memories of fear, death, dirt, and discomfort, the long, sometimes agonizing, days and nights of living in the ground like an animal were replaced by the delightful aura of his dreamworld.

"If this is a dream, I'm sure as hell going to enjoy it!" he swore aloud, startling the New Zealander sitting opposite him.

"I certainly hope we're not dreaming, Mike. I don't think I could stand the shock of waking up and finding myself back in some dirty Korean hole. Incidentally, old chap, about this business of sitting here drinking ourselves into a complete stupor—it's not that I object to your company, mind you—wouldn't you like to enjoy some female company at this stage?" Ron Burton, the New Zealand subaltern inquired hopefully.

"You took the words right out of my mouth, Ron," Mike replied. "But where do we start? Maybe our best approach is to ask some of the guys who have been around here for a few days, they'll know where to look. What do you say we try the two Yanks sitting over there in the corner? They didn't get to look that tired from sightseeing, I'll bet."

The two American officers readily made room for Mike and his friend; a broad grin creased both their faces when Mike broached the subject of finding suitable women.

"That's no problem, cousin!" the taller member of the American duo drawled. "Why, this city is loaded with fetching females. If you're not fussy, just walk along the Ginza and you won't have to wait very long. In this burg, you don't have to chase them, they chase you! Now, if you're fussy and don't mind the expense, there's two pretty good places in town, here's the cards, the Mioshi and the Ichakawa. They're good joints, eh, Mitch?" he added, nudging his companion.

"They sure as hell are! Boy, what luscious dolls! They sing and dance too," Mitch responded, licking his lips. "Come on, Rick," he pleaded. "Let's go back to the Mioshi tonight."

"Good god, man, no! Why, another night in that snake pit would kill me. Oh, my aching back!"

"Sounds like rather a good spot, Mike. What do you say we give it a go?" Ron asked eagerly. "It sounds like a prince of a place."

"You mean princess, don't you?" Mike laughed then turned, addressing the two Yanks, "How much does it cost to spend the night in either of these sin bins?"

"Oh, about ¥5000. Let me see, at ¥360 to the buck, it works out to about $14 American," Mitch replied. "But believe you me, it's well worth the dough. You guys want a drink?

"Hey, Charley! Hubba-hubba chop-chop, four whiskey soda—no, three whiskey soda and one whiskey water, okay? You fixee fast.

"Now as I was saying, these joints are really the cat's ass. Take the Mioshi, for instance. When you go in, an old doll all dressed up in a Jap kimono, wig and what have you, meets you at the door, leads you through a small patio into a big paper-walled room, but before you go in, off come the big boots! You put on a pair of paper sandals—that's right, paper—then you go in the main room sitting around a small table set in the middle of the floor. They don't have chairs, just mats to sit on.

"As you sit there, Mama-san, that's the old doll who runs the joint, asks you what you would like to eat and drink, so you orders some beer and maybe a sukiyaki dinner with some hot sake. Don't order liquor! They charge too damn much, it's better to bring your own. Then she claps her hands and out come a bunch of dolls to wait on you and keep you entertained. But don't get any funny ideas, there's no monkeying around with these dames! The drinks come first then Mama-san claps her hands and out come the dolls you have fun with, and I'm not fooling, am I, Rick?

"When I tell you these girls have real class, you just sit there and take your pick. The gals you pick are real happy about it, the ones you don't start to cry. These kids really take their business seriously! Well, man, the little bundle of joy you select sits beside you and makes you real comfortable, while the first bunch of dolls do the work and provide the music, these luscious things you picked are busy with you. Still no fooling around though! Maybe a little hug, squeeze, but that's all.

"When you get tired of eating, drinking, and dancing, you give old Mama-san the eye and she gets the ball rolling. Oh yes, I forgot to mention, right after you get your girls, Mama-san packs them off and you outs with the yen then the dolls come back. Well, as I was saying, the old doll gets the ball rolling, and your little Chichi-san will whisper in your ear and lead you off to have a bath, and I really mean a bath! You take off your clothes as she stands there, not batting an eyelash, then takes your duds as soon as you peel them off. You leave the dressing room and into the shower room, where you'll see a little wooden stool and two buckets. You squat down on the stool and your doll scrubs you from head to toe, both of you naked as the day you were born! She rinses you off, using the little buckets. Then into the bath tub you go. The bathtubs here are different from ours, they're deep, instead of long—you can't sit down in them, you have to stand, and is the water ever hot! Hottest thing I ever felt, eh, Rick?

"While you stand in the tub, boiling like a lobster, the gal gives herself the same scrubbing she gave you, and then—bang!—she jumps in the tub beside you! Don't get that idea, mister! Still no nonsense. When you've had enough of that, you get out and your girl puts a bathrobe on you and gives you a fresh pair of sandals, no towel, just the bathrobe and sandals. Mama-san is usually waiting outside and takes you and your doll to your room. When you get there, she slides open your door. Inside is a mattress right in the center of the floor, covered with fresh bedding, a hibachi in the corner and a few other odds and ends. When Mama-san closes the door, your girl is all yours. She'll lock up your valuables, if you like, and you don't have to worry, those kids are honest.

"Next morning, about nine o'clock, in comes Mama-san with a girl with breakfast, another dame comes in with your uniform all nicely pressed and your boots all shone. About ten, your taxi comes and your doll says goodbye, begging you to come back and really means it, eh, Rick?

"You know something, Rick, I just talked myself into it. Let's go to the goddamn Mioshi," Mitch finished, asking, "You coming, fellas?"

"You're bloody right we are," Mike answered excited. "A guy would be crazy to pass up a deal like that!"

During the daylight hours, Reardon and Burton spent their time sightseeing in the fabulous city, visiting the outer fringes of the Imperial Palace, shopped at the American post exchange and at the many bazaars and shops found on the Ginza. The offbeat strains of the combined Oriental and Western music bombarded their ears from loudspeakers situated at all the principal intersections of Tokyo's main street, the Ginza. They visited Buddhist shrines and Mikimoto's world-famous cultured pearl emporium located in the arcade of the Lloyd Wright architectural masterpiece, the Imperial Hotel. At night, they returned to the sensual pleasures so effectively provided by the Mioshi. Korea rapidly became a dim memory in the minds of the two young sybarites.

CHAPTER 26

The Trap

The Eighth Army high command decided to straighten out the bulging, irregular UN defensive line to achieve greater depth and greater ease in coordinated defense over the broad Korean front. The operational plan was to be carried out in two distinct phases: the first, called Operation Scorpion, was designed to firmly establish the First U.S. Corps across the Imjin River; the second, called Operation Python, was intended to seize and hold a number of strategic hills and ridges further north. Unknown to the planners of the massive operation was the coincidence the line running through the objectives of Python, code named the Jamestown line, constituted the main winter defensive line of the Chinese armies in that area.

On September 8, 1951, the Canadian brigade was transported across the Imjin River over a pontoon bridge built for the operation by U.S. Army engineers. The Canadians were preceded by a screen of Commonwealth division forces, enabling them to advance rapidly and without opposition. The Royals soon reached their initial objective; a series of small hills and ridges occupied by Australians was lying immediately north of a small brackish, partially dried-out reservoir. The Aussies reported limited enemy activity in their immediate area but excessive activity in the area of two hills to their front where their patrols had been harassed by accurate, heavy mortar fire. After wishing the Royals the best of luck, the Australians left. Operation Scorpion was over.

Preparatory to launching the next phase, Python, divisional HQ issued orders for a vigorous patrol program for all brigades to test the enemy's defenses in the area of the proposed Jamestown line. The brigade commander changed the position of the Royals twice before satisfied with the battalion's defensive positions. These irritating moves had no tactical significance to the grumbling men in the ranks. To them, it was just more unnecessary digging and wiring. Making matters worse, it started to rain.

Paul, Monty, and Mike were sitting, talking in Chuck Dearing's command post, awaiting his return from a battalion orders group. Outside, a steady cold rain was beating incessantly on the sandbagged roof of A Company headquarters, the afternoon sky dark with scurrying rain clouds, the air was damp and chill to the skin. Mike was retelling his leave experiences in Japan to his still-interested audience.

"You'd never believe that a girl could be so beautiful. No kidding, fellas, I've never seen a girl with a more beautiful body or face than Michiko, we spent five glorious nights together. Why, I even got to like taking hot baths! I wish to hell I could take one now. Boy, I can still feel her long dark hair in my fingers. What a woman!"

"Oh, come off it, Mike," Monty chaffed. "Surely she wasn't that good. Besides, she's probably making up to some other chap this very minute the same way she made up to you."

"So? Tell me, Monty, does a good horse's value decrease because someone else has ridden it?"

"Good lord, man! You can't compare a horse to a woman! Well, in truth, old cock, I'm just envious. I can scarcely wait for my turn. How about you, Paul? Can't you just see the lights, the luxury of a modern city again? Just to smell it, the streets, the restaurants, having a drink in the comfort of a first-rate bar, enjoying the company of a beautiful woman!"

"To be perfectly honest with you, I'm not particularly interested in trying to live a lifetime of sex in five days then spending the rest of my time desperately trying to keep the memory alive. Memories can be a curse as well as a blessing," Anderson answered, frowning.

"Here comes the boss," Mike informed his friends, his uncanny hearing identifying Dearing's footsteps.

"Lord, it's cool out today. Goes right through your bloody clothes. I hate to think what the damn winter will be like," Dearing commented, entering the semidarkness of his bunker.

Shaking the rain from his poncho, he began fumbling in the breast pockets of his battle dress jacket, saying, "I've got a letter here some bloody place, for you, Paul. Ah, here it is."

Dearing pulled out a bulky envelope, handing it to the eagerly expectant Anderson. His hopes were fulfilled; it was postmarked Saint Paul, Minnesota. Dearing waited patiently by as Paul frantically ripped open the envelope; it was a letter from Anne. Chuck, sensing this particular letter was very important, drew Monty and Mike aside, allowing Anderson to read his letter in privacy.

"My Darling," it began. *"Will you ever be able to forgive me for what I've done to you? Please believe me, Paul, dearest, I thought it would be the best thing for both of us if we never saw or heard from each other again. My father was so certain that nothing could ever come of our love, that everything was far too complicated. Oh, darling! It was hell when they found out. They made me feel so cheap. They wouldn't let me alone unless I agreed and promised to forget you and never write to you. I'm so ashamed to admit this, but after a while, I began to believe them. I felt so lost, alone, confused. I began to hate myself, and I suppose I even grew to hate you.*

"My aunt and uncle have been wonderful—you see, they planned to adopt our baby. Oh, darling, when my sister forwarded Monty's letter to me, telling her of how miserable and upset you've been, I cried for shame. I knew they had been wrong and that my heart had been right. I showed Monty's letter to my aunt and uncle and then told them all about us. They were wonderful, dear. Uncle Jack immediately wrote to Dad and told him that what he and Mother were doing to us was a sin. They've arranged for me to stay here with them for the birth of our baby and wait for your return. They've been simply wonderful and want very much to meet my Canadian! Our baby is due in late November, dear. I am so excited . . ."

Paul read and reread Anne's letter with tears of happiness in his eyes. He was finally interrupted by his grinning companions.

"Good news, kid?" Dearing asked quietly.

"It certainly is . . . Thanks to you, Monty," Paul replied gratefully, turning to face his friends. "In fact, I guess this is the happiest moment of my life!"

"I hate to put a damper on this happy scene, lads, but we have a job to do," Chuck reminded them.

"I guessed as much, sir," Mike replied with an air of false resignation. "I know. Our company is being sent home to put on demonstrations for the active force on how the war is being fought in Korea."

"Good lord! What have you been drinking, old cock? Or have you pinched some dead Chinaman's opium?"

"Okay, let's cut the comedy for a few minutes and get down to business," Chuck commanded. "There's a big push on within the division to get a prisoner at all costs. Recent intelligence reports indicate the area ahead of us might be the location of a main Chink line of defense. The intelligence wheels are really hot to get a few prisoners to confirm this. The CO has decided to send a platoon strength patrol out every night from the companies in rotation. We get the first one. Now all we have to decide is who gets the honor from our outfit." He paused looking at the expectant faces of his platoon commanders.

"I'll take the first crack at the job, if you like," Reardon volunteered halfheartedly.

"No, you won't, old cock. I suggest we toss for it," Carr-Wilson said.

"That sounds fair to me, except that we haven't anything to toss. I have an idea—I'll put three slips of paper in my hat and mark one." Dearing added.

"I say, Mike, you should be happy. You're fabulously lucky at draws," Monty chided his friend.

Throughout the bantering among his companions, Paul remained silent, feeling a throbbing knot of fear clutching at his insides. "It won't be me, surely to God, it won't be me. Not now!" he breathed prayerfully to himself.

The three subalterns stood around their company commander, each drawing a folded slip of paper from Dearing's hat. Monty drew first.

"Blank," he called out, trying to hide his relief.

"Mine's blank too," Mike announced, flashing his slip around for the others to see.

"Not much point in my looking at mine," Paul said ruefully.

"We'd better get down to business then," Dearing suggested practically. "We haven't very much time left. Paul, you'd better call up your platoon, warning them to get ready. Then I'll give you the gen."

When Paul returned, the major continued, "Intelligence has reason to believe that the Chinos are concentrated in the area of hill 187. That's the dominant feature you've all seen about a mile to our front. We know the Chinese have an outpost set up on hill 152. Here it is on the map. As you can see, it's about two thirds the distance from here to 187. The Chinks haven't been manning their outposts during the day, only at night. The Aussies sent out a night reconnaissance party to check the strength of the outpost, estimating that it's occupied by roughly a section of Chinese. I think your best chance to snatch a prisoner is there. If the damn rain continues, it'll be dark by seven o'clock. If we hit them early, we should catch them by surprise, so I'm sending you out at last light, which means you should be back sometime before midnight . . ."

As Dearing continued to give Anderson his orders for the patrol, he was too occupied to notice the color draining out of Paul's face. Mike and Monty, aware of their friend's condition, looked at each other apprehensively. Chuck, suddenly aware of the stares of the two men, looked up from his map board, gazing directly into Anderson's face, shocked by the unmistakable evidence of fear he saw there.

"Anything wrong, Paul?"

"Ah no. Of course not, sir. I guess I'm still a little shaken up," he replied, trying to smile.

"Pardon me for interrupting, sir," Reardon pleaded, "let's forget the draw and let me take this one out."

"No!" Paul snapped at Mike. "I drew the job, so my platoon is going to do it. Besides, what difference does it make? If I don't take this one, I'll just have to take the next one, or the one after, so I might as well get it over with now. Sorry for the interruption, sir."

Dearing continued giving his orders, covering the details regarding routes out, routes in, report lines, success signals, and the many other details necessary in the planning of a patrol operation. As he spoke, Paul was only half listening, his mind filled by a confused muddle of unrelated thoughts. Two emotions predominated—his love of Anne and cold fear.

Oh, Anne, Anne! I just have to come home to you. I can't let anything happen to us now. Oh god, if only I could leave this forsaken place! Haven't I suffered enough? Can't let them see I'm frightened . . . got to keep from shaking. I'm turning into a coward. That's it—I'm turning yellow, yellow, yellow . . .

Anderson's map case fell from his trembling hands and struck the hard packed dirt floor of the command post with a loud clatter, bending over quickly to pick it up in a futile attempt to hide his nervousness from the others.

Dearing reached under his camp bed, searching for a bottle of rum. He handed it to Anderson, saying, "Have a belt of this. It'll steady your nerves."

Does he know? Is it that obvious? Paul wondered frantically as he gratefully accepted the bottle and took a deep draught of the burning liquid.

The major looked down at Anderson's hunched figure speculatively. "Any questions, Paul?"

"No, sir. I've got the picture."

"How about you, Mike? Monty?"

"None, sir," they both replied.

"Fine. Check in with me before you take your boys out, Paul, in case I should have some last-minute information for you. Well, gentlemen, if you have no questions, that's all I have."

After wishing Anderson success on his patrol, Mike and Monty remained behind briefly, discussing the startling change that had taken place in their friend.

"I've never seen the likes of it before, Monty. Honest to God! One minute, he stands there saying he couldn't care less. Then he gets a bloody letter and becomes as nervous as a flea in a fit. No kidding, he looked scared."

"I think there's more to Paul's situation than meets the eye, Mike. We both know him too well not to know that he's not afraid for himself. He's had enough, and Lord knows he's done more than his share. The sooner they pull him out the better."

"Do you think we should speak to the major?"

"I hardly think so, Mike. I'm sure Dearing is as much aware of the situation as we are. Besides, Paul wouldn't appreciate our interfering.

As Monty spoke, Dearing was sitting in his command post thinking about Anderson. He finally made up his mind: he was going to speak to Graves as soon as possible and recommend Paul be sent to Japan as an instructor there at the Canadian battle school.

When he had taken leave of his friends, Anderson made his way along the narrow muddy track that led to his platoon area. Despite the poncho he wore, the streaming late afternoon rain soon soaked through his clothes, making him shiver. His feeling of well-being, created by the large shot of rum, soon disappeared as he stumbled along the slimy path toward his platoon headquarters, once again filled with the grim reality of his situation.

"I've got to take a hold of myself. I mustn't let the men see me upset. If they discover I'm afraid of this patrol, there'll be hell to pay."

Anderson was too busy to worry about himself the remainder of the dismal afternoon. Having to brief his platoon on the object and details of their patrol that night, he took his section commanders on a reconnaissance to show them the route they would follow to the objective, the objective itself, hill 152, the route they would take back, his plan of action relatively simple, easily understood by his corporals. He finished his preparations, carefully inspecting the person and weapons of every man in his platoon, then collected their personal effects, such as letters, pay books, and other articles that could prove useful to the enemy should any of them be captured. He removed his treasured letter from Anne from the pocket of his battle dress jacket, looked wistfully at it, and shrugged his shoulders, placing it in the canvas bag along with the other effects belonging to his men.

Darkness was spreading over the rain-swept Korean hills as Anderson, his senior corporal, Gord Frost, and his signaler, Len Peters, sat in the headquarters bunker. Paul was twisting the cap off a bottle of rum.

"Now that the boys have received their issue of the old black magic, we'd better have a nip ourselves," Anderson grunted to his silent companions eagerly watching the pleasant ritual. "Ah . . . there we are. Pass over your cups, chaps."

The gurgling of the dark liquid was a most satisfying sound to the three men. As they drank liberally of the stomach-warming liquid, Frost commented, "No wonder the Yanks are willing to pay up to twenty bucks a bottle for this stuff. It's the real answer to a tired infantryman's prayer."

"Yeah, almost better than women!" Peters added, smacking his lips in appreciation.

"The patrol should be a snap. We'll be in and out of their blasted position before they know what hit them," Frost offered optimistically.

"There's no guarantee that we'll even find any Chinks in the vicinity. We know that they don't occupy 152 by day, so it's quite possible they've given up occupying it by night," Anderson added hopefully.

The effect of the rum was to spread a feeling of relaxed contentment over the three men. The more they drank, the more they became assured of their patrol's success.

"It had better be a snap! I go on leave next week, and I sure as hell would hate to disappoint all those beautiful Jap dolls just waiting to get laid by getting knocked off by some SOB of a Chino," Frost offered jokingly.

"That's enough of that kind of talk, Frost," Anderson snapped. "There won't be anyone knocked off if we do our jobs properly."

"I'm sorry, sir, I didn't mean—"

"All right, all right, just remember what I said," Paul continued in an irritated tone.

Keerist! Is he every jumpy. Oh well, I guess he's just as pissed off with this goddamn war as the rest of us, Frost thought, watching Anderson drain the last of the bottle.

Paul checked out with Dearing then proceeded to lead his platoon through Reardon's platoon area, Mike waiting for him to wish him luck once again, standing watching the straggling line of figures make their way down the slippery hillside until disappearing into the moonless void of the rainy night.

As the Canadians approached the long narrow ridge leading to the top of their objective, the staccato patter of the driving rain ceased to be an enemy, becoming a friend to the cautiously advancing patrol by muffling the sounds they made. When they arrived at the base of their objective, Anderson halted his patrol, sending two scouts up the broad slope of the low feature to detect any signs of enemy movement. He signaled the two sections lying in wait behind him to stay put, as prearranged, with Frost's section, and began to follow the path traced by his scouts.

They had no sooner passed over the summit of the shell-pocked, napalm-blasted hill when they were met by a fusillade of small arms fire and popping bowling-pin grenades. The Chinese, spotting the movement of the Royals' patrol, moved out of their forward slope positions, cleverly concealing themselves on the reverse slope some twenty yards from the summit, craftily allowing the scouts to move over the skyline unmolested, anticipating the main body of the patrol would soon follow. They were right: Anderson fell into their trap.

As soon as the first line of Chinese opened up with automatic fire, their comrades farther down the hill began to rain a hail of light mortar bombs on to Anderson's other two sections still waiting at the base of the feature, their accurate mortaring having a deadly effect. The main body of the patrol was forced to withdraw back along the ridge, dragging their dead and wounded with them, leaving their platoon officer and Frost's section trapped on the summit.

The whole engagement lasted less than ten minutes, but the costs to the Canadian patrol was frightful, every member of Frost's section killed or wounded by the first Chinese fusillade. Many of the patrol members waiting at the base of the objective were killed or wounded by the accurate mortar fire; Peters was killed instantly as he stood beside Anderson. As Paul turned, he was shot through the right thigh then knocked unconscious by a flying rock thrown up by an exploding Chinese grenade.

As Anderson regained consciousness, slowly becoming aware of a dull throbbing in his right leg, he rubbed his eyes hard in a frantic attempt to clear away the black void surrounding him. *Good god, I'm blind!* he thought in panic.

He began to carefully feel the ground around him and discovered he was lying on a rough-surfaced rice mat, his sharpening senses detecting the garlic-tainted, musty smell characteristic of the interiors of Korean huts.

"Someone has carried me here . . . I wonder . . . Oh my god!" he groaned aloud. "My leg, my leg," he moaned as the dull throbbing changed to a pulsating agony now that he was fully conscious.

Immediately after his involuntary groan, a low-powered flashlight was snapped on and beamed into his face, blinding him completely. The figure holding the flashlight muttered some unintelligible sounds to another invisible person who answered briefly then disappeared into the inky blackness of the night.

A few moments later, the door of the hut was roughly thrust open, followed by the sound of scuffling feet, the door secured as one of the newcomers struck a match, lighting the wick of a battered oil lamp. It took Anderson some time to become accustomed to the light. When he had done so, he recognized the figures of three Chinese soldiers standing only a few feet from his prostrate form, one of the Chinese covering him with a Russian burp gun. Anderson, trying to shift his weight, raising himself on one elbow, fell back in agony as a searing shaft of pain lanced up his right leg. It was then he noticed the blood-saturated ragged tear in his pant leg caused by the Chinese machine-gun bullet now lodged in his thigh. Cold beads of sweat covered his forehead, his heart pounded uncontrollably, still managing a wry smile as he asked, pointing at his right leg, "Can any of you do something for my leg?"

To Anderson's astonishment, the Chinese soldier standing in the center of the group answered in lilting but perfect English, "Your leg will be attended to in due course, Canadian. You are an officer?"

In spite of his befuddled mind and extreme pain, Paul became mentally alert at this question and did not answer.

"Come, come, Canadian! You are allowed by your country to give your name, rank, and number."

"Anderson, Paul, Lieutenant . . . B2450. For god's sake, man, do something for this leg, the pain is unbearable! A shot of morphine . . . I . . ."

"We have no morphine, Andahson," his interrogator cut in.

"Damn it, man, you must have! I had three shots of first-aid morphine on me earlier tonight."

"Indeed? You must have lost them. Now tell me, what was the object of your patrol?"

"None of your damn business. My name is Anderson, my rank is—"

"Yes, yes, I understood you the first time," the Chinese snapped then changed his approach, saying in a more friendly tone, "My name is Liu Han, and my function is to, shall we say, ask questions. If you will answer my questions, I'm quite sure some morphine can be found, we may even have a doctor look at your wound. When are your forces planning to attack? Ah, you still prefer to remain stubborn. Then answer me this, why are the Canadians fighting for the Americans?"

"Why are the Chinese fighting for the Russians?" Anderson countered.

"We do not fight for the Russians. We fight for the future of international communism and the future of China!"

"I don't give a damn what or who you fight for . . . Please, do something for my leg!" Paul pleaded through clenched jaws.

Liu Han spoke a few curt words in Chinese to the soldier holding the flickering lamp. The man he addressed immediately knelt beside the pain-racked Canadian and began, roughly but efficiently, cut away the blood-soaked cloth from around the bleeding wound. He poked his fingers around the festering flesh manipulating Anderson's right thigh, the resulting pain so acute he gave an agonized shuddering scream. The crouching soldier looked up at Han, speaking in Chinese, who in turn spoke to Paul.

"Andahson, your femur is broken. My comrade thinks you will lose your leg. As we have no way of caring for you, we may have to shoot you. I will check with my superiors," he said sympathetically.

Mentally and physically exhausted, Paul fell into a troubled sleep.

It was still dark when Anderson regained his senses, knew by the cool, sweet smell in the air that morning was not far off. Strangely enough, his leg no longer ached, a numbing paralysis having spread over the shattered member. He could make out the form of his guard squatting on the floor by the doorway, the alert manner in which his captor sat up when Paul shifted his weight sufficient proof to the Royals officer he was well guarded. The jumbled nightmarish events of the previous night began penetrating the clouded recesses of Paul's pain-numbed mind, and he thought, rationalizing uncertainly, *He must have been bluffing. Surely they won't shoot me, an officer is too valuable to them.*

Grey streaks of dawn light had cut through the night's blackness, infiltrating through the cracks in the window and tracing a shapeless pattern on the floor. Anderson's thoughts were interrupted suddenly as Liu Han and two companions entered the hut.

"I see you're awake, Canadian. I bring you some food."

Anderson accepted the small bowl of dirty half-cooked rice from Han, began to eat hungrily.

Maybe he was bluffing after all. He wouldn't bother to feed me if he was going to have me killed, he thought hopefully.

"Eat heartily, Canadian, it is your last meal on this earth! We must soon leave this place, you will not be coming with us, my superiors do not choose to leave you behind alive," Han said quietly.

A sudden thought struck Paul. "What happened to the other men who were with me?"

"If you mean the men at the bottom of the hill, they went back. If you mean the men with you, they are all dead. We saw no point in keeping the wounded alive after we identified you as their leader. Unfortunately for you, having proven to be of little use to us and in terrible condition, will soon be joining them." he replied almost sympathetically.

"You rotten filthy murderer! You didn't have to kill those men!"

"Your concern is touching, Canadian, but do not worry yourself unduly, you shall soon be with them," Han snapped.

Giving some instructions to his two companions who immediately moved to where Paul lay and began lifting his limp body.

Anderson's mind became a morass of confused unrelated thoughts as the two squat Chinese dragged him to his feet and placed his arms over their shoulders. He couldn't concentrate on the faces of anyone he had ever known, not even Anne Martin's. He tried to think of his mother. He tried futilely to pray. "Dear God, forgive them, they know not what they do. No . . . That's not it . . . Just words, words, don't mean anything. Oh Christ, I don't believe! I don't believe!"

Anderson was half dragged, half walked to the center of the rain-lashed courtyard outside the hut, a group of Chinese soldiers standing in a rough semicircle around him, their faces impassive, their voices stilled. One of his escorts forced his protesting body to kneel as his brain churned. "This is fantastic! These things just don't happen . . . This . . ."

His escort began to tie his hands tightly behind his back with a piece of thin metal wire; the wire cut deeply into his flesh, saturating his hands with blood. The lines of an almost forgotten poem suddenly came into his mind, erasing everything else—the dread, the confusion, the present—as the short black muzzle of a burp gun pressed against the back of Anderson's head. Paul instinctively flinched from the pressure of the unyielding steel.

Suddenly, he straightened his back, looking directly at the wall in front of him; the rain mixed with the tears streaming down his face as he mouthed the words

> Help me, O God, when death is near,
> To mock the haggard face of fear,
> That when I fall—I fall I must—
> My soul may triumph in the dust . . .

The rain-drenched members of a British reconnaissance patrol from the Royal Ulsters cautiously made their way down the slippery reverse slope of hill 152. The combination of the slate grey sky of early morning and the pulsating rainfall had completely obscured their view of the Korean village of Sogon-ri lying in the valley below. The men were moving in a manner characteristic of patrols. Two scouts were barely visible in the gathering mist, slipping and sliding down the mire-covered hill well ahead of their comrades. The remaining members of the patrol were taking cover, awaiting the all-clear signal from their scouts before following them. The youthful patrol commander, fearing that some of the Chinese nighttime defenders of the hill might still be lurking in the area, frequently ordered his bitterly cursing men to be quiet.

Finally, the mud-covered Ulstermen reached the network of overflowing paddy fields covering the valley floor. The officer commanding the patrol expertly positioned his men along the edge of the main dike bordering the apparently deserted village. After whispering a few detailed instructions to his second in command, the young officer joined the scouts, proceeding with them on a reconnaissance of the area. Tensely alert for a strange movement or sound that might reveal the presence of an enemy trap, the stealthily moving trio approached the edge of the desolate village and proceeded to move through it. Carefully inspecting each of the thatched mud huts that lined their route, they cautiously approached the most imposing structure in the village, the former home of the village leader. As they entered its circular walled courtyard, they froze to a sudden halt; lying in the center of the compound was the half-kneeling body of a man. The suspicious trio gingerly approached the still form. The corpse's face, half submerged in a pool of water, lay turned away from them, revealing a large gaping hole in the back of the blond-haired skull. It was obvious to the three silent men that, from his dress and insignia, the dead man was a Canadian officer. It was also quite apparent that the unfortunate Canadian had been ruthlessly executed by the Chinese, his hands wired behind his back, the swollen puffy flesh of his wrists almost completely obscuring the confining wire coils.

After turning the body over, one factor about the dead man perplexed the Ulsters' lieutenant, the look of intense concentration still evident on the corpse's once handsome face.

What on earth could this poor bastard have been thinking about to die with a look like that? he wondered.

CHAPTER 27

Operation Python

Major Dearing gave Monty Carr-Wilson the disheartening task of gathering together Paul Anderson's personal effects. Sorting out his friend's belongings, he came across Anne's letter, and although not in the habit of reading other people's mail, Carr-Wilson felt obliged to read the crumpled letter held in his hand. Reading it, he was shaken by a depth of emotion unusual for him. Finishing, he thought, *I'll have to write to her and let her know. God! What a terrible thing to have to tell her at a time like this. She was so full of hope and happiness . . . Ah, well,* c'est la vie.

Anderson's death had greatly shocked his friends, and it seemed so unfair that Paul should die at a time when he had so much to live for. However, there was little time for grieving—the big one was coming up, Operation Python.

The assault to secure the Jamestown line was to involve the entire First Corps, with the First ROK Division attacking on the left, the First Commonwealth Division hitting the center, the Fifth U.S. Cavalry Division striking from the right. The Canadian brigade was made responsible for the right flank of their division. To the left lay the broad Samichon Valley and the ROK Division, to their right, the British twenty-eighth brigade.

The main objective of the Royals was hill 187 and its associated ridges, spreading out like tentacles from the octopus-head-shaped summit. Dearing's company was given the task of attacking the hill from the left, securing the summit and a ridge lying along a line directly west of the main objective. D Company was to attack 187 from the right, joining Dearing's forces on the summit. B Company was designated to pass around the hill and to secure a finger-shaped ridge that ran due north from the dominating feature. C

Company was given the relatively easy task of securing hill 152, serving as a firm base and start line for D and B Companies. A Company was detailed to pass through the Royal Ulsters, who had been given the special task of seizing a series of ridges lying approximately one thousand yards from the top of 187, the Ulsters' position serving as the start line for Dearing's attack.

The commander of A Company gave Reardon the responsibility for assaulting the summit, Carr-Wilson the job of capturing the ridge called the Brown Bastard by the men of the company because of its peculiar coloration, holding Anderson's platoon, now under command of his sergeant, in reserve.

The men of A Company didn't have to be told by their commander the attack on the Chinese winter line was going to be the toughest thing they had yet tackled; they seemed to sense, indeed accepting the fact faced a strong possibility of being either killed or wounded in the assault. Fighting in Korea had long ceased to be a novelty for them, the aggressive challenge of "Let me at those Chinamen" substituted by "Only five more months until we're rotated home."

Reardon's men were unusually quiet and thoughtful, mechanically going through the motions of cleaning their weapons in preparation for the assault the following morning. His section commanders were checking their men, ensuring they had the full complement of equipment necessary, not only to capture their objective but also holding it in the face of anticipated Chinese counterattacks. This check included ammunition, grenades, concentrated rations, filled water bottles, picks or shovels, first-aid dressings, and other items that make up a fighting soldier's kit. Early that same morning, after moving across the narrow valley separating their positions from the firm base held by the Ulsters, the long straggly line of the Royals A Company was strangely quiet. There was little conversation among the men, most of them were preoccupied with their own thoughts; the only sounds made were caused by the rattling of their equipment and the occasional order barked imperatively by one of the NCOs. There was no laughter, no brave singing, just a line of quiet men squinting against the glare of the sun.

Sitting together in the night, the mood of the men was surprisingly calm, their conversation subdued, meaningless, living in a suspended state, afraid of making plans, afraid of what the morning might bring.

Mike left his platoon area, moving up a ridge defended by the Northern Irish battalion. Checking in with their outpost, he sat on top of the ridge observing the summit of 187 barely one thousand yards away. Staring at the hilltop objective, his objective, he wondered what the Chinese defenders holding the position were thinking at this moment.

They must know we're coming, he mused. *They can't possibly have missed seeing our preparations. I wonder if they're making peace with their gods as some of our men are doing. It looks so damn quiet up there, hard to believe that it's crawling with Chinks. It looks so beautiful in the moonlight. I wish to hell this was tomorrow night and that the bloody thing was over!*

Carr-Wilson found Mike sitting with his knees clasped in his arms, staring ahead in the night. "Gad, Mike, I've never seen you look se pensive. Quite a peaceful-looking panorama, don't you think?" he said as he sat beside his friend then, not waiting for an answer, continued, "I wish this was tomorrow night and that the nasty business facing us was over."

"Funny that you should say that, Monty, because I was just thinking the same thing. What did you think of the major's happy little talk to the boys, telling them he expects we'll have about half our company knocked out as casualties?"

"I thought it was a stupid thing for him to say. I can't understand whatever prompted him to do it. He certainly didn't raise the morale of my chaps one damn bit. In fact, most of them are bloody depressed."

"My guys feel the same way. In fact, my corporals were pissed off about the whole deal. They seem to think we were given the dirty end of the stick."

"To be perfectly honest with you, old cock, I don't envy you your task of linking up with Dog Company at the top of 187, especially if they happen to get held up somewhere along the way. They have a lot further to go than we do, you know," Monty agreed.

"I certainly do know. Imagine having to advance at the ridiculously slow rate of a hundred yards in five minutes! Why, that's barely crawling along, just so that another blasted company will be able to get there the same time we do."

"Tactically sound, Mike, old chap."

"Sure but as dangerous as hell too! Nothing like giving the Chinks a good shot at you. Listen to those bloody guns, will you? We must be pounding Little Gibraltar. I didn't think it was supposed to start until midnight."

"I think the twenty-eighth brigade attacks at midnight, Mike. The barrage starts an hour earlier."

"Well, I sure as hell wish them luck because we won't get very far if they don't capture their objective. Listen! By god, I'll swear I can hear bagpipes! Listen closely."

"I haven't your hearing, Mike. I can't hear—wait, yes, I can hear it now. The King's own Scottish borderers must be going into their attack."

"If nothing else scares the living hell out of the Chinos, the bagpipes certainly will." Mike laughed. "How do you feel about tomorrow, Monty?"

"I really don't know, Mike. To be perfectly honest with you, I haven't given it much thought. Should be all right though. Why, we're being given bags of artillery support. In fact, the whole of the New Zealand artillery regiment is going to shoot our company on to the objective. Mind you, a lot depends on how quickly Dog Company advances. If they are held up for any length of time, we're for it."

"I know—that's what's bugging me! I hope to hell I don't end up at the top of that goddamn hill all by myself."

"Well, I suppose, old chap, 'the die is cast,' as the old Roman said, and all we can do is to hope for the best. At least we have one consolation," he went on.

"Oh? And what would that be?"

"Well, Mike, old friend, it couldn't possibly be any worse than our dear major has predicted."

"I hope you're right, I hope you're right."

"What's the matter, keed, feel a little jumpy?"

"Yeah, I suppose so. Take Paul for instance, no one would have ever thought he'd get it the way he did. All he had to do was take out a perfectly routine patrol, and look what happened—he gets the old smokie express. Tomorrow we know what to expect, we know they're sitting there waiting for us. If you start working out the odds, it doesn't look too good."

"Ah but that's just it, Mike! You can't work out the odds in war as you would in a game of chance—there are far too many variables to be considered. At any rate, I wouldn't let it get me down if I were you. Remember the old proverb, 'Only the good die young,' and as far as I'm concerned, that sure as hell lets us out!"

They continued talking together for a short time longer then parted company and returned to their platoons.

Cpl. Jack Harvey had gathered his men around him and was giving them a last-minute briefing on their part in the impending attack. He finished by saying, "Now even if you forget everything else I just told you, I want you to remember this: no matter what happens tomorrow during the attack, keep going when the Chinks open up. Even if you see some guy get hit, forget him. Even if he's your buddy, keep going! You'll have a hell of a lot better chance to live if you do. The stretcher bearers and medical types will look after him. Okay, hit the pit and get some sleep. We got a big day tomorrow."

In spite of their fears and uncertainty, most of the men of the Deuce slept. Morning came; the time had come.

Reardon formed up his platoon in a tight arrowhead formation, with Harvey's and Whitefoot's sections forming the barbs, and platoon headquarters, followed by Blackie's section, forming the shaft. Mike decided to move directly behind the point with his signaler rather than stay with his headquarters group. Following behind the Deuce was Carr-Wilson and his platoon, Chuck Dearing and his headquarters, and in the rear, the third platoon, now commanded by Sergeant Bush. The company had to line up in this manner to conform to the narrowness of the steep ridge serving as the axis for A Company's advance. The men of the company were becoming increasingly tense and nervous as they waited for the signal to advance. In the distance, the sounds of heavy small arms fire could be heard coming from the direction of hill 355 as the twenty-eighth brigade fought desperately for the summit of Little Gibraltar. The troop of tanks assigned to Dearing to help support his company on to its objectives rumbled noisily into position. At intermittent intervals, the skirl of bagpipes could be heard over the sounds of the vicious firefight still occurring on the upper slopes of 355. Finally, at ten o'clock, two hours behind schedule, the Brits captured their objective, and the Royals were ordered to attack. By now, they had lost the element of surprise; the Chinese were waiting, and the Canadians knew it.

At the precise moment, Dearing relayed the order to advance to his platoon commanders; the artillery began to fire a concentrated barrage of shells on the summit of 187. The slowly advancing men could see the screaming blue blurs made by the shells as they thudded into the top of 187, the heavier whine of falling mortar bombs added to the din. Mike checked his watch frequently as he advanced, too preoccupied to notice the shells and bombs exploding violently on the objective ahead. Three shells, sounding like an express train speeding through a railway tunnel, fell directly in front of the Deuce and exploded within twenty yards of Harvey's section. Fortunately, there were no casualties as the shrapnel sprayed forward. Reardon began to shout above the din of the detonating shells.

"Jack! Hey, Jack! The left flank of your section has moved too far down the ridge. George . . . Whitefoot! You're moving ahead too fast . . . Jack, Hey! You look like Superman with that air-recognition panel on your back."

"Yeah? I feel like a goddamn target at a sideshow too," he snapped back.

Only three hundred yards to go and still no fire from the Chinese on top of the hill. Two hundred yards. The burning cordite and the heavy dust pall kicked up by the explosions covered the Canadians. Closer and closer they came to the exploding inferno ahead, but still no retaliatory fire from the enemy on the summit.

Maybe they've taken off, Mike thought hopefully. *Most likely, they're waiting until we get right on top of them . . . Hope the goddamn artillery doesn't cut off too soon. Wonder how Dog Company is doing? Can't see a damn thing over on their side—too much crap in the air. Keerist! I could have sworn that I could have reached up and touched that last bloody shell . . . Come on, you yellow little bastards, start shooting!*

Less than two hundred yards to go but still nothing from the waiting enemy. Reardon felt a gnawing sensation in the pit of his stomach; his pistol felt slippery in his sweaty hand.

"They must be waiting to shoot down our bloody throats," he snarled, both in rage and fear.

The summit of 187 now loomed directly in front of the Deuce; they had less than a hundred yards to go. The air was so filled with dust and black smoke that the sun was completely obscured from sight of the steadily advancing men. The mortars had been cut off, but the artillery shells were still screaming in, almost on top of the Royals. To Reardon's relief, the Chinese began firing upon his men from their crawl trenches.

Waving his pistol in the air Mike shouted, "Come on, you bastards! You can't live forever! Charge!"

As if pulled by an invisible string, the forward sections of the Deuce began to run in the wake of their leader. Their faces grim, their heads bent, they ran relentlessly forward toward the chattering Chinese machine guns. Just before the Canadians reached their objective, the Chinese stopped firing and began to flee in wild disorder, the Deuce sweeping over the hilltop in wild pursuit of the fleeing reds. One of Harvey's men, forgetting completely that he had his rifle slung over his back, was swinging his pick high in the air, overtaking one of the fleeing Chinese. As the unfortunate commie looked wild-eyed behind him, he stumbled and fell. The Canadian swung his pick with vicious force, pinning the Chino's squirming body to the ground. Three Chinese ran out of their hilltop bunker directly into the muzzle of Freddie Frome's machine gun; their bodies twitched spasmodically as their blood soaked into the powdered sand. A hysterically screaming Chinese soldier ran blindly toward Reardon who shot his face away. As the Deuce was reorganizing on the position, five Chinese trapped in a deep bunker refused to surrender. Reardon ordered Whitefoot's section to flush them out with phosphorus grenades. The victims, covered with the hot white burning metal, ran screaming out of the bunker to be mercifully cut down by Whitefoot's Sten gun. In a few minutes, it was all over.

Carr-Wilson and his platoon were not nearly as fortunate as the Deuce. While Mike and his platoon were assaulting the summit of 187, Monty had led his men along the Brown Bastard. Roughly halfway to their objective, they encountered fifty or sixty Chinese who had fled from the summit of the hill in the face of Reardon's and Dog Company's coordinated attack. The result was a confused mêlée of vicious hand-to-hand fighting—no organized attack or defense, just killing.

Monty had just shot a shrieking Chinese in the chest when his body was lifted slightly by a blast under his left foot, stepping on a Chinese bowling pin grenade just as it exploded, blowing the boot of his left and foot, filling his thighs with needlelike slivers of shrapnel, the force of the blast knocking him sideways to the ground. He looked amazedly at the shredded remnants of his left foot and his blood-soaked pants, dragging himself to the gnarled stump of a nearby tree to gain some support so that he could stand up. As he reached the stump, he came face to face with a startled Chinese defender who suddenly appeared out of the dirt-smoke pall hanging over the area. Before the weakened Carr-Wilson could raise his pistol, the enemy soldier riddled his wounded leg with submachine fire. As Monty fell backward, the Chinese was shot dead by Preston, Carr-Wilson's signalman.

When the "fog of war" finally cleared, Dearing's company was in command of its objectives; the Royals had successfully occupied hill 187 and its adjacent ridges. Operation Python was over, but the important task of establishing strong defenses against expected enemy counterattacks had just begun. Even though the Canadians were exhausted, mentally and physically, they dug trenches, strung barbed wire around their positions throughout the remainder of the day and all that night.

CHAPTER 28

Outpost

The day following the Commonwealth Division's successful attack, the Canadian brigade commander, accompanied by Colonel Graves, visited the Royals' newly established company positions. On reaching Dearing's locality, becoming concerned over a long fingerlike ridge projecting from the main ridge occupied by A Company and running in a northwesterly direction toward the Chinese-occupied hills, he turned to Graves, saying, "John, I don't like to see that ridge unoccupied. It provides a natural avenue of approach for the Chinese should they decide to attack in this area."

"I agree with you, sir, but it will leave Dearing overextended. He has a lot of ground to cover as it is," Graves commented.

"True, John, but on the other hand, it will give you more defensive depth and provide a means of early warning if a platoon strength outpost is set up on that feature."

"Do you have any suggestions, Chuck?" asked Graves.

"No, sir, not a present. It will certainly leave me vulnerable on the Brown Bastard itself," Dearing answered.

"I suggest you try it anyway. If it proves impractical, it will be a simple matter to withdraw the platoon and to reestablish it in your main defense perimeter," the brigade commander insisted.

"Surely we won't be staying here long, sir? We should be able to drive the Chinks at least as far as Pyongyang."

"I'm not certain of this, Major Dearing. There is a strong possibility we may stay here for some time. It really depends on events at Panmunjom. Evidently, the communists are taking a greater interest in the peace negotiations as a result of our attack. In any case, it would be prudent to set up first-class defenses in the event we don't move any further.

When the brigadier and Graves had finished their tour of inspection, they left to visit C Company, which had been moved up from its firm base position to occupy the ridge that lay to the right of A Company. Chuck suddenly cursed himself for not asking Graves if he had any word on Carr-Wilson's condition, recalling how pale and weak Monty had been when evacuated, remembering how Monty tried to be bluff and cheerful while he was being loaded into a jeep ambulance, his last words to Daring had been, "Give my regards to Mike, sir. Tell him to look me up when he comes home."

Dearing decided to have Sergeant Bush's third platoon set up the outpost position at the location suggested by the brigade commander, calling Bush over to brief him on his new task. The ridge in question, called the Songgok on the map, was six hundred yards long, bare of vegetation along its spine, heavily treed at its base. It rose abruptly at its far end then quickly dipped and rose again into a pimple-like formation. At its far extremity, to the right of the Songgok and across a wide paddy field, lay C Company's position; to the Songgok's left, across a narrow rice paddy, lay an unoccupied ridge; to its front lay the menacing slopes of hill 166 some 1,200 yards away, soon to become one of the communists' main defensive positions. The part of the ridge suggested by the brigadier for the outpost was the far tip, including the pimple.

Bush looked at the location indicated by Dearing. "Good lord, sir! It seems a hell of a long distance away. It almost looks as if we want to give a platoon away to the Chinks!"

"It won't be as bad as all that, Jim. If the outpost is properly set up, dug in, and wired, it'll be a pretty hard nut for the Chinos to crack, especially when you consider the support it'll get from our medium machine guns, mortars, and artillery," Chuck added, smiling. "Besides, I'll be rotating the platoons around regularly. I'm sending you out first because you have the most men and you had it easy yesterday."

"Right, sir. I'll call an O group and get my men started as soon as possible."

"Try to get dug in and at least one fence of wire around your position by tonight. I suggest that you post a four-man listening post on that pimple off the end of the Songgok . . . Let me see . . . Here it is on the map, point 97. Yes . . . Man 97 with a listening post. That way, the Chinks won't be able to sneak up on you from 166."

After Sergeant Bush left, Chuck moved toward Reardon, busy supervising his men as they set up their defenses.

The Chinese forces, soon recovering from their initial setback, began patrolling actively along the whole of the First Corps front, launching a full-scale attack against the ROK Division on the left, only to be repulsed with heavy losses. A stream of reports of active enemy patrol action began coming in to divisional headquarters from the Commonwealth's forces in the front line. The activity of the communists could mean only one thing—counterattack.

Two days after they commenced setting up the outpost on Songgok, Sergeant Bush's platoon was engaged by a raiding force of Chinese, some sixty strong. They managed to overrun the pimple, point 97, killing two of its four members. When they tried to do the same thing against the main body of the third platoon, they were sharply repulsed with heavy losses. Two weeks later, they tried again, this time with over a hundred strong supported by light mortars and machine guns.

The Deuce was occupying the outpost when the Chinese tried a sneak attack shortly after midnight. After cutting the platoon's telephone line to A Company headquarters, they moved up on the ridge to cut the defenders off from the rest of the company. It was Freddie Frome who first detected the silently advancing Chinese moving toward his position, alerting Jack Harvey, patiently waiting until they had reached the barbed wire fence forty feet from him before opening up with his Bren, killing four with his first burst of fire. After a vicious three-hour engagement, the Chinese withdrew, taking as many of their dead and wounded as they could with them. The cost to the Canadians was unbelievably light, only two men wounded.

The following two weeks were relatively quiet as the men occupying the outpost position took advantage of the lull in the fighting to build up their defenses against the attack they were certain was to come. The Canadians stayed alert throughout the long nights, maintaining a 50 percent stand to from dusk to dawn.

Each day's routine was much the same. After first light, the men breakfasted, washed, and shaved, and then most of them would catch a few hours' sleep. Their workday started around ten o'clock. While a lookout was maintained, the rest of the men worked, improving the defenses, cleaning grenades and weapons, cutting wood, and fetching water. Contrary to normal practice, Dearing set up his company's kitchen directly behind his position to provide his men, including those at the outpost, with hot meals. The meals for the men at the outpost were transported in special containers by members of the Korean Corps attached to the company. The men looked forward most to supper because it was at this time their beer, cigarettes, and mail were brought out to them.

When the last burdened Korean had struggled up the ridge, the hay boxes were quickly opened and the rations distributed by the outpost commander and his section leaders. Afterward, the mail was passed out and the beer issued. When the men finished eating and the Koreans returned to the company lines, the sober task of preparing for the night began.

The communists stepped up their mortaring and shelling of the outpost toward the end of October, the long dark nights now lit up by ceaseless strings of brilliant chandelier flares fired into the air by the Chinese in the rear of their lines. When the wind was blowing from the north, the rumble of trucks and tanks could be heard moving south to the Chinese lines. The reason for this activity was obvious: the Chinese were building up for an attack. The big question in the minds of the Canadians was "Who are the poor bastards that are going to get it?"

Mike Reardon was worried; the activity taking place behind 166 was too close for comfort, the ceaseless bombardment carried out by the Commonwealth artillery against the area behind the towering Chinese-held hill seeming to have very little effect in stopping or even slowing down the communist buildup. As he looked into the setting sun at the slopes of 166, he wondered about Carr-Wilson, having heard from Doc Patrick that Monty was in a hospital in Kure, Japan—that was all, not a word about his condition. His thoughts were interrupted by Bernie Viau's voice, calling from below the command post.

"Sir! Mr. Reardon! The meal train is on its way up the ridge. Looks like they're bringing some mail too!" he shouted, excited at the prospect of hearing from Dorothy.

"Thanks, Bernie. I'll be right down. Hey, Jack! Blackie! George! Get your boys ready for chow. We've got only about twenty minutes before the Chinks open up with their daily supper music."

Viau's letter from his wife dealt mainly with their coming baby and the loneliness she felt at his absence, her letters generally full of plans for their future, plans that Bernie dared not think about. All his private thoughts were about his wife, loving her very much.

"Hey, Blackie, only two more weeks and I'll be a father! What do you think of that, eh?"

"That's swell, Bernie. Nothing like being a father, I guess . . . Say, you're pretty lucky, at that. You won't have to be around when all the excitement starts. Keerist, you wouldn't get any more sleep at home than you're getting here."

"I don't know about that. I think I'd sooner wake up hearing a baby crying in my ear than a screaming Chinaman."

"Hey, Bernie, come over here and get your beer," Harvey called.

At ten o'clock the next morning, the Chinese artillery and mortars began to engage the outpost in earnest. Twice, while he was making his rounds, Reardon was thrown off his feet by the force of nearby explosions. The men didn't work that day, staying sheltered in the safety of their bunkers. Mike knew that the Deuce were in for trouble when, just before dark, three Chinese tanks rumbled to the forward slope of 166 and began to blast large holes in the barbed wire entanglements surrounding his position. When it grew dark, the enemy bombardment intensified at eight o'clock, the Chinese began climbing the unoccupied ridge situated between the outpost and A Company's main defenses.

CHAPTER 29

The Attack

Jack Harvey, returning to his position from the command post, detected the Chinese moving up the ridge behind the Deuce's position. Running to his slit trench, he bellowed out, "Chinks! Behind us!"

Fortunately, the unmanned ridge had been partially mined the previous day. Loud explosions, mingled with screams of agony, shattered the black silence of the Samichon Valley.

At almost the same moment, George Whitefoot shouted, "Hey, boss! Chinks moving up on the pimple!"

In the command post, Reardon felt a cold fist twist his guts; his worst fears were being realized. "My god!" he cried out. "We're it . . . They're going after us!"

Momentarily, he didn't feel Kal, his signaler, urgently shaking him by the shoulder. "Sir! Sir, the major wants to know the score."

Reardon, not answering, stood there staring.

"Are you okay, boss?" Kal demanded, apprehensive at his platoon commander's strange behaviors.

Reardon jolted to his senses by the snapping of bullets as a Chinese machine gun opened up. "Yeah, I'm okay," he rasped, grabbing the handset from Kal.

"What in hell is happening out there?" Dearing's voice crackled in Reardon's ear.

"Don't know for sure yet. They're still moving on the ridge and digging in on 97. Setting up machine guns, I think."

"Watch that goddamn pimple!" Dearing warned. "They'll probably mount an attack under covering fire from the top."

Reardon, now in complete control of himself, in a matter-of-fact tone, demanded, "Get me some heavy stuff on the pimple and the ridge."

"Wilco . . . Out," Dearing acknowledged.

Reardon left his command post, stumbling over the twenty yards separating him from Corporal Whitefoot's slit trench facing the pimple.

"Where are the bastards?" Mike demanded in a hoarse whisper, sliding into the trench beside George.

"I can't see them. I can sure as hell hear them though. Listen! They're really digging in now."

Reardon, unable to see anything in the inky darkness, turned to his corporal, "George, get one of your guys to tell our mortar team I want a flare above the pimple."

Whitefoot sent Parsons, one of his riflemen, to relay the order.

"We've got some heavy stuff coming up shortly, front and back, that should slow the little bastards up," Mike added.

Suddenly, they heard a loud metallic clank followed by a chorus of loud curses.

In a short time, Parsons returned, reporting, "Bloody firing pin in the mortar broke on the first round, sir."

"Of all the friggin' luck!" Mike swore. "I'd better let Dearing know . . . We've got to get some damn light out here to see the bitches."

On returning to his command post, he smelled an unmistakable smell of urine. "My god, Kal . . . are you pissing yourself?"

"Sorry, sir," the embarrassed signaler replied. "I can't seem to help myself."

Reardon was going to comment further but thought better of it, remembering his own initial reaction. "Get me the major," he said instead.

Blackie Balaski's section was facing the main enemy position across the valley, hill 166. The only activity detected by his section so far was some movement near his barbed wire defenses.

"The Chinks are just probing the wire for gaps," Blackie concluded shrewdly.

Hearing a rustle behind him, he whirled, bringing his Sten submachine gun to bear on the source of the noise.

"Take it easy with that goddamn plumber's nightmare!" a voice demanded nervously. "It's only me, Doc." Doc Sturgess, the Deuce's first-aid man, was dropping down beside Balaski. "Blackie! Did you just fart? Smells awful in here."

"You don't smell no hot yourself," Blackie retorted.

"Brought you some extra field dressings . . . just in case."

"Thanks. We might need them," Blackie replied quietly then asked, "What's doing with Jack and the chief?"

"Things are quiet in front of Jack. Lots going on around the pimple. George told me they're digging in machine-gun emplacements. Reardon figures the Chinks are going to hit us from there."

Their conversation was interrupted by the unmistakable booming of the Canadian artillery located a few miles behind the front. Shortly after, they heard the screeching whine of the twenty-five-pound shells as they exploded on top of the pimple and the ridge in front of Harvey.

"Keerist! They're really zeroed in!" Balaski shouted happily, clapping Sturgess on the back.

"That should keep their heads down for a while," Sturgess added.

Their joy was short-lived. Six Chinese tanks, lined up on the skyline on hill 166, started shooting directly at the outpost. Their high-velocity shells cut the air overhead with a sharp "pfffft," which preceded the arrival of the sound of the tank guns by a fraction of a second. The pffft-bang sound of the firing continued for ten minutes as the tanks tried to destroy the wire defenses fronting the outpost and any Canadians who might be unfortunate enough to get in the way. Two of Blackie's men were wounded by a hit near their slit trench.

In the command post, Reardon and Kalamazoo ducked instinctively as each shell thudded into the position, in spite of realizing they would never hear the one hitting them.

Mike called to Dearing, "It won't be long now. They're blowing my wire apart!"

"Any casualties yet?" Dearing asked anxiously.

Mike gave him a coded response reporting two wounded in Balaski's section. To Reardon's surprise, Colonel Graves's voice boomed in his ear.

"We think we have the picture now. It looks like the Chinese will try to take out your position before launching a major attack against the brigade with one, maybe two divisions, formed up behind 166. Reardon, you've got to hold! We'll give all the help we can."

Reardon was dumbfounded. It was like a bad dream. He was supposed to hold off God knows how many Chinese because there were even more ready to attack. His introspection was interrupted by three red star-shaped flares popping far above his heard, followed by a torrent of machine-gun fire raking George Whitefoot's position.

"Here they come!" Whitefoot yelled.

Above the din, Reardon could hear the rattling of the Chinese soldiers' equipment as they ran up the steep slope in front of George's position.

"Hold your fire until I give the order!" Reardon shouted at the top of his lungs. "Hold! Hold!" As soon as he saw the shadowy figures of the attackers break out of the darkness, he roared, "Fire!"

Whitefoot's section opened fire with machine guns, rifles, and grenades with devastating effect. Bullets and shrapnel cut the Chinese down as they stumbled through the torn barbed wire defenses. As soon as Whitefoot opened fire, Reardon called for a major artillery bombardment at a prearranged target area in front of George's section, the artillery responding with remarkable speed and accuracy, the pinpoint bombardment falling in the middle of the attacking enemy column, forcing most of the Chinese back to the safety of the pimple, leaving their comrades in the front of the charge to the mercy of Whitefoot's deadly fire.

Reardon was elated, his Indian corporal hadn't suffered a single casualty in beating off the attack. His euphoria was short-lived, above the ear-shattering noise created by the Canadian artillery fire on hill 166, as the guns tried unsuccessfully to knock out the menacing tanks, the men of the Deuce heard the ominous sound of a tracked vehicle clanking across the valley toward the pimple.

"Good god!" Reardon exclaimed. "Surely the bastards aren't sending a tank after us?"

He alerted his two-man rocket-launcher team to get ready to take on this new threat.

"Hey, Gerry! We're finally getting a chance to shoot this goddamn thing at a real target!" Larry Kirkpatrick, the team leader, exclaimed excitedly to Gerry Marlow, his crewman.

Reardon briefed the team, "Kirk, keep your eyes and ears open. If that tin can comes close enough to engage, you better be sure you don't miss, you'll probably only get one shot at the bastard! Remember, as soon as you fire your rocket, get the hell out of the way and take up a new position in case you get another chance."

"Right, sir!" the two men chorused.

The rattling roar of the tracks became increasingly loud as the vehicle shuddered its way up the reverse slope of the pimple. Reardon moved down to Whitefoot's position to have a better view.

"Sure can hear the bastard, but I can't see a goddamn thing," Whitefoot complained nervously to Mike.

"There it is!" someone shouted.

About fifty yards away, a medium-sized self-propelled gun had positioned itself in the middle of the saddle, linking Whitefoot's position with the pimple, and was training its gun on the wire defenses.

Mike called Kirkpatrick over and pointed it out to him. "See it? No! Over to your right . . . That's it—now go and get that son of a bitch!"

Kirkpatrick and Marlow half ran, half stumbled to a position near the wire, giving them a good view of the Chinese gun silhouetted in the gloom. Kirk knelt on one knee as Marlow helped fit the light but cumbersome tube of the 3.5-inch launcher on his right shoulder. As Kirk looked through the optic sight, trying to keep his nervous sweat from clouding the eyepiece, Marlow hooked up the ignition wires to the rocket.

Reardon was cursing, "Keerist! Won't those stupid bastards ever fire that goddamn thing?"

He had no sooner spoken when the rocket launcher emitted a tremendous blast of flame—they missed. The self-propelled gun traversed and fired into the center of the burning debris. The two Canadians, transfixed by disbelief at missing their target, forgot Reardon's caution and were seriously wounded.

"Jesus Christ! Did you see that?" Whitefoot shouted in horror.

"Poor buggers," Reardon replied then added under his breath, "Now we're in for it."

Mike's prediction was only too true, unopposed, the Chinese gun began blowing large holes in the Canadians' defensive wire. The number of machine guns on the pimple had doubled, and they started pouring a withering hail of fire on Whitefoot's and Balaski's positions; the tanks on 166 started shelling the entire forward slope of the outpost. Once again, the sky was illuminated with red flares; the Chinese buglers began blasting their rallying signals for the assault, a mass of Chinese dog trotting up the slope, splitting into two groups nearing the wire. By this time, the guns of the Canadian artillery regiment were providing a circle of defensive fire around the besieged outpost.

The combined Chinese and Canadian fire blanketed the outpost with a pall of acrid, lung-searing smoke and dust, the surrounding air resonating with a crescendo of ricocheting bullets, blasting grenades, and exploding shells. The only source of illumination within the outpost was Reardon's flare pistol feebly illuminating the areas immediately in front of his sections by moving around his command post and shooting his short burning one-inch flares above them.

Meanwhile, a large enemy force had gathered in front of Jack Harvey's position, preparing to attack the outpost from the rear. Lacking the fire support provided to their comrades attacking from the pimple, they were preparing to blow a hole in Harvey's wire, using long bamboo tubes filled with explosives. Frome watched three Chinese place one of the tubes on the wire directly in front of him less than forty feet away. Holding his fire, not wanting to give away his position, he was waiting for bigger game, the large enemy force he knew was waiting to come through the hole. Frome, sweating profusely from nervous anticipation, ducked as the charge exploded, blowing a six-foot-wide hole in the wire. The Chinese, screaming at the top of their voices, charged forward, Frome catching them as they bunched up in the gap. Tapping his Bren gun gently from side to side, he fired short deadly accurate bursts into their midst. The shocked Chinese broke off their attack, running back to cover, leaving a twisted pile of their screaming, cursing comrades caught in the gap. Frome kept up this controlled, concentrated fire until the writhing human mass plugging the gap lay still.

The firing from Whitefoot's and Balaski's sections were so deadly, the Canadian artillery fire so effective, only a few Chinese managed to break through the wire; the attack stalled. However, the Deuce paid the price, nine more of the defenders casualties; they were dangerously low in ammunition, were nearly out of grenades. Harvey, who up to this time had been only lightly engaged, was requested to send some of his ammunition to Whitefoot's section.

"Hey, Bernie, take a full box of ammo to Whitefoot and get right back."

"Okay, Corporal," Bernie replied. Viau, crouching low as he moved, grunting from the exertion of slugging the heavy ammo box over the battered ground, cursed as he almost fell into the outpost latrine.

Bernie had just been challenged by Kalamazoo, on watch in the command post, when he saw a figure loom out of the blackness below him. Thinking it was someone from Whitefoot's section coming to meet him, he called out, "Hey! It's me, Bernie. I brought your ammo."

The figure did not answer, seeming to raise a hand in greeting, a Chinese grenade bounced at Viau's feet, lunging sideways, the wrong way, rolling over on his face on top of the exploding grenade, blowing a hole in his guts. Though too late, George, seeing the grenade thrown at Bernie, shot the Chinese. Kal helped Whitefoot carry Bernie, who was miraculously still alive, up to the command post. Viau, in a state of shock but conscious, was propped against a wall of the bunker in a sitting position. Amazed at how little pain he felt, he began hoping his wound wasn't too serious.

Doc Sturgess handed his first-aid kit to Kal as he dropped over the side of the command post, moving beside Bernie. His face was grim, having seen enough blood letting this night to last his lifetime.

"Where's he hit?" he asked Kal tersely.

"In the guts" was the equally short reply.

"Bernie, for Christ's sake, let me move your hands away so I can have a look at the goddamn thing," he demanded impatiently.

He flashed his small light on the torn mass of intestines and bloody clothing spilling through Viau's fingers. Gently moving Bernie's hands away, he expertly applied a large abdominal field dressing to the foul-smelling nauseating wound.

"I'm not too bad, hey, Doc?" Bernie pleaded.

"No, kid . . . You'll be fine—take it easy," Sturgess replied, smiling sadly.

As he got to his feet, he looked at Kal. He shook his head, handing him two morphine syrettes, saying, "It's going to hurt like hell when the shock wears off. Give him a shot as soon as he starts hurting bad. I've got to look at some other guys."

Reardon, returning from checking the other sections, asked who the slumped figure was.

"Viau, sir."

"Is it bad?"

"Yeah . . . he's had it."

"Damn it to hell!"

There was no stopping the next attack. Even though the advancing Chinese were being decimated by shells from both the Canadian and their own guns, they charged right through the hail of fire overrunning the outpost. A Chinese bugler placed himself a few feet from the command post, seemingly oblivious to his surroundings, blowing a rallying call for the attackers. Reardon leaned over the parapet shooting the bugle through the back of the man's neck. The Chinese started milling around, not certain where the defenders were located in the murky darkness.

Reardon called Dearing, shouting, "They're overrunning the position. We can't stop them anymore. I want a 'Mike' target!"

"No! You'll all be blown to hell!" Dearing shouted back.

"Goddamn you!" Mike cursed his commander. "I want all the guns zeroed in on us. We'll be under cover. It's our only chance!"

"Okay, Mike. When it's over, try and pull back over the ridge. I'll have Bush's platoon cover you . . . Good luck!"

Graves, who by now had moved forward to Dearing's position, approved the request, relaying the order to the divisional artillery commanders, who immediately had all their guns zero in on the outpost, shown as a small oval on their battle maps.

Poor bastards! they thought, barking the order, "Fire!"

All seventy-two guns began raining shells on top of the outpost; Dearing and Graves watched with fascinated horror as the torrent of shells gouged out the surface of Reardon's position with exploding tongues of flame.

"Oh my god! What have we done?" Dearing cried aloud, turning his head away from the carnage, tears streaming down his cheeks.

Graves turned, facing Dearing, putting his hand on his shoulder. "We probably saved the battalion, Chuck."

CHAPTER 30

Aftermath

The nerve-searing noise of the violent shelling suddenly stopped; an eerie calm settled over the whole battle area, the ominous death-like stillness occasionally broken by the spine-tingling shrieks and moans of the wounded and dying, Canadians and Chinese, the dense, acrid pall of smoke blanketing the ridge slowly dissipated by a frigid Siberian wind, the pitch-black quiet shattered by the loud pop of an exploding parachute flare. During the few brilliant seconds of the flare's whirring flight, many torn and twisted bodies, some still writhing in agony, could be seen sharply outlined against the finger-shaped ridge, the flare's blinding light also revealing the shell-shattered remains of the once formidable oval-shaped barbed wire barricade that had enclosed the defenders. The scrambled wire entanglements, blasted by the tremendous Chinese and Canadian artillery barrages, were filled with huge torn gaping holes, the bent and twisted steel pickets supporting the wire giving mute testimony to the destructive force of the heavy shelling.

As the first flare spat out its last flickering light, a second popped, illuminating the battle scene, at first looking as if the defensive position was deserted, except for the many motionless forms sprawled around it. However, as the cordite haze drifted away, small groups of Chinese soldiers could be seen stealthily dragging their dead and wounded comrades down to the base of the steep ridge. One such group, breathing heavily from the exertion of crawling through the tangled maze of shattered wire, was greeted by a chattering burst of machine-gun fire from the outpost. The Chinese flattened themselves against the unyielding earth, cursing loudly from fright and rage.

Miraculously, many of the Canadian defenders had survived the saturation shelling. The command post, manned by five defenders, each armed with an automatic weapon, positioned around the broken sandbagged walls of the X;shaped command post. Bernie Viau was still sitting bent over on the dirt floor, obviously in great pain, his young puckish face streaked with dirt and dried blood, his hands spasmodically clutching the blood-soaked field dressing covering his lower abdomen.

Bernie was rocking his pain-racked body gently, quietly crooning to himself in French, completely unaware of the shadowy figures of his comrades standing beside him in the blackness. In his delirium, he was home, a boy of seven, suffering from a burst appendix, being comforted by his mother. His mind cleared suddenly as he thought of Dorothy and the baby he might never see.

"Soon, help will come. I must get out of this," he wheezed to himself, lapsing into the French of his boyhood.

"Bernie's in bad shape, sir," Kalamazoo informed Reardon.

"I know, Kal, but there's not a goddamn thing we can do for him, Doc Sturgess gave him the last of our morphine a half hour ago," Reardon replied helplessly.

Kal turned his attention to the shattered radio, saving his life by absorbing the impact of a piece of shrapnel during the intense shelling.

Bernie suddenly screamed, "Oh Christ! Oh Christ! How much longer do we have to wait for those Chinese bastards?" A punishing spasm of pain shook his whole body. "I can't stand it—I can't . . ."

Reardon involuntarily clamped his hand over the wounded man's mouth, hissing, "Shut up, Bernie! Do you want every Chink in North Korea on our tails?"

"There's a bunch of Chinos trying to sneak through the wire," whispered Frome then snarled, "Try this for size, you sons of bitches!" as he let go a burst from his Bren. An answering cry of pain confirmed that some of his bullets had found their mark.

"Surely they can't be getting ready to attack again, not after that god-awful shelling?" questioned Reardon.

"Don't think so. Probably just another one of them Chink rescue parties."

"Jack! How are George and Doc coming along with the wounded down in the saddles?"

"Can't tell, boss, it's too bloody dark down there. Hey, George . . . George, how are you coming?"

"Used the last on Viau."

Blackie called out from his position on the far side of the command post, "Can I come over and see Bernie, sir?"

"Sure thing, Blackie. Fred! You go over and cover Blackie's spot for a minute."

"Keerist! He looks awful, sir," whispered Blackie. "Isn't there something we can do for him?"

"I'm afraid not, Blackie. I don't think he's got much longer to go."

"The poor little bugger. It's going to be rough on his wife." Mike bent over Bernie's still form, feeling for his pulse. "He's cashed in, Blackie. It's all over for him."

"Maybe he's the lucky one," Blackie snapped, moving back to his position.

"How many men do you figure we have that can still fight, Jack?"

"Seven, maybe eight, depends on how many guys George has got left."

"Is everyone in the picture as to what they're to do when we pull out, Jack?"

"Yeah, I think so. George seemed to get the message when I passed the dope on to him. I sure hope Bush knows it's us coming in, not the Chinks," he added.

"Okay, just remember this, either we all go out together or nobody goes! I figure that once we get on that bloody ridge behind us we'll be home free."

"Do you figure we got a chance, boss?"

"Jack, you've always got a chance as long as you're mobile. Don't forget . . . if the Chinks start attacking, make for that bloody ridge with whatever men you have left. Doc and George will follow with the wounded. Blackie, Frome, Kal, and I will look after the rear. Okay?"

"Check!"

"Okay, you guys. We're going out. Good luck!"

Passing the wounded through the wire proved to be a slow painful task as some of the injured men caught themselves on the shattered barbs. The four men constituting the rearguard were forced to leave the command post, in danger of being cut off from the others.

For a moment, Mike missed Kal and, thinking his signaler had not heard the order to withdraw, had run back to the command post. To his relief, he saw a solitary figure standing at the top of the parapet. Mike was about to call out when the shadowy figure was joined by two others.

"Chinks!" he snarled as he cut them down with a burst of fire from a burp gun he'd taken from a dead Chinese.

Meanwhile, Jack and his men, seizing their objective with surprising ease, were covering the slow withdrawal of the wounded along the ridge when Harvey, deciding to return to the outpost to give Reardon a hand, had just reached the wire, seeing the four men rearguard stumbling toward him, some shadowy figures following them. "Look out behind you, boss! Chinks!"

Startled by Harvey's shout, Reardon turned around and saw three or four Chinese calmly setting up a machine gun a scant thirty feet away. He shouted to the others to cover Harvey and himself as they charged the commies, the lethal bursts from their submachine guns either killing or scattering the Chinese, except for one, crouching on one knee, fired his burp gun directly at Reardon.

Mike, feeling the white hot slugs ripping into his right side and shoulder, spun around in a crazy pirouette before crashing to the ground. Jack Harvey shot the kneeling Chinese, dragging Reardon's unconscious body down the slope toward the ridge.

In the distance, the searchlight protecting the site of the truce talks from attack could be seen probing the black sky over Panmunjom.

CHAPTER 31

Journey Home

Reardon regained partial consciousness in the Royals' battalion aid post as Steve Patrick injected blood plasma into his veins in a desperate attempt to keep him alive. Mike's morphine-clouded brain registered sounds but not words and figures but not faces, his eyes slowly focusing on the face of the Royals' medical officer. Patrick's drawn, tired expression relaxed a little when he saw Mike's half-closed eyes open in recognition, knew he had got him just in time, and there was a fighting chance Reardon might live. Mike tried to speak, but his words were soundless.

Patrick saw Mike's lips moving, shrewdly guessing what he was trying to say. "Take it easy, Mike, don't try to talk. It's important you save your strength. If it's your men you're worried about, relax. They got out, including the wounded."

A slight smile appeared on Reardon's lips, signifying he understood Patrick's words.

Another familiar face came into view; it was Colonel Graves who bent over his stretcher to speak to him. "Good show, Mike! You had your lads did a wonderful job. Every man in the brigade is proud of you. Now you take it easy and get well."

Mike saw a plasma bottle being raised high over Patrick's head, wondering idly who the plasma was for, lapsing into unconsciousness.

For the next few days, Reardon lived in a dreamworld of semi-awareness, not knowing what was happening to him nor caring. Mike was unaware of his bumpy trip in a jeep ambulance to the brigade field dressing station, nor did he regain consciousness during his helicopter trip to the Seoul and subsequent ride by ambulance to the large military hospital located in the heart of the city. He seemed to have a fuzzy awareness of hospital smells, of mostly masked figures, some dark, some light, of buzzing, subdued conversation. It never really occurred to him he was the reason for all the activity he sensed around him, feeling like a detached observer, a spectator.

It was a full week before Mike completely regained consciousness, awakened by a ray of bright sunshine streaming through his window, striking his haggard, colorless face. His mouth felt dry as if someone had swabbed it out with cotton wool. *At least, I can see*, he thought to himself.

When his eyes became accustomed to the bright morning light, he started to experiment in an effort to determine how badly he had been hurt, relieved finding he could move his head slightly, both his legs and his left arm, but not his right arm and shoulder, which were tightly bound, his chest seemed to be ringed with a steel band, making breathing difficult. Trying to shift his weight, he found himself too weak to move.

"Welcome to the fold, stranger. Now you just lie still and take it easy there," a cheery voice called out.

Turning his head with great effort, he saw the smiling face of a smartly dressed American nursing sister.

"You certainly gave us a very difficult time for a while, soldier."

"Where am I?" he croaked, surprised at the trouble he had in speaking.

"In Seoul military hospital" was the reply. "Now don't try to talk anymore. I'm going to call the surgeon who operated on you. He told me to call him when you woke up."

When his nurse left, Mike slowly turned his head from side to side, looking over his room; it was quite small but clean and attractive. The sight of the intravenous feeding bottle on a stand at the head of his bed brought a faint memory of the plasma bottle held over his head in the Royals' first aid post. He was wondering about the fate of his men when a young-looking bespectacled American major entered his room. He said a breezy "hello" as he picked the temperature chart hanging at the foot of the bed, asking, "How do you feel?"

"Hard to say, Doc. I feel awfully weak, though," he wheezed. "Tell me, what day is this?"

"November 8. Now you take it easy and keep your talking to a minimum. It's amazing how exhausting talking can be. You've just finished experiencing a very difficult operation, so it's important at this stage that you don't overdo it. We don't want to see our hard work tossed out the window. Well, I really must go now. I'll be in to see you when the nurse changes your dressings, and meanwhile, if there is anything you want, just ring for the sister. So long!"

The following day, the young surgeon gave Mike a detailed account about his injuries. "You came very close to not making it. In fact, at one stage, we just about gave you up. We had to extract four bullets from your right arm and shoulder and one from your right lung. It was the one in your lung that gave us the most trouble and nearly finished you. Fortunately, you're as strong as an ox! It was your good physical condition and strong heart that carried you through."

"I sure as hell don't feel very strong right now, Doctor."

"You'll get your strength back in time, but that isn't your main trouble right now."

"What do you mean?"

"Well, your arm and shoulder are in bad shape. You need a specialist in neurosurgery familiar with your particular problem. Consequently, we're sending you to the Kure Military Hospital where they'll take over where we've left off."

"Will I lose my arm, Doc?" Mike wheezed worriedly. "Tell me the truth!"

"No, you certainly won't lose your arm, but to be perfectly honest with you, there is some doubt as to just how much use you'll get out of it. The nerves and tendons have been badly damaged. Just what are the problems involved in restoring your arm to its full use, I can't say, but the chances of a full recovery are definitely in your favor. That's why we're sending you to Kure as soon as we feel you're strong enough to make the trip. The sooner they can get started, the better your chances are."

The following week, as Mike's stretcher was being loaded onto a casualty evacuation Dakota aircraft, he remembered ruefully how happy he had been the last time he had boarded a Dak at Kimpo airfield.

"No booze and geisha girls this trip," he muttered unhappily.

During the course of his flight, the combination of the bouncing motion of the aircraft and his difficulty in breathing caused Reardon to fall into a partial coma; he was unconscious when he arrived at the hospital. His awakening the next morning was a repetition of his return to consciousness at the Seoul hospital, with the exception that this time he felt much stronger and had a clear memory of the events of the preceding week.

A tall redheaded Australian nursing sister entered his room, greeting him, "It's jolly well about time you woke up, Mr. Reardon! Can't sleep all day, you know. By the way, you have a visitor," she said affably as she fluffed up his pillows and checked his pulse.

At first, he was unable to distinguish the features of the person sitting at the left of his bed, his attention focused on the gaudy colors of the dressing gown his visitor was wearing, and then the smiling blond-haired newcomer's mustache-wearing face became clear; it was Monty Carr-Wilson!

"Monty! Monty! You old bastard!" Mike wheezed, his eyes brimming with tears.

Carr-Wilson reached over and grasped Mike's left hand in a tight emotional grip. "Good to see you, old cock! From what I've heard and read, you've had a pretty rough go, but you're in excellent hands now," he said huskily.

The combination of exhaustion after the strip and his excitement at seeing his friend again proved to be too much for Reardon. Closing his eyes, he fell into a deep sleep, a trace of a smile on his colorless lips.

The next day, Mike was sufficiently strong to have Monty stay for a longer visit. "How's your leg, Monty? I was too knocked out to ask you yesterday. I heard from Dearing that it was kind of bad."

"Not too bad at all, old chap. Fact is I don't feel a thing."

"What in hell are you doing here then? Swinging the lead?" Mike asked half seriously.

Monty's smile vanished as he stood up, reaching from his crutches, hopping back to the wall. Turning around so that Reardon could see his full length without raising his head, he opened the front of his long dressing gown, revealing he was standing on one leg, his left pajama leg was neatly folded at the knee, its cuff pinned at the thigh.

"I'm terribly sorry, Monty," groaned Mike. "I didn't know it was that bad! I feel like a fool! I've been lying here, feeling sorry for myself, and you've been sitting there all the time trying to cheer me up, without even mentioning you'd lost a leg," he gasped painfully.

"Oh, don't trouble yourself on that account, Mike. Why, the chap who did the job said that as soon as the stump thoroughly heals and I return to Canada, the boys at Sunnybrook will be able to fix me up with an artificial leg that will make me nearly as good as new," he retorted with forced cheerfulness.

"The peculiar thing I can't become accustomed to is the feeling I have sometimes that my bloody leg is still there! I'll admit I felt very depressed at first, but after I saw the condition of some of the other chaps here, I began to feel damn fortunate."

In the ensuing weeks, Reardon was under constant observation. His chest, shoulder, and arm wounds were healing nicely, but the tendons and nerves presented a more difficult problem. After carefully considering his case, Mike's consulting surgeon recommended that the young Torontonian be turned over to one of the recognized experts in the field of neurosurgery, a prominent Toronto surgeon, who in addition to his normal practice, did consultant work for the Sunnybrook Military Hospital.

Recognizing the therapeutic value the two friends would have for each other, the commandant of the hospital decided to send Mike and Monty home together. A week later, they started on their long voyage home. Arriving at Tokyo's Haneda Airport, they were transferred from their twin-engine Dakota to a huge four-engine North Star, bearing the roundel of the Royal Canadian Air Force. After the two Royals officers were comfortably settled in their bunks on the specially equipped aircraft, the broad-winged North Star took off, heading for the island of Hokkaido, its last refueling stop before proceeding on its Pacific journey.

Reardon was lying on his back, staring at the top of his two-tiered bunk, preoccupied with his own thoughts. Carr-Wilson propped up in his bunk directly across the aisle, reading an American exposé magazine.

Mike suddenly broke the silence. "Do you have anything special in mind when you finish at the hospital, Monty? Any special plans?"

"No, nothing special . . . I haven't given it much thought, to be perfectly honest, old cock. One thing is certain—any hope I may have had of following an army career has certainly been fritzed," he replied regretfully, looking at his stump.

"Well, I never planned to stay in the bloody army in any event," said Mike, "and now that I've got a bum arm, they wouldn't keep me even if I wanted to stay. I thought I might take a flier at my father's real estate business and figure it would be nice if you came in with me," he suggested hopefully.

Carr-Wilson, thinking over his friend's proposition for a moment, replied enthusiastically, "You know something, old cock? You might have something there! In fact, the more I think about it, the better it sounds. A bad arm or an artificial leg couldn't matter less in that business, it's personality that counts, and we've lots of that commodity! With your father to show us the ropes and my experience in the insurance business, real estate might prove to be a highly profitable venture."

"Why, sure it would, Monty! We should be able to make a lot of money if we have any luck at all. We'll need only one car between us to start," Mike went on. "Then we'll line up a nice comfortable apartment where we can entertain without getting in each other's way and—"

"Hold on now! Haven't we forgotten something?" Monty interjected, smiling broadly.

"No . . . I don't think so. Why?"

"Our wives, old chap. Our wives!"

"Damn it to hell, yes! I'd almost forgotten that little detail."

The two friends, looking across the aisle at each other, began laughing so hard Monty started choking, Mike's chest and shoulder aching.

"We go through nearly a year of hell, get all smashed up. Then as a nice juicy reward for our trouble, we go home facing the same damn thing we left! Boy, is that ever great? Lord, give me strength!"

Later, when their laughter had subsided, Mike asked quietly, "Do you think it was worth it, Monty? You, me, Paul and all the others?"

Carr-Wilson sat up in his bunk, looking through the gathering darkness at his friend whose face clearly reflected the many weeks of pain he had suffered. He glanced at the bandaged remnant of his left leg. His mouth twisted into a cynical grin as he thought of the many young men who had died and who were yet to die on the bleak Korean hills while the peace talks at Panmunjom dragged endlessly on. He thought of Anne Martin and Dorothy Viau.

"That's one question I'd rather not try to answer, Mike."

The End

CPSIA information can be obtained at www.ICGtesting.com
Printed in the USA
LVOW10s2024251215

467859LV00002B/477/P